Frommer's

Seattle
day BY day®

2nd Edition

by Beth Taylor

WILEY

John Wiley & Sons, Inc.

Contents

Published by:

John Wiley & Sons, Inc.

111 River St.
Hoboken, NJ 07030-5774

ISBN 978-1-118-02744-8 (paper); ISBN 978-1-118-13257-9 (ebk); ISBN 978-1-118-13258-6 (ebk); ISBN 978-1-118-13259-3 (ebk)

Editor: Jessica Langan-Peck
Production Editor: Lindsay Conner
Photo Editor: Alden Gewirtz
Cartographer: Liz Puhl
Production by Wiley Indianapolis Composition Services

For information on our other products and services or to obtain technical support, please contact our Customer Care Department within the U.S. at 877/762-2974, outside the U.S. at 317/572-3993 or fax 317/572-4002.

Wiley also publishes its books in a variety of electronic formats. Some content that appears in print may not be available in electronic formats.

Manufactured in China

5   4   3   2   1

A Note from the Editorial Director

Organizing your time. That's what this guide is all about.

Other guides give you long lists of things to see and do and then expect you to fit the pieces together. The Day by Day guides are different. These guides tell you the best of everything, and then they show you how to see it *in the smartest, most time-efficient way*. Our authors have designed detailed itineraries organized by time, neighborhood, or special interest. And each tour comes with a bulleted map that takes you from stop to stop.

Hoping to explore Seattle's iconic Pike Place Market, or tour the city's eerie underground past? Want to try some of the country's finest coffee while strolling through Seattle's hip shopping districts? Whatever your interest or schedule, the Day by Days give you the smartest routes to follow. Not only do we take you to the top attractions, hotels, and restaurants, but we also help you access those special moments that locals get to experience—those "finds" that turn tourists into travelers.

The Day by Days are also your top choice if you're looking for one complete guide for all your travel needs. The best hotels and restaurants for every budget, the greatest shopping values, the wildest nightlife—it's all here.

Why should you trust our judgment? Because our authors personally visit each place they write about. They're an independent lot who say what they think and would never include places they wouldn't recommend to their best friends. They're also open to suggestions from readers. If you'd like to contact them, please send your comments our way at feedback@frommers.com, and we'll pass them on.

Enjoy your Day by Day guide—the most helpful travel companion you can buy. And have the trip of a lifetime.

Warm regards,

Kelly Regan

Kelly Regan, Editorial Director
Frommer's Travel Guides

About the Author

Beth Taylor is an Air Force brat who roamed the world before finding her heart's home in Seattle. She's reported and edited at newspapers and magazines in Florida and the Pacific Northwest, and written a variety of travel articles and guides. Degrees in journalism and political science have been helpful in understanding and describing the lands she's explored, but as any traveler knows, the tools that really count are curiosity and a sense of adventure.

Acknowledgments

Many thanks to Scott and Molly for joining in enthusiastically on many of my explorations, and for their patience during the writing process. And much gratitude also goes to my editor, Linda Barth, whose unflappable, upbeat outlook kept the book on track and made the project a pleasure.

Advisory & Disclaimer

Travel information can change quickly and unexpectedly, and we strongly advise you to confirm important details locally before traveling, including information on visas, health and safety, traffic and transport, accommodations, shopping, and eating out. We also encourage you to stay alert while traveling and to remain aware of your surroundings. Avoid civil disturbances, and keep a close eye on cameras, purses, wallets, and other valuables.

While we have endeavored to ensure that the information contained within this guide is accurate and up-to-date at the time of publication, we make no representations or warranties with respect to the accuracy or completeness of the contents of this work and specifically disclaim all warranties, including without limitation warranties of fitness for a particular purpose. We accept no responsibility or liability for any inaccuracy or errors or omissions, or for any inconvenience, loss, damage, costs, or expenses of any nature whatsoever incurred or suffered by anyone as a result of any advice or information contained in this guide.

The inclusion of a company, organization, or website in this guide as a service provider and/or potential source of further information does not mean that we endorse them or the information they provide. Be aware that information provided through some websites may be unreliable and can change without notice. Neither the publisher nor author shall be liable for any damages arising herefrom.

Star Ratings, Icons & Abbreviations

Every hotel, restaurant, and attraction listing in this guide has been ranked for quality, value, service, amenities, and special features using a **star-rating system.** Hotels, restaurants, attractions, shopping, and nightlife are rated on a scale of zero stars (recommended) to three stars (exceptional). In addition to the star-rating system, we also use a **kids icon** to point out the best bets for families. Within each tour, we recommend cafes, bars, or restaurants where you can take a break. Each of these stops appears in a shaded box marked with a coffee-cup-shaped bullet ☕.

The following **abbreviations** are used for credit cards:

AE	American Express	DISC	Discover	V	Visa
DC	Diners Club	MC	MasterCard		

Travel Resources at Frommers.com

Frommer's travel resources don't end with this guide. Frommer's website, **www.frommers.com**, has travel information on more than 4,000 destinations. We update features regularly, giving you access to the most current trip-planning information and the best airfare, lodging, and car-rental bargains. You can also listen to podcasts, connect with other Frommers.com members through our active-reader forums, share your travel photos, read blogs from guidebook editors and fellow travelers, and much more.

A Note on Prices

In the "Take a Break" and "Best Bets" sections of this book, we have used a system of dollar signs to show a range of costs for 1 night in a hotel (the price of a double-occupancy room) or the cost of an entree at a restaurant. Use the following table to decipher the dollar signs:

Cost	Hotels	Restaurants
$	under $100	under $10
$$	$100–$200	$10–$20
$$$	$200–$300	$20–$30
$$$$	$300–$400	$30–$40
$$$$$	over $400	over $40

How to Contact Us

In researching this book, we discovered many wonderful places—hotels, restaurants, shops, and more. We're sure you'll find others. Please tell us about them, so we can share the information with your fellow travelers in upcoming editions. If you were disappointed with a recommendation, we'd love to know that, too. Please write to:

Frommer's Seattle Day by Day, 2nd Edition
John Wiley & Sons, Inc. • 111 River St • Hoboken, NJ 07030-5774

16 Favorite
Moments

16 Favorite **Moments**

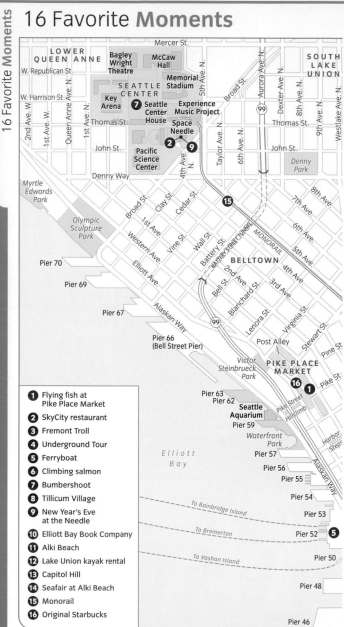

1. Flying fish at Pike Place Market
2. SkyCity restaurant
3. Fremont Troll
4. Underground Tour
5. Ferryboat
6. Climbing salmon
7. Bumbershoot
8. Tillicum Village
9. New Year's Eve at the Needle
10. Elliott Bay Book Company
11. Alki Beach
12. Lake Union kayak rental
13. Capitol Hill
14. Seafair at Alki Beach
15. Monorail
16. Original Starbucks

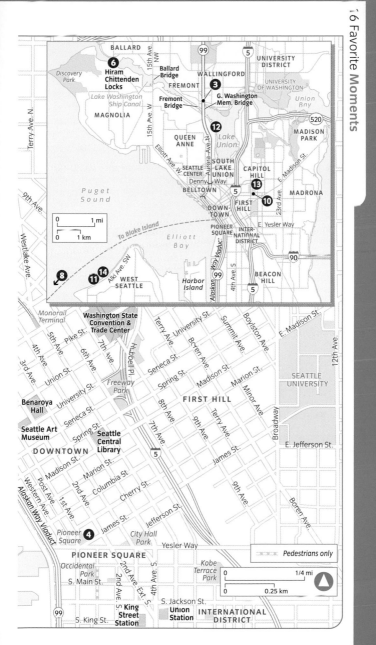

Detail map (lower portion):

Monorail Terminal

Washington State Convention & Trade Center

Benaroya Hall

Seattle Art Museum

DOWNTOWN

Seattle Central Library

Freeway Park

FIRST HILL

SEATTLE UNIVERSITY

Pioneer Square ❹

City Hall Park

PIONEER SQUARE

Occidental Park

Kobe Terrace Park

King Street Station

Union Station

INTERNATIONAL DISTRICT

Pedestrians only

**Main map labels:**

BALLARD

Discovery Park

❻ Hiram Chittenden Locks

Ballard Bridge

WALLINGFORD

Lake Washington Ship Canal

FREMONT

❸

Fremont Bridge

G. Washington Mem. Bridge

MAGNOLIA

QUEEN ANNE

❶❷ Lake Union

UNIVERSITY DISTRICT

UNIVERSITY OF WASHINGTON

Union Bay

MADISON PARK

Puget Sound

SEATTLE CENTER

SOUTH LAKE UNION

BELLTOWN

Denny Way

CAPITOL HILL

❶❸

❶⓪

FIRST HILL

MADRONA

DOWNTOWN

E. Yesler Way

To Blake Island

Elliott Bay

PIONEER SQUARE

INTER-NATIONAL DISTRICT

❽ ❶❶ ❶❹

WEST SEATTLE

Alki Ave. SW

Harbor Island

BEACON HILL

Perched near the edge of the continent, Seattle is a town that has always reached for the future. A land of extremes, the Emerald City is caffeine-driven yet laid-back, practical yet dreamy, soggy yet obsessive about the great outdoors. This pioneer-spirited town is a mix of the old and the new: from the former brothels of the Gold Rush era to the take-your-breath-away architecture of the Central Library. And where else will you find folks planted at a crosswalk in the pouring rain, nary a car in sight, clutching their lattes and waiting patiently for the crossing signal? Seattle is a quirky, endearing town, and here are a few things I like best about it.

❶ **Dodging the flying fish.** Working the crowds just behind Rachel, the giant piggybank that guards Seattle's beloved Pike Place Market, fishmonger-entertainers noisily toss salmon back and forth across the counter. Watch out for the "snapping" monkfish—and the Pike Place Fish Market staffer hiding behind the counter, string in hand, waiting for the next unsuspecting tourist. *See p 54.*

❷ **Spinning at the Space Needle.** On a clear day—or even a cloudy one—head to the Space Needle's SkyCity revolving restaurant for a uniquely Seattle dining experience. A trip to the observation deck is included in the price of your meal. Diners view the Emerald City from

The Space Needle has become a Seattle icon.

every angle as they rotate their way through lunch or dinner. Top off your meal with a fudgy Lunar Orbiter—complete with dry-ice Seattle "fog." *See p 132.*

❸ **Climbing on the troll.** Hunkered under the Aurora Bridge in the funky Fremont neighborhood is a menacing, shaggy-haired troll, clutching an actual Volkswagen Beetle in his gnarly left hand. Ill-tempered he may be, but he's never harmed any of the tourists who scramble up for photo-ops. *See p 78.*

❹ **Going down under.** Seattle wasn't always on the level—at least not the one folks walk on today. Down below historic Pioneer Square, Underground tour guides will lead you through subterranean passages that were once Seattle streets and relate spicy tales of the city's quirky and occasionally naughty early history. *See p 44.*

❺ **Riding a ferryboat.** Gliding across the Puget Sound is one of the best ways to enjoy this city, which is all about water. The passengers tapping away at their laptops are local commuters, taking advantage of the free Wi-Fi. Grab a scone and a latte on board, then head out one deck and enjoy the view. You can walk aboard or drive your car. *See p 18.*

❻ **Watching the fish climb.** At the Hiram M. Chittenden Locks, see the world's smartest salmon climb the

The Freemont Troll may look menacing, but he tolerates photo ops.

ladders, determined to get from Puget Sound to the lakes and streams where the next generation will begin a journey of its own. Be sure to wave at the boats going up and down in the locks. It's a Seattle tradition. *See p 106.*

7 Partying at Bumbershoot. Seattle celebrates summer like nobody's business. The mother of all the non-stop festivals is Bumbershoot, held at Seattle Center on Labor Day weekend to "welcome" back the rainy season. Expect most anything at eclectic Bumbershoot, from stilt-walkers to impromptu parades to sculptures made of "junk." *See p 101.*

8 Savoring salmon at Tillicum Village. The local Native Americans greeted Seattle's pioneer families warmly, and you'll get a taste of that hospitality here. As your boat lands, you'll be handed a bowl of steaming clams, then set free to explore Blake Island while salmon roasts in the longhouse. During dinner, enjoy an entertaining show of tribal dances and legends. The high-tech special effects are not exactly traditional, but pretty cool. *See p 25.*

9 Ringing in the New Year at the Needle. You've never seen fireworks like these. Exuberant explosions of color "climb" their way up

the Needle as festive music booms in the background. Get to Seattle Center around 10:30pm and stake out the highest spot you can find on the west side of the Center House, near the front. Then send someone inside to fetch hot cocoa and popcorn. *See p 9.*

10 Curling up with a book at Elliott Bay Book Company. Get lost in Seattle's favorite bookstore, which has packed up its tomes and moved from its longtime Pioneer Square location to great new digs on Capitol Hill. You'll find the same jaw-dropping collection, same knowledgeable staff, and you can still grab a bite at the Elliott Bay Café, which now has two locations. *See p 87.*

11 Soaking up the sun at Alki Beach. The Denny Party knew a good thing when they saw it, which is why they made Alki Beach the "Birthplace of Seattle" in 1851. Today, you can gaze across the Puget Sound at the Seattle skyline as you hike, skate, or walk along a 2-mile path skirting the sandy beach. Bikes, blades, and go-carts are available for rent. Word of warning: The water's chilly! *See p 17.*

Consider scheduling your visit to coincide with Bumbershoot, Seattle's world-famous city-wide festival.

No lawn-mowing is necessary at Seattle's famed houseboats.

⑫ Visiting the "neighbors." Rent a kayak and explore the charming floating "neighborhoods" on Lake Union. About 500 Seattleites live on the water, in boats of every size and shape—including the one featured in the movie *Sleepless in Seattle*. Just like any "city," there are some upscale areas and others populated by funky little vessels. *See p 102.*

⑬ People-watching on Capitol Hill. The grunge era lives on in this colorful neighborhood, where college students and hangers-on from the '90s still cling to the heyday of Seattle's music scene. Piercings and Mohawks abound, as do funky consignment shops, great little ethnic cafes with student-friendly prices, and some of the best lattes in town. *See p 66.*

⑭ Ogling the pirates. Seafair is a month of merriment and mischief, kicked off in early July by the Landing of the Pirates at Alki Beach. That's right, pirates . . . as in Vikings, whose blood coursed through the veins of Seattle's largely Scandinavian settlers. Nearly every neighborhood has its own Seafair festival. The zany Torchlight Parade in downtown Seattle is my personal favorite. *See p 101.*

⑮ Riding the monorail. Built for the 1962 World Fair, it's only a mile-long ride, but gliding above downtown is truly a Seattle experience. The monorail starts at Seattle Center and ends on the upper floor of the upscale Westlake Center. In between, you zoom through the center of the bizarre but fascinating Experience Music Project, an innovative museum designed by Frank Gehry and inspired by Seattle native Jimi Hendrix. From the air, the EMP looks like a smashed guitar; from the ground, it's anyone's guess! *See p 9.*

⑯ Sipping lots of lattes. You can't get a better cuppa joe anywhere in the world than right here, where the nation's espresso craze began. Even if you don't know your double-tall-skinny-no-whip from your venti-soy-half-calf, it's fun to make a pilgrimage to the original Starbucks at Pike Place Market. It's standing-room-only, so carry your cup with you as you browse the market stalls. *See p 39.* ●

Glide through the super futuristic Experience Music Project on the monorail.

The Best in **One Day**

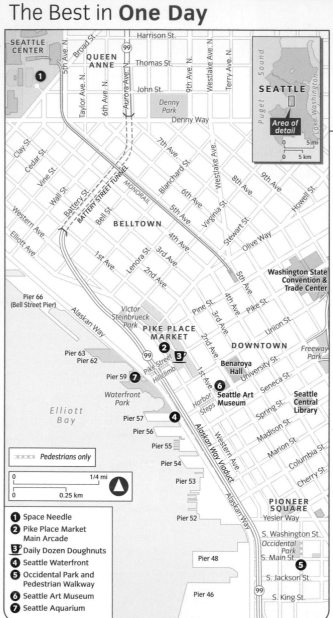

1 Space Needle
2 Pike Place Market Main Arcade
3 Daily Dozen Doughnuts
4 Seattle Waterfront
5 Occidental Park and Pedestrian Walkway
6 Seattle Art Museum
7 Seattle Aquarium

---- Pedestrians only

SEATTLE CENTER

QUEEN ANNE

Harrison St.
Thomas St.
John St.
Denny Park
Denny Way

Clay St.
Cedar St.
Vine St.
Wall St.
Bell St.

BELLTOWN

BATTERY STREET TUNNEL
MONORAIL

Battery St.
Blanchard St.
Virginia St.
Stewart St.
Olive Way
Pine St.
Pike St.

Western Ave.
Elliott Ave.

Pier 66
(Bell Street Pier)

Alaskan Way

Victor Steinbrueck Park

PIKE PLACE MARKET

Pike Street Hillclimb

Pier 63
Pier 62
Pier 59

Waterfront Park

Elliott Bay

Pier 57
Pier 56
Pier 55
Pier 54
Pier 53
Pier 52
Pier 48
Pier 46

Washington State Convention & Trade Center

DOWNTOWN

Benaroya Hall

Seattle Art Museum

Harbor Steps

Freeway Park

Union St.
University St.
Seneca St.
Spring St.
Madison St.
Marion St.
Columbia St.
Cherry St.

Seattle Central Library

Western Ave.
Alaskan Way Viaduct
Alaskan Way

PIONEER SQUARE
Yesler Way
S. Washington St.
Occidental Park
S. Main St.
S. Jackson St.
S. King St.

0   1/4 mi
0   0.25 km

SEATTLE

Puget Sound
Lake Washington

Area of detail

0   5 mi
0   5 km

Sure, you can drive, but parking spots in Seattle are scarce and pricey. One of the most compact big cities in the country, the Emerald City is easy—and just plain fun—to navigate on foot. This sampler-platter tour roams from one end of town to the other. As you wander, always check out the incline. If it's steep ahead, walk a block farther and you'll likely find flatter ground. But don't worry too much about tiring yourself out—there are plenty of places to rest your weary feet while enjoying the eclectic street scene.

START: Monorail or bus 3, 4, 8, 16, or 30 to Seattle Center.

1 ★★★ kids **Space Needle.** Part retro, part futuristic, more than a touch eccentric, the Needle is the perfect symbol for Seattle. It was built for the World's Fair in 1962 after an artist sketched out a space-age focal point for the event on a place-mat at—where else?—a local coffee shop. Lines for the glass elevator ride up to the observation deck can be long in summertime, but it's worth the wait—just try to not get shoved to the back, or you'll miss the view on the way up. The typical Seattle mist only makes the view from the top that much dreamier. Your ticket to the top includes a free digital download from the Space Needle's photography department. You can also have lunch or dinner at the revolving SkyCity restaurant (reservations highly recommended) and rotate around the town while you dine. Pick up a special dining ticket on the ground floor, and you won't have to pay to go to the top. ⏱ *1 hr. Summer weekends are busiest. 400 Broad St.* ☎ *206/905-2100. www.spaceneedle. com. Observation deck tickets: $18 adults, $16 seniors, $11 ages 4–13. Mon–Thurs 10am–11pm; Fri–Sat 9:30am–11:30pm; Sun 9:30am–11pm.*

2 ★★★ kids **Pike Place Market Main Arcade.** The heart and soul of Seattle, Pike Place is home to those famous flying fish, which you'll spot right behind Rachel, the porcine bank. With just one day, you won't have time to go Down Under, but there's plenty to overwhelm the senses on the Market's top floor. Street musicians turn junk into instruments, farmers hawk a spectacular assortment of locally grown produce—which you can taste at many of Seattle's finest restaurants—and local artists display an eclectic array of talents, from

Travel Tip

Even though Seattle's fun to walk, there may be times when your feet need a break. To get downtown from Seattle Center—home of the Space Needle (see bullet **1** above)—hop on the monorail ($4 round-trip for adults, $1.50 for ages 5–12, $2 for seniors) for the short ride to Westlake Center. From there, take a metro bus—free from 6am until 7pm—anywhere in the downtown, Pioneer Square, Pike Place Market and waterfront neighborhoods. You can catch a bus on the street, or in the bus tunnel, conveniently located underneath Westlake Center.

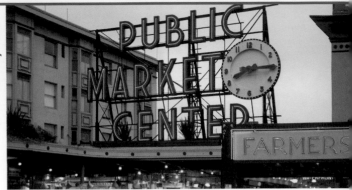

Pike Place Market is far more than a farmers market and is well worth exploring.

kazoo-making to wood-carving. The Market is a great place to sample some tasty wares and shop for high-quality souvenirs. My weakness is for the lavish bouquets of flowers, fresh from the fields in nearby lush valleys. They cost half what you'd pay at a grocery store for a much smaller spray. ⏱ *1 hr. Pike Place and Pike St.* ☎ *206/682-7453. www.pikeplacemarket.org. Mon–Sat 10am–6pm; Sun 11am–5pm.*

🖰 **Daily Dozen Doughnuts.** Around the corner from the Main Arcade, in the Economy Building, follow your nose to this heavenly kiosk. Don't let the line discourage you! These light confections, fresh from the fryer, are nothing like their heavier cousins you've encountered at some doughnut shops. Might as well buy two dozen while you're at it! *93 Pike St.* ☎ *206/467-7769.*

❹ ★★ **kids** **Seattle Water-front.** From Pike Place Market, take the elevator downhill and cross the street to Seattle's sparkling Elliott Bay, where you can amble from pier to pier. The waterfront is always lively, and the smell is a pleasant mix of saltwater and fresh

fish and chips, available at stands along the way. If you have little ones, a stop at Pier 57's Bay Pavilion is a must. Pirates Plunder gift shop has every kind of sea-scalawag item imaginable; at the back of the pavilion, an antique carousel and game room offer a fun break. But the harbor is not all about play; it's a real working waterfront, one of the busiest in the nation. To get a good look at all the action, stop by Waterfront Park, which stretches between Piers 57 and 61, and peer through the free telescopes out at the barges, tugboats and ferryboats coming and going on the bay. ⏱ *1 hr.*

The Lunar Orbiter desert, complete with dry ice "steam," at SkyCity restaurant.

—

5 Occidental Park and Pedestrian Walkway. From the waterfront, walk or take the free bus 99 to Jackson Street and Occidental Avenue. The bricked walkway occupies one block; the park claims the block to the north. In this area you'll find a sampling of Seattle's avant garde art galleries, Victorian-Romanesque buildings constructed hurriedly during the Gold Rush, and **Glasshouse Studio,** 311 Occidental Ave. S. (☎ 206/682-9939), where you can watch skilled glass-blowers at work. Several totem poles tower over visitors, and the Fallen Firefighter's Memorial pays tribute to those who have lost their lives battling Seattle's fires. ⏱ *1 hr. Occidental Ave. & Jackson St.*

6 ★★★ Seattle Art Museum. SAM's eclectic global collections include Northwest Native American, Pan Asian, African, European and American modern art. The first-rate special exhibits have included the U.S. debut of a major Picasso show. The museum offers lots of activities for kids in conjunction with the displays. Despite its world-class reputation, SAM has a friendly feel, with a passionate staff that treats visitors as honored guests. SAM's permanent collections are on display at no charge the first Thursday of every month; free to seniors the first Friday; and free for teens the second

The Seattle Aquarium offers a view into life in Puget Sound.

Friday from 5–9pm. ⏱ *2 hr. 1300 1st Ave.* ☎ *206/654-3100. www.seattleartmuseum.org. Admission $15 adults, $12 seniors over 62, $9 students & kids 13–17, free for kids 12 & under. Hours: Wed–Sun 10am–5pm; Thurs–Fri 10am–9pm.*

7 ★★ kids Seattle Aquarium. This is a sealife-lover's dream come true. The aquarium's pride and joy, a 40-foot-by-20-foot viewing window, gives visitors a glimpse of the intriguing creatures that swim in the Puget Sound. Divers interact with fish in the tank several times a day, while volunteers explain what's going on. The aquarium is perched on a pier overhanging the sound, so many of these animals are also swimming under your feet. Don't miss the giant Pacific octopus—the largest in the world. ⏱ *2 hr. 1483 Alaskan Way on Pier 59.* ☎ *206/386-4300. www.seattleaquarium.org. Admission $17 adults, $11 ages 4–13. Daily 9:30am–5pm (exhibits close at 6pm).*

Good Deal

A CityPass (888/330-5008; www.citypass.com) is one of the best deals is town. You can visit five popular Seattle destinations for half-price (if you take them all in). Better yet, you don't have to wait in line. The passes will get you into the Space Needle, Seattle Aquarium, Pacific Science Center, Woodland Park Zoo, an Argosy Cruises harbor tour of Elliott Bay, and the option of either the Museum of Flight or Experience Music Project/Science Fiction Museum. A CityPass costs $59 for adults and $39 for kids ages 4–12. You can buy them at any of the included attractions, or order them ahead from the website.

The Best in **Two Days**

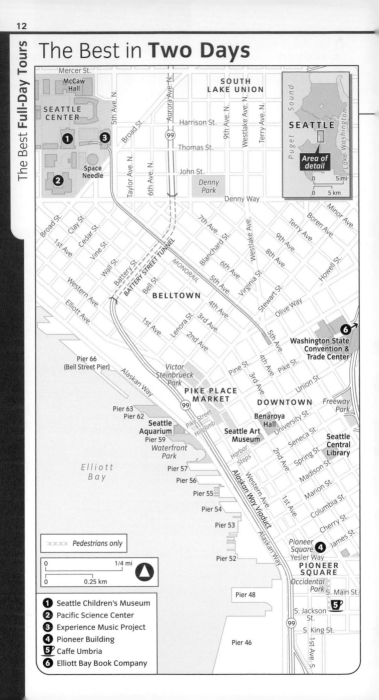

Mercer St.

McCaw Hall

SEATTLE CENTER

Space Needle

SOUTH LAKE UNION

Harrison St.

Thomas St.

John St.

Denny Park

Denny Way

SEATTLE

Area of detail

Puget Sound

Lake Washington

0   5 mi
0   5 km

BELLTOWN

BATTERY STREET TUNNEL

MONORAIL

Denny Way

Battery St.

Bell St.

Lenora St.

Wall St.

Clay St.

Cedar St.

Vine St.

Broad St.

1st Ave.

Western Ave.

Elliott Ave.

Taylor Ave. N.

6th Ave. N.

5th Ave. N.

Aurora Ave. N.

9th Ave. N.

Westlake Ave. N.

Terry Ave. N.

Broad St.

Thomas St.

Harrison St.

7th Ave.

Blanchard St.

Westlake Ave.

6th Ave.

Virginia St.

5th Ave.

4th Ave.

3rd Ave.

2nd Ave.

1st Ave.

Terry Ave.

Boren Ave.

9th Ave.

8th Ave.

Stewart St.

Olive Way

Minor Ave.

Howell St.

Washington State Convention & Trade Center

Pier 66 (Bell Street Pier)

Alaskan Way

Pier 63
Pier 62

Seattle Aquarium
Pier 59

Waterfront Park

Elliott Bay

Pier 57

Pier 56

Pier 55

Pier 54

Pier 53

Pier 52

Pier 48

Pier 46

Victor Steinbrueck Park

PIKE PLACE MARKET

Pike Street Hillclimb

Harbor Steps

Alaskan Way Viaduct

Western Ave.

2nd Ave.

1st Ave.

Alaskan Way

Pine St.

Pike St.

Union St.

University St.

Seneca St.

Spring St.

Madison St.

Marion St.

Columbia St.

Cherry St.

James St.

Yesler Way

4th Ave.

3rd Ave.

5th Ave.

DOWNTOWN

Benaroya Hall

Seattle Art Museum

Seattle Central Library

Freeway Park

Pioneer Square

PIONEER SQUARE

Occidental Park

S. Main St.

S. Jackson St.

S. King St.

1st Ave. S.

Pedestrians only

0   1/4 mi
0   0.25 km

1 Seattle Children's Museum
2 Pacific Science Center
3 Experience Music Project
4 Pioneer Building
5 Caffe Umbria
6 Elliott Bay Book Company

The first day was the sampler platter of Seattle highlights; now it's time to go back and spend some quality time at **Seattle Center,** the city's favorite place to hang out; and at two other stops that offer the quintessential Seattle experience.
START: **Monorail or bus 3, 4, 8, 16, or 30 to Seattle Center.**

❶ ★ kids Seattle Children's Museum. Inside the Center House, near the Space Needle at Seattle Center, you'll see the children's museum below, visible through a railed opening in the floor. The bright colors and enchanted forest are irresistible to kids, so hop on the glass elevator and ride down to the museum. On the fourth Wednesday of each month, the Family Fun Series offers an activity for the whole family, including a snack and a take-home project. ⏱ *60 min. 305 Harrison St.* ☎ *206/441-1768. www.thechildrensmuseum.org. $7.50.*

The dinosaurs that prowl the Pacific Science Center are fun for kids and adults alike.

adults and children, free under age 1. Mon–Fri 10am–5pm, Sat–Sun 10am–6pm.

❷ ★★ kids Pacific Science Center. *Do touch!* is the rule at this museum at Seattle Center. There's plenty here to interest all ages, but this is mainly a youth-focused museum. Kids love the animatronic dinosaurs, the butterfly garden, and the Body Works area, where they can put their own physical abilities to the test. There are buttons to press, levers to pull, animals to touch, a playground for tiny tots, and special exhibits ranging from bubbles to snakes. You can gaze at the stars in the planetarium, and watch exciting laser shows (Thurs through Sun nights, plus Sat and Sun afternoons) set to music by the likes of The Beatles, Michael Jackson, and Led Zeppelin. The IMAX theaters show movies for varying ages. ⏱ *2 hr. 200 2nd Ave. N.* ☎ *206/443-2001. www.pacsci.org. Admission $14 adults, $12 seniors, $9 ages 6–15, $7 ages 3–5. IMAX: $9–$14 adults, $8–$12 seniors, $7–$11 ages 6–15, $6–$9 ages 3–5; discounts available for combination passes. Mon–Fri 10am–5pm; Sat–Sun 10am–6pm.*

❸ ★ Experience Music Project. Microsoft billionaire Paul Allen's monument to home-grown Seattle rock legend Jimi Hendrix features lots of interactive exhibits on music ranging from soul to rock to hip-hop. You can record your own CD in the Jam Studio, using guitars, drums, keyboard, and voice. With

Be sure to explore the remains of old Seattle, which lie a full story beneath the modern city, on the Underground Tour.

www.undergroundtour.com; $15 adults, $12 seniors, $12 youth ages 13–17, $7 children 7–12; offered daily, throughout the day), which takes you beneath the sidewalks to view the remnants of the original pioneer town, a full story lower than the rebuilt city. (It seems there was a little problem with sewage coming back in with the tides.) You'll get a 90-minute lowdown (literally) on the era's get-rich-quick schemers, gold-crazy prospectors, and colorful women who listed their occupation as "seamstress," though they seldom produced a stitch. Some of the content is mature, but it should go right over the heads of the little ones. In any case, they'll be more fascinated by the stories of the rats that once roamed the streets. The guides are witty, and they know their stuff. 🕐 *90 min. 1st Ave. & Yesler Way.*

Music-lovers and fans of modern architecture will both find something to love at the Experience Music Project.

this technology, you don't need an instrument—or even talent. Through mid-April 2013, the EMP is hosting a blockbuster exhibit called "Nirvana: Taking Punk to the Masses," complete with the first guitar Kurt Cobain destroyed onstage. Within the EMP, the Science Fiction Museum is worth a look, too. Both are housed in a stunning Frank Gehry–designed building meant to look from above like one of Jimi's guitars. From the street, it looks more like an undulating blob of metal. 🕐 *90 min. 325 5th Ave. N. (at Seattle Center). ☎ 206/770-2700. www.empsfm.org. Admission $15 adults, $12 seniors/ ages 5–17. Late May–early Sept daily 10am–7pm; early Sept–late May 10am–5pm.*

❹ ★★ **Pioneer Building.** This historic grand dame now houses **Doc Maynard's Pub** and the popular **Underground Tour,** 608 1st Ave #200 (☎ **206/682-4646;**

Whether you indulge in gelato or a latte, Caffe Umbria is a haven for weary walkers.

⑥ ★★★ Elliott Bay Book Company. In its "new" location—a 20,000-square-foot historic 1917 building on quirky Capitol Hill—Elliott Bay still feels like Seattle's comfy living room. An old Ford truck service center, the space has fir floors and massive ceiling beams. Seattlcites love to while away the hours here, perusing more than 150,000 books. Your challenge: not to bring home more than you can fit in your carry-on! ⏱ *60 min. 1521 10th Ave.* ☎ *206/624-6600. www. elliottbaybook.com. Mon–Thurs 10am–1pm; Fri–Sat 10am–11pm; Sun 11am–9pm.*

5 ★ The Emerald City is not exactly known for balmy weather, but that's never kept a Seattleite from indulging in a frozen treat—like the sinfully creamy gelato at **Caffe Umbria.** My favorites are cappuccino and pistachio. Sit at the window bar and gaze out at the passersby, or grab an outside table on a sunny day. The panini sandwiches and croissants are fresh and delicious. *320 Occidental Ave. S.* ☎ *206/624-5847. Mon–Fri 6am–6pm; Sat 7am–6pm; Sun 8am–5pm.*

Get in from the rain at the Elliott Bay Book Company, housed in a historic 1917 building on Capitol Hill.

Seattle Makes Music

The Kingsmen, Jimi Hendrix, Heart, Queensrÿche, Pearl Jam, Nirvana, Alice in Chains, Death Cab for Cutie, Modest Mouse—Seattle seems to spawn great music. Since the 1950s, the Emerald City has been famous for its garage bands that end up going big-time. The "Louis Louis" phenomenon began when the Wailers from Tacoma (just south of Seattle) recorded the song in 1960 and it became a radio hit. (A couple of years later, two Northwest bands from a bit farther south—Portland, Ore.—recorded the same song: The Kingsmen and Paul Revere and the Raiders.) In the 1990s, Seattle's Kurt Cobain and his band Nirvana kicked off the grunge era that made Seattle arguably the hippest place on the planet. The tradition lives on in Seattle's contemporary rockers, like Modest Mouse.

The Best in **Three Days**

1 Harbor Tour
2 Alki Beach
3 Alki Bakery and Café
4 Ferryboat to Bainbridge Island
5 Winslow
6 Elliott's Oyster House

To fully appreciate Seattle, you need to get out on the water. After all, nearly half the city is immersed in the stuff! Plenty of fun awaits, whether you want to row, paddle, or sit back and relax while someone else navigates the lakes, canals, and bays. START: **Bus 16, 66, or 99 to Seattle Waterfront, Pier 55.**

❶★★ Harbor Tour. A lively, informative tour of Seattle's working harbor lasts just an hour—perfect to keep the kids enthralled as the boat cruises past dry docks, tugboats, and one of the world's largest shipping terminals. . . not to mention the great views of Seattle's distinctive downtown skyline. The popular harbor tour—drawing crowds since 1949— leaves at 1:30pm every day, and varying additional times depending on the day and season. If an hour isn't long enough, you can choose from a variety of other dinner and pleasure cruises. *Argosy Cruises (☎ 1-888/623-1445; www.argosy cruises.com) leaves from Pier 55, Seattle Waterfront. Prices (including sales tax): $17.25 Jan–Mar and Oct–Dec and $22 Apr–Sept for adults; $8.50 Jan–Mar and Oct–Dec and $9.75 Apr–Sept for ages 5–12.* ⏱ *1 hr.*

❷ ★★★ Alki Beach. This is the best beach in Seattle—though technically, it's in West Seattle, where the settlers first arrived. The mood is festive, the view of Elliott Bay and the Seattle skyline breathtaking, and the water is always—even in the summertime—very chilly. That doesn't keep the locals from taking a dip, even in the cooler months when a wetsuit is needed. From spring through fall you can zip across Elliott Bay from the Seattle Waterfront on the water taxi. In the wintertime, you'll need to drive over the West Seattle Bridge and take the Harbor Avenue/Avalon Way exit, then turn right onto Harbor Avenue and bear left at Alki Avenue. This wide, sandy beach has a great **promenade** for walkers, joggers, and roller-bladers, and you can rent bikes or go-carts at shops across from the beach. Cafes

The Alki Beach Promenade gives walkers and bikers a gorgeous view of the Seattle skyline.

and shops line the street across from the water, so you need never go hungry. ⏱ 2½ hr.

3 **Alki Bakery and Café**. If all the salt air makes you long for something sweet, head across the street for pastries and coffee. You can also get more substantial fare: sandwiches, pasta, or seafood. Enjoy your snack outside, with the panoramic ocean and mountain view thrown in for free! *2738 Alki Ave. SW.* ☎ *206/935-1352. $*

4 ★★ **Ferryboat to Bainbridge Island.** Washington State runs the largest ferry system in the country, and this line is very popular with commuters. You could plug in your laptop and check e-mail for free, but don't do it. Instead, grab a cup of coffee and a raspberry scone at the onboard cafe, then go out on deck and enjoy the 35-minute ride. If you walk onto the ferry, arrive 15 minutes early; if you drive your car on (not recommended), come at least 20 to 30 minutes ahead. Drive-on wait times can be much longer during rush hours. *Catch the ferryboat at the Seattle Ferry Terminal at Pier 52 (*☎ *206/464-6400; www. wsdot.wa.gov/ferries; fares $6.90 for adults, $3.45 for seniors, $5.55 for children, $14.85 for car & driver; check schedules for departure times).*

5 ★★ **Walk through Winslow.** Once you're on the island, follow the crowds walking into the charming town of Winslow, where you can roam the art galleries, taste some wine, and do some shopping on **Winslow Way**. A great place to see the work of hundreds of area artists—both new and seasoned—is the nonprofit gallery **Bainbridge Arts and Crafts** (151 Winslow Way E., ☎ **206/ 842-3132,** Mon–Sat 10am–6pm, Sun 11am–5pm). For a great cup of java, turn left (toward the water) at Madison Avenue South, then right onto Parfitt Way Southeast, and stroll over to **Pegasus Coffee House and Gallery** (131 Parfitt Way SW, ☎ **206/842-6725**), a picturesque, ivy-covered brick shop on the waterfront that roasts its own tasty beans. ⏱ *3 hr.*

6 ★★ **kids** **Elliott's Oyster House.** Back in Seattle, this is a great place to stop for fresh local seafood. Or head for the raw bar if you just need an oyster fix. It's the perfect place to wrap up a day on the water. *1201 Alaskan Way, Pier 56.* ☎ *206/623-4340. www.elliotts oysterhouse.com. $$.* ●

Riding the ferry is half the fun of a trip to Bainbridge Island.

The Best Special-Interest Tours

Seattle **Heritage**

1 Museum of Flight

2 Klondike Gold Rush National Historical Park

3 Wing Luke Asian Museum

4 Museum of History & Industry

5 Burke Museum of History and Culture

6 Nordic Heritage Museum

7 Enlighten Café & Art Gallery

8 Tillicum Village

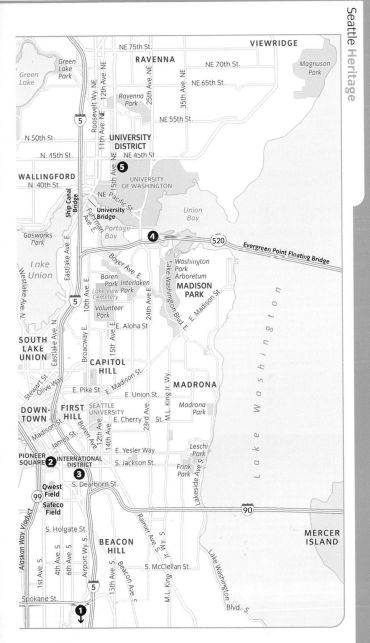

When it comes to historic roots, Seattle may not compare to a city like Boston, but the Emerald City has such a colorful past, kids and adults alike get caught up in the fun. This tour will take you on an exploration from the days before the arrival of Europeans to the birth of the aerospace industry that helped modern Seattle take flight. START: **Bus 124, 154, 173 to the Museum of Flight.**

① ★★★ **kids** **Museum of Flight.** The focus here is the contemporary era—relatively speaking, that is, since the history of aviation goes back pretty far in Seattle. This top-flight museum will amaze anyone intrigued by the human species' dream of escaping the bonds of earth. The historic Red Barn (Boeing's first manufacturing building), houses exhibits on early aviation, including the mail bag carried by William E. Boeing and Eddie Hubbard on the first international U.S. Air Mail flight from Vancouver, BC, to Seattle in 1919. The exhibit ends with the Boeing 707, which ushered in the jet age. The cavernous Great Gallery features dozens of historic aircraft, many of them hanging from the ceiling as though in flight. Visitors can climb into the cockpit of a real Blackbird, the fastest jet ever made. The Personal Courage Wing tells the stories of fighter aviators in World Wars I and II. And at the Airpark, you can view legendary aircraft including the Concorde and the first jet Air Force One. The simulator exhibit lets you try virtual flight and hang-gliding. The museum is building a 6.5-acre Space Gallery in hopes of giving one of the three retiring Space Shuttles a permanent home before the end of 2011. ⏱ *90 min.* ☎ *206/764-5720. www.museum offlight.org. 9404 E. Marginal Way S. $15 adults, $13 seniors, $8 ages 5–17, free 4 & under. Free 5–9pm 1st Thurs of every month. Daily 11am–4:30pm.*

② ★ **kids** **Klondike Gold Rush National Historical Park.** You're bound to catch Gold Fever as you listen to the tales of Yukon-bound prospectors and their families who passed through Seattle, and view personal items they left along the way. This is not only a

The aviation industry played a major role in Seattle's social and economic development.

At the interactive Klondike Gold Rush International Historical Park, you'll learn everything you ever wanted to know about the Gold Rush.

museum but also a national park. Kids can earn honest-to-gosh Junior Ranger badges by filling in an activity book based on information gleaned from the two floors of exhibits. This keeps them conveniently busy while the grown-ups enjoy the displays. Films on the Gold Rush and Seattle's role in the mania are shown frequently. In the summer, you can watch gold-panning demonstrations twice a day or take a walking tour of Pioneer Square, led by a park ranger. ⏱ *1 hr. 319 2nd Ave. S.* ☎ *206/220-4240. www.nps.gov/klse. Free admission. Daily 9am–5pm.*

❸ ★★ Wing Luke Asian Museum. The Wing Luke celebrates the many Asian cultures that have emigrated to the Pacific Northwest. Its main exhibit, "Honoring Our Journey," tells the 200-year-old story of Asians and Pacific Islanders settling in Washington. Temporary exhibits have included refugees' personal stories. "Camp Harmony

D-4-44" re-created a livestock stall converted into a family holding cell, barbed wire and all, for Japanese Americans being sent to internment camps in 1942. The museum is housed in the former home of the

Explore the influence of Asian immigrants to Seattle at the Wing Luke Asian Museum.

historic Freeman Hotel, where many early Asian immigrants lived while working in the canneries and lumber mills. 🕐 *1 hr.* ☎ *206/623-5124. 719 S. King St. (South King St. & 8th Ave. South) $12.95 adults, 95¢ seniors & students, 95¢ ages 5–12. Price includes tour of historic building/former hotel. Tues–Sun 10am–5pm, 1st Thurs of month & 2nd Sat of month 10am–8pm.*

❹ ★★ Museum of History & Industry (MOHAI).

It may not have the most exciting name, but there is nothing dull about this museum. It's a great way to learn about Northwest history through riveting, often hands-on exhibits and historic photos. You can amble along the "sidewalks" of pre-fire Seattle, which would soon be reduced to ashes by the Great Fire of 1889. The exhibit includes the very glue pot believed to have

Learn about Seattle's past, including the Great Fire that destroyed much of the city, at the Museum of History & Industry.

started the blaze. MOHAI is slated to move in 2012 to the shores of Lake Union, where the historic landmark Naval Reserve Building will be renovated to house its new tenant. 🕐 *1 hr.* ☎ *206/324-1126. 2700 24th Ave E. $7 adults, $5 ages 5–17 & seniors, free 4 & under. Also, free first Thurs of each month. Daily 10am–5pm, first Thurs 10 am–8pm.*

❺ ★★ kids Burke Museum of Natural History and Culture.

I love this museum on the tree-lined campus of the University of Washington because it's doable in a couple of hours, and it's all about Washington: from 40 million-year-old fossils to an extensive Native American arts collection. Dino Times, with its dinosaur skeletons and walk-through volcano, is enormously fun, and the cultural showcases are engaging and unique. 🕐 *1 hr. 17th Ave. NE and NE 45th St.* ☎ *206/543-5590. www.washington. edu/burkemuseum. $9.50 adults, $7.50 seniors, $6 students & youth, free 4 & under. Daily 10am–5pm. Free 1st Thurs of month.*

❻ ★ Nordic Heritage Museum.

This unassuming two-story museum is the only one in the country that celebrates the history of the five Nordic countries, many of whose descendants call the Pacific Northwest home. My favorite exhibit brings to life the arrival of early Scandinavian immigrants, via Ellis Island, to the land of their dreams. You can feel the excitement, and then the chaos of their new adventure. Each country—Denmark, Finland, Iceland, Norway, and Sweden—has a room at the museum to tell its story and show off its art and culture. Lots of kids' programs are offered, as well as classes in Nordic folk arts. 🕐 *1 hr. 3014 NW 67th St.* ☎ *206/789-5707. www.nordicmuseum.org. $6 adults,*

Seattle Takes Shape

In 1852, a windy, rain-drenched winter prompted Seattle's founders to move from Alki Point (now in West Seattle), where they had landed the previous year, to the more sheltered eastern shore of Elliott Bay. The reason for the zany layout of the town they created—now the Pioneer Square neighborhood—was the lack of agreement among the city fathers (and possibly the chronic drunkenness of at least one) about which direction the roads should go. Perhaps not surprisingly, squabbling over roads became a Seattle tradition. Thirty-five years later, Seattle struck it rich when gold was discovered in the Yukon. Would-be prospectors stocked up on supplies before they headed out to the gold fields; on the way back, those who had struck it rich dropped a large percentage of their profits here. After the fire in 1889, Seattle's businessmen, frantic at missing out on profits, scrambled to rebuild their city. They built fast, but they built to last.

$5 seniors and students, $4 children over 5. Tues–Sat 10 am–4pm, Sun noon–4pm.

7 ★ Enlighten Café & Art Gallery. Sip a cup of java or gourmet tea, or indulge in a glass of wine, as you nibble on a decadent pastry and enjoy the artsy surroundings. If you love the beautiful wood furniture—or the lamps—you can take them home! *5424 Ballard Ave. NW. ☎ 206/706-0910. $.*

8 ★★★ kids Tillicum Village. Rewind to pre-European times in the Northwest. The local Indian tribes may have lived to regret their initial hospitality to the white settlers who landed at Alki Point and who, many years later, drove the Native Americans onto second-rate reservation land. But at Tillicum Village, the hospitality is in full force as a number of local tribes cooperatively present a salmon bake in the longhouse, then perform traditional dances illustrating creation stories. Skilled tribal artists carve masks and other items, many of which can be purchased. The setting is deeply forested Blake Island, believed to be an ancient campground of the Duwamish and Suquamish tribes, and the likely birthplace of Chief Seattle. There's a playground for children, and you'll likely spot a few deer. Now a state park, it can be reached only by boat. *4 hr. ☎ 206/933-8600. http://www.tillicumvillage.com. Argosy Cruises offers rides to and from Tillicum Village, leaving from Pier 55 on the Seattle waterfront. Price with the cruise: $80 adults, $73 seniors, $30 ages 5–12; free age 4 & under. Dates & times vary by month.*

Seattle for **Art Lovers**

U DISTRICT

NE Campus Pkwy. **6**

UNIVERSITY OF WASHINGTON

N. 40th St.

N. 39th St.

N. 36th St.

WALLINGFORD

FREMONT

N. 35th St.

N. 34th St.

Gasworks Park

Ship Canal

University Bridge

NE Pacific St.

Fremont Bridge

G. Washington Mem. Bridge

Portage Bay

520

Queen Anne Dr.

Lake Union

Interlaken Park

Boren Park

Lake View Cemetery

E. Galer St.

QUEEN ANNE

Boston St.

Volunteer Park **5**

E. Aloha St.

LOWER QUEEN ANNE

Roy St.

Mercer St. **7**

SEATTLE CENTER

Valley St.

Mercer St.

SOUTH LAKE UNION

Denny Park

Denny Way

CAPITOL HILL

E. Roy St.

Broadway

E. John St.

E. Thomas St.

Olympic Sculpture Park

BELLTOWN

MONORAIL

SCCC

Cal Anderson Park

E. Pine St.

E. Pike St.

Pine St.

Pike St.

Stewart St.

Olive Way

Howell St.

PIKE PLACE MARKET

DOWNTOWN

Union St.

University St.

Seneca St.

E. Madison St.

E. Union St.

1

3

2

Waterfront Park

Elliott Bay

Alaskan Way Viaduct

FIRST HILL

SEATTLE UNIVERSITY

Madison St.

4

James St.

E. Cherry St.

PIONEER SQUARE

Yesler Way

Qwest Field

INTERNATIONAL DISTRICT

1	Seattle Art Museum
2	Cherry Street Coffee House
3	Benaroya Hall
4	Frye Art Museum
5	Seattle Asian Art Museum
6	Henry Art Gallery
7	Marion Oliver McCaw Hall

0   1/2 mi

0   0.5 km

The Emerald City has always supported the arts with its extra cash, whether from gold, aerospace- or dot-com mania. The Pacific Northwest is known for its public art, particularly sculptures, and for its Venetian-influenced glass. Renowned home-grown glass artist Dale Chihuly launched an American glass-art movement in the late 1960s that is still going strong in Seattle.

START: **Bus 212, 216, 217, 255, 256 to Seattle Art Museum.**

The Hammering Man looms over the Seattle Art Museum.

1 ★★★ Seattle Art Museum. You'll know you're there when you see the hardworking Hammering Man, a 48-foot tribute to the working classes who shaped Seattle's character. Appropriately, the arm of the animated outdoor sculpture, designed by Jonathan Borofsky, gets a rest every year on Labor Day. The recently expanded museum's first two beautiful floors are free of charge, including the Brotman Forum, which features changing exhibits and Cai Guo-Qiang's fanciful sculpture of nine cars falling across the space. Special traveling exhibits and art from around the world fill the rest of the museum. ⏱ *2 hr. 1300 1st Ave.* ☎ *206/654-3100. www.seattle artmuseum.org. Admission $15*

adults, $12 seniors 62 & over, $9 students & children 13–17, free children 12 & under. Wed–Sun 10am–5pm; Thurs–Fri 10am–9pm. See p 65.

2 ★ Cherry Street Coffee House. While you're in an artsy mood, stop for a snack at this chic cafe, which showcases the works of local artists. The coffee is great, and so are the soups and sandwiches. If you're a carnivore, try their famous BLT; if not, you'll love the home-made veggie burgers. *1212 1st Ave.* ☎ *206/264-9372. $.*

3 ★★ Benaroya Hall. Home to the Seattle Symphony, the Benaroya is aesthetically and acoustically state of the art. Check the website for concert and other event dates. If you have children, check out the Tiny Tots and Discover Music! Performances. Even if you can't attend a concert, the hall is worth a stop to ogle the

World-famous glass artist Dale Chihuly designed the dramatic chandeliers at Benroya Hall.

Olympic Sculpture Park

You won't have to be cooped up indoors to enjoy this relative newcomer to Seattle's art scene. Run by the Seattle Art Museum, the **Olympic Sculpture Park** (2901 Western Ave.; ☎ **206/654-3100**) is a unique outdoor sculpture park that features 9 acres of very large permanent and traveling exhibits. Added bonus: It's all right on the waterfront. From *Father and Son,* a double fountain by Louise Bourgeois that captures a sometimes problematic relationship, to *Eagle* by Alexander Calder, an abstract work on wings of fancy, the creations are both fun and thought-provoking. Admission is free, and the park is open daily from 30 minutes before sunrise to 30 minutes after sunset. Free hour-long tours are available through the **Seattle Art Museum** (☎ **206/654-3100**) at noon and 1pm on Saturday and Sunday.

dazzling, spiraling glass chandeliers by world-famous Seattle glass artist Dale Chihuly. 🕐 *30 min. 200 University St. ☎ 206/215-4800. www.seattle symphony.org. Ticket prices vary; free admission to see the chandeliers or browse at the Benaroya gift shop.*

❹ ★ Frye Art Museum.
Charles and Emma Frye, German immigrants who made their fortune

Kids are welcome to climb on the stone camels outside the Seattle Asian Art Museum.

in gold-mad Seattle, left their immense collection of then-contemporary art to the city to be displayed in one location. Thus was born the Frye. Its collected representational works—portraits, still lifes, landscapes—are by 19th- and 20th-century French, German, and American painters. But in recent years, the museum has re-invented itself, adding modern and abstract art to the collection. These new works are often intriguingly juxtaposed with paintings that once hung in the Fryes' living room or meat house. 🕐 *1 hr. 704 Terry Ave. ☎ 206/622-9250. www.fryeart.org. As mandated by Charles Frye, admission is free. Tues–Sun 11am–5pm; Thurs open until 7pm.*

❺ ★ kids Seattle Asian Art Museum. Set in the middle of lovely **Volunteer Park** (p 67) and operated by the Seattle Art Museum, SAAM features a stunning collection of historic and contemporary art from a variety of Asian cultures. If you love Eastern art—or want to learn more about it—this is the perfect venue. Most of the exhibits won't appeal greatly to younger kids, but they love playing in the child-size Japanese house. Shoes off first, of course! Kids also love climbing on the life-size camel statues that kneel on either side of the outside entrance. Don't miss (it would be hard to) Isamu Noguchi's captivating *Black Sun* outside the museum. A photo of the Space Needle taken through the statue's open center makes a great souvenir. ⏱ *1 hr. 1400 E. Prospect St.* ☎ *206/ 654-3100. www.seattleartmuseum. org. $7 adults, $5 seniors, students & ages 13–17, free 12 & under, Wed–Sun 10am–5pm; Thurs until 9pm, free first Thurs (& first Sat to families) of each month.*

6 ★★ Henry Art Gallery. Old world meets new at the Henry, where you can find works by masters such as Rembrandt, but also avant-garde photography and sculpture. The Henry's solid reputation has soared since its mega-expansion a few years ago. One of its most popular permanent exhibits is James Turrell's riveting *Skyspace*, which turns light—both natural and artificial—into ever-changing art. ⏱ *1 hr. University of Washington campus, 15th Ave. NE and NE 41st St.* ☎ *206/543-2280. www.henryart. org. Wed 11am–4pm; Thurs–Fri 11am–9pm; Sat–Sun 11am–4pm $10 adults, $6 seniors, free for students and ages 13 & under.*

Statues of dancers adorn the lobby of Marion Oliver McCaw Hall.

7 ★ Marion Oliver McCaw Hall. Seattle has seen a burgeoning of art houses and expansions since the '90s, and this was one of the most notable. Home to the Seattle Opera and the Pacific Northwest Ballet, the hall—resplendent with color and drama—has drawn rave reviews for its architectural beauty, acoustic excellence, and stunning art exhibits. Outside, a contemporary fountain blends in seamlessly with the walkway; at night, colored lights create swirls of color. If you're in town over the holidays, PNB's *The Nutcracker*—complete with Maurice Sendak costumes and sets—is not to be missed. ⏱ *15 min. 321 Mercer St.* ☎ *206/ 389-7676. www.seattleopera.org. Ticket prices for performances vary.*

The Olympic Sculpture Park is operated by the Seattle Art Museum.

Seattle **Film & Theater**

Seattleites spend those long-awaited summer days outdoors, but come fall, it's time to head for the theater. So perhaps the gray winters have played a role in making this an important
film and theater town. The month-long Seattle International Film Festival (☎ **206/324-9996;** www.seattlefilm.org), held in May at several
venues throughout the city, is the largest film festival in the country
and has launched a number of world premieres. The city also boasts
several magnificent theaters built in the Roaring Twenties or earlier,
as vaudeville houses, playhouses, movie palaces, or clubs. START: **Bus
9 or 49 to E. Roy St. & Harvard Ave.**

❶ ★ Harvard Exit. Tucked
away in an unassuming brick building
on a side street in the artsy Capitol
Hill neighborhood, this art theater
specializes in independent and
foreign-language
films. Built in 1925
as a clubhouse for
The Woman's Cen
tury Club, it was
converted in the
'60s to a movie the-
ater. In addition to its
cozy fireplace, grand
piano and comfy chairs,
the huge lobby houses a
1919 movie projector
used for silent films.
Parking can be tricky, so
leave yourself plenty of
time if you come for a
show. ⏱ *15 min. 807
E. Roy at Harvard.*
☎ *206/781-5755.*
*www.landmarktheatres.com/Market/
Seattle/HarvardExitTheatre.htm. Free
admission to see the lobby.*

*A detail from the Egyptian
Theatre's elaborate lobby art.*

❷ Julia's on Broadway. The
spotlight is on Broadway at this light-
hearted themed restaurant, complete with show-monikered cocktails.
It's the perfect spot to grab a bite
during a theater tour. I love their
"afternoon breakfast"—try the Hue-
vos Rancheros. The emphasis is on
fun—and fresh, healthy ingredients.
300 Broadway E. ☎ *206/860-1818. $.*

❸ ★ Egyptian Theatre.
Though built in 1915, this former
Masonic Temple didn't adopt its
Egyptian theme until the '80s, when
it became home to the Seattle International Film Festi-
val. Still one of the
main SIFF venues,
the Egyptian
shows classic, for-
eign, and indepen-
dent films the rest of
the year. You can usu-
ally find parking along
the street or in one of
several nearby lots, or
in the Seattle Central
Community College
garage across the street.
⏱ *15 min. 805 E Pine St.*
☎ *206/781-5755.*

**❹ ★★★ Paramount
Theatre.** My one
complaint about this opulent theater. I often find myself transfixed by
the ceiling instead of the stage. Not
that the shows aren't riveting. The
Broadway series, silent movies,
comedy, and diverse range of concerts are first-rate. It's just that the
French Renaissance architecture is
so lavish, and the intricate ceiling so
intriguing, that the architecture can
almost steal the show. Built in 1928
as Seattle's most spectacular theater, the Paramount treated guests
to stage shows and silent films,
shown to the accompaniment of a

A detail from the 5th Avenue Theatre's elaborate ceiling.

custom-made Wurlitzer organ. Not a bit of its former splendor has been lost, a fact often noted by affluent Seattle brides, who make their entrances down the grand staircase in the lobby. At wedding receptions, the theater's sloped seating area converts to a flat hardwood floor for tables and dancing. ⏱ *15 min. 911 Pine St.* ☎ *206/467-5510. www.stg presents.org. Free admission to the lobby.*

❺ ★ ACT (A Contemporary Theatre). The focus at this nationally recognized theater is on presenting contemporary and new plays, a number of which have gone on to New York. However, one of its most popular performances is the classic *A Christmas Carol.* The audience sits in a semicircle around the central stage. The beautiful 1924 terra-cotta building became home to the ACT in 1973. The theater doesn't have a parking lot, but ample parking is available across the street, in the Convention Center Garage. ⏱ *15 min. 700 Union St.* ☎ *206/292-7676.*

❻ ★★★ 5th Avenue Theatre. The 5th was one of the first vaudeville houses built with an Asian design in the 1920s, when all things Eastern were in vogue. Architect Robert Reamer intended the magnificent interior to look like three Imperial Chinese masterpieces: The Forbidden City, The Temple of Heaven, and The Summer Palace. The theater has undergone two transformations since the vaudeville days: first, to a movie palace; then, after a major renovation in the '80s, to a playhouse. Its stage has been graced by stars the likes of Katharine Hepburn, Robert Goulet, and Carol Channing. The 5th hosts more than 100 live performances each year, including touring Broadway musicals and Broadway-bound shows. Nearby parking garages offer evening discounts. ⏱ *15 min. 1308 5th Ave.* ☎ *206/625-1900. www.5thavenue.org.*

❼ ★ Cinerama. Remember the old wraparound cineramic films? You can still see them at the historic Seattle Cinerama Theatre, one of only three venues in the world that can show the classic three-panel Cinerama films. Once sentenced to be torn down, Cinerama was saved in 1999 by former Microsoft co-founder Paul Allen. And, as you might expect, the renovation was done in high-tech fashion, with a 90-foot-long louvered screen and cutting-edge acoustics. There's also a smaller screen for contemporary films. And the theater recently underwent a major renovation that brought better digital sound and a 3-D experience. ⏱ *15 min. 2100 4th Ave.* ☎ *206/441-3080. www. cinerama.com.*

8 Seattle Repertory Theatre. This Tony Award-winning regional venue has two stages, both housed in a graceful curved building in the northwest corner of Seattle Center. The focus here is on serious artistic theater. ⏱ *15 min. 155 Mercer St.* ☎ *206/443-2222.*

9 Intiman Theatre. Specializing in international drama—both classics and contemporary plays—this

ACT features mostly modern works.

intimate Tony-winning regional theater has launched world premieres. It is sandwiched between the Seattle Repertory Theatre and the Pacific Northwest Ballet's McCaw Hall. ⏱ *15 min. 201 Mercer St.* ☎ *206/269-1900.*

The Paramount Theatre is not to be missed.

Seattle for **Kids**

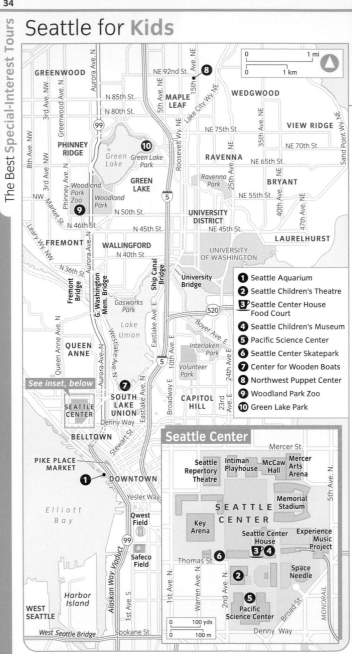

1 Seattle Aquarium
2 Seattle Children's Theatre
3 Seattle Center House Food Court
4 Seattle Children's Museum
5 Pacific Science Center
6 Seattle Center Skatepark
7 Center for Wooden Boats
8 Northwest Puppet Center
9 Woodland Park Zoo
10 Green Lake Park

Seattle Center

Though Seattle is heavy on young professionals with relatively few kids, it is an unusually child-friendly town. Glaring shopkeepers and condescending waiters are rare. Kids love the natural beauty of the Puget Sound, the mountains, and parks; and there is a wealth of activities to keep youngsters busy any time of the year. START: Bus 99 to Pier 59.

Experience the beauty of underwater life at the Seattle Aquarium.

1 ★★ kids **Seattle Aquarium.** A perennial favorite of children, the aquarium offers stories for tots, crafts for older kids, and animal feedings and presentations. Most special programs are included with admission. At the tidepool exhibit, kids love to get their hands on anemones and sea stars. ⏱ *2 hr. 1483 Alaskan Way on Pier 59. ☎ 206/386-4300. www.seattle aquarium.org. Admission $17 adults, $11 ages 4–13. Daily 9:30am–5pm (exhibits close at 6pm).*

2 ★★★ kids **Seattle Children's Theatre.** It's hard to say who's having more fun, the kids or their parents. The sets are clever, the costumes ingenious, and the acting first rate. The season runs September through June. You can get a healthy snack at intermission, but hurry or you'll spend the whole time waiting in line—in which case you'll miss out on the gift area, stocked with books and clever items that relate to the show. Afterward,

Even adults will be entertained by the inventive performances at the Seattle Children's Theatre.

the characters chat with kids and give autographs. *201 Thomas St. at Seattle Center.* ☎ *206/441-3322. www.sct.org. Ticket prices vary.*

3 kids **Seattle Center House Food Court.** You'll find lots of quick and tasty options here, from Thai noodles to fish and chips. There are plenty of treats as well, from warm, sugar-dusted beignets to homemade taffy. The perfect "grown-up" outing for kids is dinner at the Seattle Center House food court, followed by a play at the Seattle Children's Theatre. *305 Harrison St.* ☎ *206/684-7200.* **$**

4 ★ kids **Seattle Children's Museum.** Most of the special exhibits are geared toward the 6-and-under set, but children up to 10 will enjoy the hands-on science section and Imagination Studio, where they create art projects. Make that an early stop, in case paint needs to dry, then pick up the finished product on your way out. In the new Lil' Green Thumbs outdoor exhibit, kids can learn about growing flowers and veggies and plant their own seed to take home. ⏲ *90 min. 305 Harrison St.* ☎ *206/441-1768.*

5 ★★ kids **Pacific Science Center.** Older kids will love the interactive exhibits, such as Adventures in 3Dimensions, which shows how 3-D technology involves our brains to create special effects. Younger siblings will enjoy the crawl-and-climb area, which includes a treehouse and a table-height "stream" for water play. At the Insect Village, kids of all ages will thrill and chill to the giant robotic insects and live animal displays. ⏲ *90 min. 200 2nd Ave. N.* ☎ *206/443-2001. www.pacsci.org. Admission $14 adults, $12 seniors,*

$9 ages 6–15, $7 ages 3–5. IMAX: $9–$14 adults, $8–$12 seniors, $7–$11 ages 6–15, $6–$9 ages 3–5; discounts available for combination passes. Mon–Fri 10am–5pm; Sat–Sun 10am–6pm. See p 116.

6 ★ kids **Seattle Center Skatepark.** Let the kids loose at this 10,000-square-foot, cutting-edge skateboard park. Known to local skateboarders as Seask8, it features a fully skateable vertical glass wall. ⏲ *1 hr. 2nd Ave. N. & Thomas St.* ☎ *206/684-7200. Free admission. Daily during daylight hours.*

7 kids **Tugboat Storytime at the Center for Wooden Boats.** Stories about the sea are even more entertaining when told on the deck of a boat like the historic tug *Arthur Foss.* These maritime tales are geared for ages 2 to 5. ⏲ *1 hr. 1010 Valley St.* ☎ *206/ 382-2628. Free admission. 11am second & fourth Thurs.*

8 ★★ kids **Northwest Puppet Center.** The Carter Family Marionettes, a local multi-generational family of puppeteers, present

Little ones will be thrilled to be let loose in the interactive Seattle Children's Museum.

The Northwest Puppet Center.

high-quality performances geared toward children of various ages. The artistry is remarkable, the genial Carters bring in puppeteers from around the world, and the stories are often based on books or folk tales. After the show, puppets are often brought out on stage for children to come up and touch. *9123 15th Ave. NE.* ☎ *206/523-2579. www.nw puppet.org. Tickets: $11 adults, $9 seniors, $8.50 children. Public shows are on Sat–Sun afternoons.*

⑨ ★★★ kids Woodland Park Zoo. Woodland Park has won awards for several exhibits, including the primate area and the African Savanna. The newest exhibits are the Humboldt penguin habitat, where an underwater viewing area gives guests a close-up view of frolicking penguins from Peru, and the fun-loving meerkats area. At the Zoomazium, an indoor play area, kids 8 and under can explore nature, listen to stories, and generally burn off energy. Special programs are offered for toddlers in the morning and school-age children in the afternoon. The zoo also has a beautiful 1918 carousel; rides cost $2. ⏱ *2 hr. 750 N. 50th St.* ☎ *206/684-4800. www. zoo.org. Admission May–Sept: $17 ages 13–64, $11 ages 3–12; Oct–Apr: $11 ages 13–64, $8 ages 3–12. May–Sept daily 9:30am–6pm; Oct–Apr: daily 9:30am–4pm.*

⑩ kids Green Lake Park. Seattle's favorite place to walk, the 2.8-mile path around lovely Green Lake draws moms with strollers, joggers, dog-walkers, bicyclists, and nature-lovers. An **indoor warm-water pool** (☎ *206/684-4961;* $4.85 ages 18–64, $3.25 ages 1–17 and 65+, free under 1) offers family, public and lap swimming. Tots can splash away in a large outdoor wading pool, open daily 11am–8pm from mid-June to Labor Day. This is a great playground for younger kids, because it's divided into separate areas for toddlers and their rowdier older siblings ⏱ *1 hr. 7201 E Green Lake Dr. N.* ☎ *206/684-4075. www. seattle.gov/parks. The park is open 24 hrs.*

The Woodland Park Zoo is famous for its tigers, among other things.

Caffeinated Seattle

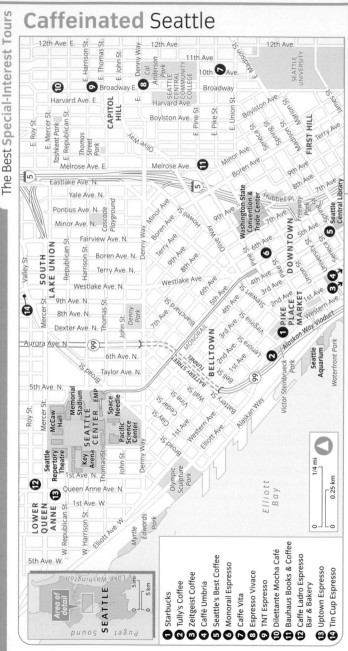

1. Starbucks
2. Tully's Coffee
3. Zeitgeist Coffee
4. Caffè Umbria
5. Seattle's Best Coffee
6. Monorail Espresso
7. Caffe Vita
8. Espresso Vivace
9. TNT Espresso
10. Dilettante Mocha Café
11. Bauhaus Books & Coffee
12. Caffe Ladro Espresso Bar & Bakery
13. Uptown Espresso
14. Tin Cup Espresso

ven inveterate tea-drinkers like myself can't help but get
caught up in the coffee frenzy that permeates Seattle.
Pumpkin-spice lattes, peppermint mochas, white chocolate lattes
with raspberry, caramel macchiatos—who could resist their favorite
flavors blended tastefully with the drug that keeps Seattleites going
through the drizzle? Purists may opt for espresso or Americanos. If
you just don't like coffee, try a chai tea latte. There's no coffee in it,
just creamy, delightfully spiced tea that makes the world seem warm
and cozy. In the summer, order your favorite drink served over ice.
Don't worry about being picky; the person in line ahead of you is
likely to demand a double short half-calf extra-hot soy no-foam latte.
Watch the barista's face; he or she won't miss a beat. **START: Bus 10,
99, 113, 121, or 122 to Pike Place Market**

1 ★ Starbucks. You must begin,
of course, where Seattle's coffee
culture itself really began back in
1971. The very first Starbucks, at
Pike Place Market, still features the
chain's original mascot, the topless
mermaid with a double fish tail,
which has been toned down over
the years in other locations. Many
coffee-lovers gripe that Starbucks
stores are ubiquitous; but I think
their flavored drinks are hard to
beat, and consistently good from
store to store. *The original: 1912
Pike Place.* ☎ 206/448-8762.

2 ★ kids Tully's Coffee.
With shops in several Western
states—including a number in
Seattle—Tully's still roasts its coffee

*Zeitgeist offers an urbane oasis from
busy city life.*

*Love them or hate them, this is the site
where the Starbucks phenomenon began.*

painstakingly, in small batches in
antique roasters. The stores are
friendly and welcoming, the drinks
and baked goods terrific, and they
usually have tables where kids can
read and draw while the grown-ups
sit by the fireplace and chat. My
favorite is the one near Pike Place
Market. *2001 Western Ave. # 110A.*
☎ 206/443-1915. *The original: 1401
4th Ave.* ☎ 206/625-0600.

3 ★★ Zeitgeist Coffee. This
spacious, hip European-style coffee-
house serves up film screenings and
rotating works by up-and-coming
artists along with its popular Italian
beans, illy Caffe. *See p 52.*

④ ★ Caffe Umbria. The Bizzarri family has been roasting beans since Emanuele's grandfather Ornello opened his first shop in Perugia, Italy. Five blends are available, including fair-trade beans. Umbria's Italian-style coffee is served by many demanding establishments, including the Bellagio Hotel and Resort in Las Vegas. You can enjoy a heavenly extra-foamy cappuccino right here in Pioneer Square. *See p 15.*

⑤ ★ Seattle's Best Coffee. An early player on the local coffee scene, Seattle's Best Coffee was bought out by Starbucks a few years ago. But SBCs are still allowed to serve their own coffee blends. The chain got its name many years ago, after winning a contest for the best cuppa joe in town. *Downtown: 1100 4th Ave.* ☎ *206/623-0104. Pike Place Market: 1530 Post Alley.* ☎ *206/ 467-7700.*

⑥ ★ Monorail Espresso. Back in 1980, even before Starbucks began selling coffee drinks at its original store, Chuck Beek came up with the idea of running a little espresso cart in Seattle. He peddled his wares underneath the monorail

Uptown Espresso's signature Velvet Foam.

track. Fifteen years later, with a greatly expanded coffee menu, he opened a permanent shop a few blocks away. It's a great spot to drink in a little history with your double latte. *520 Pike St. (at 5th).* ☎ *206/625-0449.*

⑦ ★ Caffe Vita. This roastery also claims many devotees who swear by its beans and blends from around the world. Vita forms relationships with coffee growers in Africa, Indonesia, and the Americas,

Is it really Seattle's best? After this tour, you'll be able to make an educated decision.

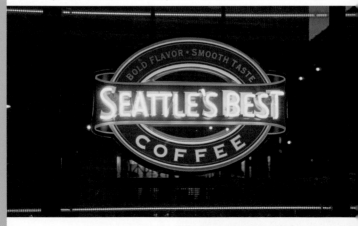

and offers a wide variety of tastes. *Locations include: Capitol Hill: 1005 E. Pike St. ☎ 206/709-4440. Queen Anne: 813 5th Ave. N. ☎ 206/285-9662.*

8 ★★ Espresso Vivace. David Schomer's slow-roasting process is designed to produce a sweet caramel flavor, and the roasting is stopped early to keep the oils in and prevent a burned flavor. For many coffee aficionados, this is as good as it gets. *Capitol Hill cafe location: 532 Broadway Ave. E. ☎ 206/860-2722. Capitol Hill Stand: 321 Broadway Ave. E.*

9 ★ TNT Espresso. This small, friendly Capitol Hill stand serves Zoka coffee, which is roasted in Seattle using beans from around the globe, including an organic chocolaty fair-trade blend of beans from Java and Yemen. Zoka's Paladino blend is sweet and nutty, and is a favorite of many baristas at competitions. *328 Broadway Ave E. ☎ 206/323-9151.*

10 ★★ Dilettante Mocha Café. Silky-smooth, top-quality chocolate makes for sinfully rich mochas, and the presentation is style. The chocolate melts in pots right beside the espresso machine. Locations include: *538 Broadway E. ☎ 206/329-6463. www.dilettante.com. Map p 88.*

11 ★ Bauhaus Books & Coffee. This hip spot in a very diverse neighborhood is stacked with books, which makes it seem very cozy. The people-watching can't be beat, either inside or at the outdoor tables. Nor can the dramatic views of the Space Needle. Best of all? You can drink coffee every night till 1 am! *301 E. Pine St. ☎ 206/625-1600.*

12 ★ Caffe Ladro Espresso Bar & Bakery. Serving only organic, fair-trade, shade-grown coffee, Caffe Ladro has about a dozen locations around metro Seattle. The urban-hip shops serve delicious quiche and baked goods. Try a Medici latte with orange peel. *600 Queen Anne Ave. N. ☎ 206/282-1549. Downtown: 801 Pine St. ☎ 206/405-1950.*

13 ★ Uptown Espresso. This is a serious coffee shop, with rough wood tables occupied by quietly chatting friends and furiously typing computer-users. The coffee and baked goods are excellent. Lattes come topped with a layer of Uptown's heavenly Velvet Foam. *525 Queen Anne Ave N. ☎ 206/285-3757. Belltown: 2504 4th Ave. ☎ 206/441-1084.*

14 ★ Tin Cup Espresso. You might think a town known for its showers would boast lots of covered drive-throughs for its favorite beverage. Not so. This is the only one, and fortunately the drinks, made with Caffe Appassionato beans, are great. I love to start the day sipping a Rush cafe—flavored with vanilla and cinnamon. *900 Broad St. ☎ 206/464-7296.*

The drinks at Espresso Vivace look like works of art.

Seattle **Architecture & Design**

1 Safeco Field
2 Qwest Field
3 Union Station
4 King Street Station
5 Pioneer Building
6 Pioneer Square Pergola
7 Smith Tower
8 Arctic Building
9 Specialty's Café & Bakery
10 Seattle Central Public Library
11 Seattle Art Museum
12 Banana Republic
13 Experience Music Project
14 Space Needle

Though a city this young may not have the widest range of architectural styles, there are many historic gems to be found, and Seattleites have put a great deal of cash into preserving their colorful past. Most of the renovations have been undertaken with care, and it is delightful to see the modern uses to which these old buildings have been put, with all due respect paid to their history. But architecture here is also moving forward. The city's rapid growth and penchant for adventure has attracted world-renowned architects, who have designed a number of cutting-edge buildings.

START: **Bus 106, 123, 124, 131, or 132 to Safeco Field.**

❶ ★ kids Safeco Field. The Seattle Mariners' stadium, erected after the team demanded a new facility to replace the not-so-old but leaky Kingdome, was built amid even more controversy than usual in Seattle. But it has won over Seattleites' hearts, partly because it keeps the rain off but lets the fresh air in. It has one of the few retractable stadium coverings in the country, and the only one that doesn't fully enclose the field. On a perfect sunny day when the roof is open, baseball doesn't get better than this. If you can't make a game, take the hour-long tour—you'll get to see off-limits areas such as the private suites and press box, if they're not in use. Even if you're not a sports fan, you'll enjoy the views of the city and sound, and the baseball-inspired art on display by Northwest artists. ⏱ *1 hr. 1250 1st Ave. S.* ☎ *206/346-4001. www.mariners. mlb.com. Ticket prices for games*

Check out a baseball game at the ultra-modern Safeco Field.

vary. Tour: $9 adults, $8 seniors, $7 ages 3–12, free under 3.

❷ ★ Qwest Field. The Mariners weren't the only sports team to demand a new stadium. The Seahawks also insisted on moving

The tour of Qwest Field gives a behind-the-scenes look at the stadium.

A totem pole guards the entry to the Pioneer Building.

out of the ill-fated Kingdome. So it was destroyed in a fantastic implosion and replaced by Qwest Field. Its graceful double-arched roof, studded with blue lights that glow as you fly into the city or drive along I-5, has become a treasured part of the city's skyline. The roof also overhangs most of the bleachers, keeping about 70% of the fans dry. The field is open-air, and so is the north end, which allows drop-dead views of downtown. If you want to taste the luxury suite experience—and walk right onto the field—take a tour. They're offered all year long. ⏲ 90 min. 800 Occidental Ave. S. ☎ 206/381-7555. www.qwestfield. com. Tours: $7 adults, $5 seniors & ages 4–12; Sept 1–May 30, Fri–Sat 12:30 & 2:30pm; June 1–Aug 31, daily 12:30 & 2:30pm.

❸ ★ Union Station. Opened in 1911, this was a transcontinental train station for 60 years. Sadly, the vast Beaux Arts building was then abandoned and sat around deteriorating until Microsoft billionaire Paul

Allen came to the rescue in the 1990s. It landed a National Preservation Award in 2000, and now it serves as the headquarters for Sound Transit, a regional commuter train. Its spectacular hall, which features a beautifully lighted barrel-vaulted ceiling, is rented out for weddings and other grand occasions, and it's easy to see why. In the daytime, natural light pours in through an enormous semi-circular window. The elegant architecture is worth an admiring look. ⏲ 15 min. 401 S. Jackson St. ☎ 206/682-7275. Free admission.

❹ King Street Station. This bustling Amtrak and Sound Transit commuter station was built in 1906 for the Great Northern Railway and Northern Pacific Railway. An extensive restoration is gradually returning it to its former glory. Its elaborate high ceilings were recently uncovered—hidden since the 1960s by drab suspended tiles. The entry hall, dubbed the Compass Room because of marble-tiled directional points on the floor, has also been refurbished, as has the station's clock tower, once the tallest structure in Seattle. And its clock is once again keeping time. ⏲ 15 min. 303 S. Jackson St. ☎ 206/382-4125. Free admission.

❺ Pioneer Building. This elegant, Romanesque-style structure, hurriedly built right after the Great Fire, was named the "finest building west of Chicago" by the American Institute of Architects when it was completed in 1892. **Underground Tour** (see p 4) offers a fascinating look at the building and at Seattle's colorful history, if you have the time. (Tours are 90 min.) ⏲ 15 min. 1st Ave. & Yesler Way. Underground Tour, 610 1st Ave., #200. ☎ 206/682-4646. www.undergroundtour. com. $14 adults, $7 children 7–12.

Tours offered daily, throughout the day. See p 51.

❻ ★ Pioneer Square Pergola.

You wouldn't know it today, but Seattle's eye-catching iron-and-glass pergola gained its fame for what once lay beneath: elegant public restrooms made of marble and bronze, widely considered the most luxurious in the world in 1910. People would enter the restrooms on stairways leading from the pergola. It was a project in keeping with Seattle's traditional egalitarian ethics. The "comfort stations" have long since closed, and the graceful Victorian pergola itself was crushed by a veering truck in 2001. Fortunately, it was restored using as many of the original materials as possible. ⏲ *15 min. 1st Ave. & Yesler Way.*

❼ Smith Tower.

The tallest building west of the Mississippi when it was built in 1914, this 42-story neoclassical office building is a grand old lady, worth a visit if only for a ride in its 1914 brass-caged elevators. They're the last manually operated ones on the West Coast. The elaborate Chinese Room, with its carved blackwood furniture, is on the 35th floor, as is the observation deck. The panoramic view is spectacular. ⏲ *30 min. 506 2nd Ave.* ☎ *206/622-4004. www.smithtower.com. Observation deck admission $7.50 adults, $5 kids 6–12, free 5 & under. Apr & Oct daily 10am–5pm; May–Oct daily 10am to sunset; Nov–Mar Sat-Sun only 10am–3:30pm. (Check first to make sure no private events are scheduled.)*

❽ Arctic Building.

Fondly dubbed the "Walrus Building," this eight-story Art Deco structure was once an exclusive club for the relatively few gold-miners who struck it rich in the Yukon. In homage to the land where the riches were made, the building featured Alaskan marble hallways and a row of sculpted walrus heads around the third floor of the colorful terra-cotta exterior. Members could do everything from sip tea to go bowling here. A few years ago, investors transformed it into a charming hotel, the Double-tree Arctic Club, featuring period decor. ⏲ *15 min. 700 3rd Ave.* ☎ *206/340-0340. Free admission to the lobby. See p 157.*

After being crushed by a truck in 2001, the Pioneer Square Pergola is back to its former glory.

Say hello to the walruses who adorn the Arctic Building.

9 Specialty's Café & Bakery.
Grab a hearty sandwich or a healthy Cobb salad, followed by a delicious, fresh-from-the-oven peanut butter cookie. For the bargain-minded, the day-old baked goods are a good value. *1023 3rd Ave.* ☎ *206/264-0882. $.*

10 ★★★ kids Seattle Central Public Library. The most talked-about design in Seattle—since the Experience Music Project museum, at least—is the $165-million central public library, an avant-garde showpiece by Dutch architect Rem Koolhaas. This is not your third-grade teacher's library. Tourists from around the world have been coming specifically to see this building since its 2004 opening. Outside, its odd, asymmetrical glass and steel angles jut powerfully over the sidewalk. Inside, patrons walk up a spiraling floor that gradually leads to the top floor. Elevators and electric-hued

escalators are another option. On your way up, stunning views of the surrounding downtown buildings can be seen through the netlike steel structure. ⏱ *30 min. 1000 4th Ave.* ☎ *206/386-4636. www.spl.org. Free admission. Mon–Thurs 10am–8pm, Fri–Sat 10am–6pm. Sun noon–6 pm.*

11 ★★★ Seattle Art Museum.
This gem of a museum was designed by Pritzker Prize–winner Robert Venturi. It moved to this location after spending its first 60 years in an Art Deco building in Volunteer Park, which now houses the Seattle Asian Art Museum. Fifteen years later, the museum was again bursting at the seams, and a large expansion was undertaken. The outside of the building—the upper 12 floors of which are office space—is short of spectacular, but the harmonious blending of old and new is impressive. The "wow" factor was reserved for the lovely interior, where exhibit spaces have doubled, prompting donations of 1,000 new pieces of art. ⏱ *1 hr.* ☎ *206/654-3100. www.seattleartmuseum.org. Admission $15 adults, $12 seniors over 62, $9 students & kids 13–17, free for kids 12 & under. 1300 1st*

Wooden carvings overlook Smith Tower's old-fashioned elevators.

The Seattle Central Public Library.

Ave. Wed–Sun 10am–5pm, Thurs–Fri 10am–9pm. See p 65.

⓬ Banana Republic. Yes, it's a chain store, but it's set in a stunning building that once housed the old Coliseum Theatre. It was built in 1916 by renowned Seattle architect B. Marcus Priteca for wealthy local property owner Joseph Gottstein. The Coliseum was one of the first elegant movie palaces built for showing silent films. Priteca also designed the Pantages theaters, including California's famous one at Hollywood & Vine. After the boom in suburban theaters in the '70s, it stood empty until its reinvention as a clothing store. The original grandeur is preserved, and the white terra-cotta exterior is striking. ⏱ *15 min. 500 Pike St.* ☎ *206/622-2303.*

⓭ ★ Experience Music Project. Without question, this is the oddest structure in Seattle, built by eccentric Microsoft co-founder Paul Allen, a huge fan of the late local guitar legend Jimi Hendrix. At ground level, the museum looks, well, rather like amorphous blobs of colorful sheet-metal, but from the air, designer Frank Gehry's building is supposed to resemble one of Hendrix's famed smashed guitars. The inside, also architecturally engaging, showcases the history of rock 'n' roll, including its roots in soul, jazz, and other genres. Your ticket will also get you into the **Science Fiction Museum and Hall of Fame** (see p 13), under the same

Heads Up!

One of the best ways to sample the city's architecture is to take one of the many popular walking tours offered by the Seattle Architecture Foundation. Most tours last about 2 hours and showcase a wide variety of styles and locations, from the Seattle waterfront to the Art Deco district to the Craftsman bungalows north of the city. There are even tours for families, "Eye Spy Seattle" geared at adults and kids ages 5–10, and the Family Tour for grown-ups with kids ages 8–14. Check the website (www.seattlearchitecture.org) for dates and times. Most tours cost $15 in advance or $25 for same-day tickets, $10 for children 5–12 (Family Tour only).

The Experience Music Project is one of Seattle's most fascinating buildings.

roof. 🕐 *1 hr. 325 5th Ave. N. (at Seattle Center).* ☎ *206/770-2700. www.empsfm.org. Admission $15 adults, $12 seniors/ages 5–17. Late May–early Sept daily 10am–7pm; early Sept–late May 10am–5pm.*

⑭ ★★★ kids Space Needle. In typical Seattle style, there was much disagreement over what the centerpiece for the 1962 World's Fair should look like and where it should go. The futuristic design

The Space Needle defines the Seattle skyline.

morphed considerably from the original "Needle" sketched out on a paper placemat by a hotel chain president. By the time architect John Graham (designer of Seattle's Northgate, the first shopping mall in the world) and his team came up with something everyone agreed on, the fair was only 1½ years away. Finding a site was even trickier, and was finally accomplished with just 13 months to go. Construction went at breakneck speed, and the last elevator car arrived the day before the fair opened. The Space Needle went on to become the world-recognized symbol for its city, and a decade ago got a snazzy $20-million face-lift. 🕐 *1 hr. 400 Broad St.* ☎ *206/905-2100. Observation deck tickets: $18 adults, $16 seniors, $11 ages 4–13. Mon–Thurs 10am–11pm; Fri–Sat 9:30am–11:30pm; Sun 9:30am–11pm. See p 9.* ●

Pioneer Square

0   100 yds
0   100 m

🔺🔺🔺 Pedestrians only

Area of detail

SEATTLE

Puget Sound
Lake Washington

0   5 mi
0   5 km

Columbia St.
3rd Ave.
Cherry St.
2nd Ave.
1st Ave.
Post Ave.
Western Ave.

James St.

★ start here
Pioneer Building
❶
❷
Pioneer Square

❺ Smith Tower

Prefontaine Place

City Hall Park

❸
Yesler Way

S. Washington St.

finish here
★ ⓫
⓾

Occidental Park

Occidental Ave. S.

Waterfall Park

❻
S. Main St.

99

Alaskan Way Viaduct

Alaskan Way S.

1st Ave. S.

❾

❽
S. Jackson St.
❼
To the International → District

2nd Ave. S.
2nd Ave. Ext. S.
3rd Ave. S.

Union Station Square

S. King St.

Occidental Ave. S.

King Street Station

❶ Pioneer Building
❷ Pioneer Square Park
❸ Merchants Cafe
❹ Seattle Mystery Bookshop
❺ Smith Tower
❻ Waterfall Garden Park
❼ Zeitgeist Coffee
❽ Klondike Gold Rush National Historical Park
❾ Glasshouse Studio
⓾ Grand Central Bakery
⓫ Globe Bookstore

For a taste of Seattle's quirky past, wander the oddly angled streets of Pioneer Square, where some of the city's finest art galleries intermingle with the shops and restaurants. The charming Victorian brick and stone buildings were slapped up after the Great Fire of 1889 by local fat cats, eager to get back to selling supplies—and services of every kind—to prospectors en route to the Yukon. At night, the district's clubs still spring to life. START: Bus 10, 11, 16, 66, or 99 to Pioneer Square.

❶ ★★ Pioneer Building. Begin your tour at the very spot where pioneer Henry Yesler built his sawmill in the 1850s, then rebuilt after the Great Fire. He hired famed architect Elmer Fisher—who designed more than 50 post-fire structures—to create the stylish building. Go inside and check out Doc Maynard's Pub and the entertaining Underground Tour, which gives you the insider scoop on Seattle's colorful past. This is one of my favorite ways to amuse visitors. Some younger kids may find it boring, as much of the spiel will (thankfully) be over their heads. ⏲ 90 min. 1st Ave. and Yesler Way. Underground Tour, 608 1st Ave. ☎ 206/682-1646. www.undergroundtour.com. $15 adults, $12 seniors & students, $7 children 7–12; offered daily, throughout the day.

❷ ★ Pioneer Square Park. The pergola (see p 45), Seattle's most beloved hunk of iron, graces the south end of this triangular park—really more of a courtyard—directly in front of the Pioneer Building. It's popular with tourists, but also with vagrants looking for a bench to while away the day. Another rebuilt item in the park is a 60-foot Tlingit totem pole, a replacement for one stolen from an Alaskan village in 1938 by a group of prominent Seattle citizens. When the pole burned years later, the city hired the descendants of the original Native

American carvers to produce its replacement. ⏲ 15 min. 1st Ave. & Yesler Way.

❸ Merchants Cafe. Step back in time at the oldest watering hole in Seattle. Back in the day, prospectors would quaff a brew at the saloon, then head upstairs to the brothel, now converted into apartments. So much gold was dropped here by prospectors on the weekends, it came to be known as the Sunday Bank. Today, you can enjoy lunch, dinner, or a beer in the remodeled restaurant. ⏲ 15 min. 109 Yesler Way. ☎ 206/935-7625. www.merchantscafeandsaloon.com Sun–Wed 11am–midnight; Thurs–Sat 11am–2am.

❹ Seattle Mystery Bookshop. Whodunit aficionados can spend hours tracking down mystery books, both collectable and current, at this terrific little shop. There are frequent author signings, and if you miss one you like, check with JB—he keeps a large number of autographed volumes on hand. ⏲ 15 min. 117 Cherry St. ☎ 206/587-5737. www.seattlemystery.com. Mon–Sat 10am–5pm & Sun noon–5pm.

Seattle Mystery Bookshop is the perfect place to while away a few hours.

5 ★ **Smith Tower.** Ride the antique caged elevators up to the 35th floor observation deck for a fabulous view of downtown Seattle and Mt. Rainier, though the building is now dwarfed by more modern 'scrapers. ⏱ *30 min. 506 2nd Ave. ☎ 206/622-4004. www.smithtower. com. Observation deck admission $7.50 adults, $5 kids 6–12, free under 6. Apr & Oct daily 10am– 5pm; May–Oct daily 10am to sunset; Nov–Mar weekends only 10am– 3:30pm (check first to make sure no private events are scheduled). See p 45.*

6 ★★ **Waterfall Garden Park.** This little-known oasis is my favorite place to hang out with a latte. You'll know you're there by the crash of water tumbling 22 feet down a wall of boulders, drowning out the urban bustle. Waterfall Garden Park is a two-level gem of a park, built in honor of United Parcel Service employees. At lunchtime, office workers sit among its trees and flowers to escape the concrete. ⏱ *15 min. 219 2nd Ave. S.*

7 Drop by **Zeitgeist Coffee** for a Muffaletta sandwich and espresso, then enjoy people-watching or discussing world events. If the conversation turns contentious, a world globe and a monster-size dictionary are on hand to help resolve matters. *171 S. Jackson St. ☎ 206/ 583-0497. $.*

8 ★ **kids Klondike Gold Rush National Historical Park.** In 1897 and 1898, 120,000 fortune-hunters stampeded north to Canada's Yukon Territory, where gold had recently passed through Seattle, and the impact on the city was enormous. This park tells the story of the Klondike Gold Rush with great attention to detail. One in 10 of those headed for the gold fields were women. ⏱ *1 hr. 319 2nd Ave. S. ☎ 206/220-4240. www.nps.gov/ klse. Free admission. Daily 9am– 5pm. See p 22.*

9 ★★ **kids Glasshouse Studio.** Seattle is home to some of the world's finest glass artists. (Dale Chihuly, famed for his outrageously colorful, fanciful works, has a studio on Lake Union.) In Pioneer Square, you can watch artists at work in Seattle's oldest glass-blowing studio as they shape glowing globs of color into the most amazing things of beauty. You can buy their vases, chandeliers and jewelry in the adjacent shop. ⏱ *30 min. 311 Occidental Ave. S. ☎ 206/682-9939.*

Waterfall Garden Park is one of Seattle's best-kept secrets.

Watch artisans at work at the Glasshouse Studio.

www.glasshouse-studio.com. Mon–Sat 10am–5pm, Sun 1am–4pm.

10 Grand Central Bakery. You'll smell it before you see it. Some of the best pastries, sandwiches, and soups in town come from this gem of a bakery, which you can enter from Occidental Park or the Grand Central Arcade on 1st Avenue. Start with a basil egg sandwich, followed by a sweet-tooth-pleasing chocolate croissant, then take home a Como Loaf, one of Seattle's original artisan loaves. *214 1st Ave. S. ☎ 206/622-3644. $.*

11 ★ Globe Bookstore. PIONEER SQUARE From Beowulf to Harry Potter, you'll likely find what you're looking for in this wonderful, musty bookshop. The focus is on used and collectable books, but you'll find new titles as well. The cookbook section is specially tantalizing, and the children's book section is impressive as well. The owner really knows his stuff, and the prices are right. He tracked down a cookbook I'd been hunting for years—and charged me less than half the price I'd seen on eBay. ⏱ *30 min. 218 1st Ave. S. ☎ 206/682-6882. Mon–Sat 10am–6pm; Sun noon–5pm. Map p 88.*

First Thursday Gallery Walk

The country's first art walk, this monthly event is great fun, and a terrific way to catch all the latest exhibits. Best of all, it's free. First Thursday showcases the Pioneer Square area's eclectic array of avant-garde galleries. The best new artists and exhibits are featured, and the art ranges from paintings to sculptures to blown glass. It all starts at Main Street and Occidental, in Occidental Park, where vendors hawk their art and street musicians entertain. Skip that big dinner before you come, because some of the galleries serve wine and cheese (www.firstthursdayseattle.com, noon–8pm the first Thursday of every month).

Pike Place Market

1 Information Booth
2 The Crumpet Shop
3 Gum Wall
4 Rachel the Pig
5 Main Arcade
6 Athenian Inn
7 Economy Building
8 South Arcade
9 Down Under
10 Pike Place
11 Post Alley

B uzzing with tourists, savvy locals, and finicky restaura-
teurs, Pike Place Market is the heart and soul of Seattle. Kids
love the street performers and the "flying" fish; adults are mesmer-
ized by the mind-boggling variety of shops, food, and entertainment.
You can find just about anything you want here, from salted herring
to $4,000-a-pound Piemontese truffles to handmade mandolins. It's
a wonderful place to spend the day—or two. Plus, it's the only
neighborhood in town where jaywalking won't get you a ticket!
START: **Bus 10, 99, 113, 121, or 122 to Pike Place Market.**

❶ **Information Booth.** Make
this your first stop—not just to pick
up a market newspaper and map,
but to arm yourself with coupons
for tours, including the popular
Argosy Cruises of the harbor and
Seattle's lakes and locks, and discounts on current theatrical shows
in town. (Also check www.goldstar.
com and click on "Seattle" at the
bottom of the page for deals on tickets.) *Pike St. & 1st Ave.* ☎ *206/228-
7291. www.pikeplacemarket.org.*

❷ ★ **The Crumpet Shop.** Start
your day off here at this British-fla-
vored spot. As a tea fanatic in a java
town, I especially appreciate the
variety of tasty global teas served
daily, with free refills. Of course,
there are also the mouth-watering
crumpets, baked fresh daily. Crumpet purists can get one with just
marmalade, but I love them with
smoked salmon, cream cheese, and
cucumber. Come early and you can
watch the bakers at work. *1503 1st
Ave.* ☎ *206/682-1598. $.*

❸ **kids Gum Wall.** If you're not
too easily grossed out, take a
detour down the ramp from the
Information Booth before you tackle
the Market proper. Hang a left and
be careful not to lean against the
wall—It's covered in several inches'
worth of chewed gum. After years

Pike Place Market's Gum Wall.

of futile efforts to clean it off, the
city dubbed it a tourist attraction.
1530 Post Alley.

❹ **kids Rachel the Pig.** Seattle's
beloved bronze porker stands just
under the famous neon "Public Market Center" sign and clock. I like to
drop a few coins in the piggybank to
help support the Market Foundation's charities. The civic-minded
folks who saved the Market in the
1970s decided the revival should
include social services, such as low-
income apartments for seniors.
Rachel has quite a cult following.
Pike Place & Pike St.

Go ahead, climb up on Rachel for a photo.

5 ★★ kids **Main Arcade.** Get ready for sensory overload! The most tender asparagus, freshest daffodils, richest sockeye salmon,

and most unusual Northwest crafts can be found here. Start right behind Rachel the Pig and elbow your way through the North Arcade. Everything sold here is required to be grown, caught, or created locally. From the world-famous fish throwers at **Pike Place Fish Market** to the tulip-growers from Snoqualmie Valley, the North Arcade is alive with scents, sounds, and colors. Salad greens with edible flowers? Chocolate pasta? Pepper jelly? You'll find it here. Try the tasty free samples at **Sosio's Fruit & Produce,** and stop for a complimentary cup of specially blended Market Spice Tea at **Market Spice,** which has been in the market since 1911. Head to the back of the shop and look for the carafe. On the north

Spirit of the Market

Tales abound of ghosts and ghouls wandering among the old narrow halls, stairwells, dusty corners, and nooks and crannies of Pike Place Market, looking for closure—or at least their old haunts. So many ghosts have been reported by workers and visitors to the Market that a few even have names—like Jacob, supposedly a horse groom in real life, back in the days when the Market had stables. Now, he's fabled to haunt the Down Under, where he reportedly mixes up the bead colors at the Bead Zone shop. Jacob favors red beads. Then there's Frank, who supposedly introduces himself to guests at the Alibi Room nightclub before fading away. And more than one ghost has been reported hanging around Kell's Irish Pub on Post Alley, the former site of a mortuary. The Market's colorful history includes brothels, orphans who worked for pennies, a deadly flu epidemic, and the old mortuary. It all adds up to fertile ground for spirits. Even if you don't believe in them, you'll enjoy taking a 75-minute Market **Ghost Tour** (1410 Post Alley; ☎ **206/805-0195;** www.seattleghost.com). Tours start at 5 and 7pm Thursday through Sunday, but check the website, because more times and dates may be added due to popular demand! Reservations are required via phone or website. The 5pm tours are more family friendly for the younger kids. Tickets cost $15; free for accompanied children 9 and under.

from around the world and magazines of every ilk. You're likely to find your hometown paper here. **DeLaurenti's Specialty Food Market** is a favorite spot for Seattle-ites to buy wine, cheeses, and olive oil. It also has a terrific deli. What I like best is being able to pick the brains of the knowledgeable staff. On your way to the Economy Atrium, you'll pass by the nut, crepe, and doughnut kiosks. Then stop and play at **The Great Wind-Up,** which specializes in (what else?) wind-up toys. The try-out table is generally monopolized by adults with big, goofy grins on their faces. ⏱ *30 min.*

8 South Arcade. The Economy Building opens onto a newer row of shops and restaurants, including **Pike Pub & Brewery,** one of the area's many excellent micro-breweries. **Northwest Tribal Art** is

Be sure to dodge the flying fish as you head through the fish market.

One of the many street performers at the market.

end of the Main Arcade, you'll find the handmade-craft booths, where you can buy anything from clay oca-rinas to watercolor paintings of umbrellas. ⏱ *90 min. Mon–Sat 10am–6pm; Sun 11am–5pm. (Fine-dining restaurants stay open later.)*

6 The Athenian Inn. Tucked off the Main Arcade, this is a favorite hangout of longtime Seattleites, and also of tourists who remember it from *Sleepless in Seattle.* You can get all-day breakfast here, or sea-food straight from the Market. The Athenian, which recently celebrated its centennial, is a dark, homey kind of place with a long bar. Sit upstairs for the best views of Puget Sound. *1517 Pike Place.* ☎ *206/624-7166. athenianinn.com. $$.*

7 Economy Building. On the corner of this building, beside the Information Booth, is **First And Pike News,** where the shelves groan under the weight of newspapers

Pike Place Market features farm fresh fruit and veggies from all over the Northwest.

a great place to find colorful masks, totem poles, soapstone figurines, and silver jewelry crafted by local Native Americans. ⏰ *30 min.*

9 ★ Down Under. Pike Place Market is perched on the top of a hillside, with a labyrinth of eclectic stores sprawling beneath the Main Arcade. It's worth venturing down the staircase to explore them. The shops are jammed with gems, books, ethnic clothing, and jewelry,

and there's even an old-fashioned barbershop. A variety of craft stores sell unusual items, including **Afghani Crafts** women's clothing; **Hands of the World,** featuring folk art mainly from developing nations; and **Polish Pottery Place,** where beautifully detailed items are made by a handful of families who've been at it for generations. ⏰ *30 min.*

10 ★★ Pike Place. Once you've jostled your way through the market and out into the fresh air (or drizzle), you're far from done. A brick street runs between the Main Arcade and several facing blocks of shops, food stands, restaurants, and yet more produce. The "Big Ass Grapes" at the corner shop are appropriately named. This area is just as lively as the inside Market, with street performers entertaining the crowds. Someone could well be tickling the ivories of a full-size piano on a street corner. The ethnic food stands are great places to grab a snack. Try the steamed-pork humbow and red bean sesame balls at **Mee Sum Pastries.** Or, for more substantial fare, **Piroshky Piroshky** serves an array of

MORE SHOPS

You'll find the perfect souvenir at one of the many shops Down Under.

Dining at the Market

You'll never go hungry at Pike Place Market, where dining options range from booths of sausage, noodles and pastries to first-rate restaurants like **Place Pigalle** (p 130), perched over the water and serving mussels to die for. For a budget lunch, I like to pick up sandwiches in the market, then head toward the water from Rachel the Pig, where there's a tucked-away indoor sitting area with the same panoramic view of the sound that you'll get in the high-end restaurants.

Tour the Market

There's no happier place in Seattle than the Market, where every turn brings a kaleidoscope of produce, crafts, garrulous vendors, and shoppers from around the world. On the hour-long **Market Heritage Tour** (☎ **206/322-2219;** $10 for adults, $7 for seniors and children 17 and under), you can pick up some great insider tips on shopping the market, plus history on how it came to be in 1907, and how it almost came not to be in the 1970s. (Happily, Seattleites decided they couldn't bear to see their market turned into parking garages and office buildings.) This tour only operates June through August, starting at Rachel the Pig at 9am Saturdays. Reserve by noon the day before your tour by calling or e-mailing (jogliore@gmail.com). Or how about a food tour to sample some of the best offerings of the market? **Seattle Food Tours** (☎ **206/725-4483;** www.seattlefoodtours.com) offers a daily 2½-hour walk, all year long. The delectable edibles may include smoked salmon, homemade gelato, to-die-for clam chowder, and locally grown fruit.

delicious savory and sweet pastries. I usually order the potato and mushroom, with a marzipan piroshky for dessert. Then stop in at the original **Starbucks** for a latte to wash it all down (see p 39). ⏱ *30 min.*

⓫ **Post Alley.** Hike east up the hill a block and you'll find yourself on a winding little street where the din is lower but the shops and cafes still delightful. **Perennial Tearoom** (1910 Post Alley) is a lovely place to stop for a spot of tea, then pick out a few varieties from the wall of teas

Stop by First and Pike News (p 57) and see what they have in stock.

Post Alley is the perfect spot to escape the hubbub of Pike Place Market.

to take home for later. The shop stocks teas and teapots from around the world. A block farther south on Post, you can find classy souvenirs—no kidding—at **Made in Washington.** ⏱ *30 min.*

Downtown

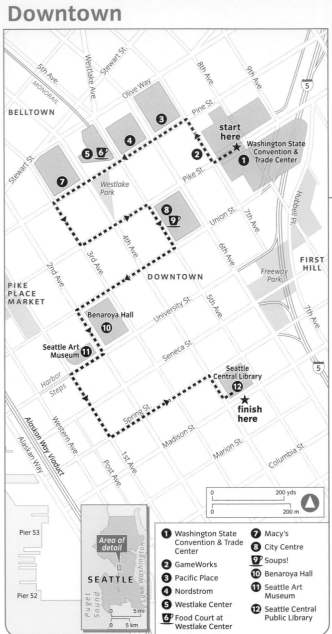

5th Ave.
Westlake Ave.
Stewart St.
MONORAIL
Olive Way
8th Ave.
9th Ave.
5

BELLTOWN

Stewart St.
Pine St.
3
4
5 6
7
start here
★ Washington State Convention & Trade Center
1
2
Pike St.

Westlake Park

Hubbell Pl.

Union St.
7th Ave.

8
9

3rd Ave.
4th Ave.
6th Ave.

FIRST HILL

2nd Ave.
DOWNTOWN
Freeway Park

PIKE PLACE MARKET

University St.
5th Ave.

Benaroya Hall
10

7th Ave.

Seneca St.

Seattle Art Museum
11

Harbor Steps

Seattle Central Library
12

Western Ave.
Spring St.
★ **finish here**

Alaskan Way Viaduct
Alaskan Way
Post Ave.
1st Ave.
Madison St.
Marion St.
Columbia St.

0 ————— 200 yds
0 ————— 200 m

Pier 53

SEATTLE
Area of detail
Lake Washington
Puget Sound
0 — 5 mi
0 — 5 km

Pier 52

1 Washington State Convention & Trade Center
2 GameWorks
3 Pacific Place
4 Nordstrom
5 Westlake Center
6 Food Court at Westlake Center
7 Macy's
8 City Centre
9 Soups!
10 Benaroya Hall
11 Seattle Art Museum
12 Seattle Central Public Library

S eattle's downtown core is a world-class destination, bustling with shoppers and gawkers from all over the globe. Once declining, this neighborhood was livened up more than a decade ago by the dot-com millionaires. That came right on the heels of the grunge rock era, which had already focused the world's attention on the Emerald City. Downtown tenants include Nordstrom, the world-famous department store that started here as a humble shoe store way back in 1901; the world's first GameWorks, dreamed up in part by Steven Spielberg; and Pacific Place mall, boasting high-end retailers such as Tiffany. Today, Seattle's downtown is vibrant, colorful, and one of the most walkable in the country. But if you're loaded down with packages, why not hop on a metro bus? They're free in the downtown area. **START: Bus 10, 11, 14, 306, or 312, to the Washington State Convention & Trade Center.**

① Washington State Convention & Trade Center. Space was an issue when Seattle's convention center was built in 1988, and it was solved with a unique freeway-straddling design. Look up if you're driving on I-5 and you'll see the center's greenery draping along the overpass. Just a few years later, when the city's economy began to skyrocket, it became clear that the convention center needed yet more elbow room. The problem? There was nowhere to expand, except across Pike Street. So that's just where the other half went in 2001, connected to the original building by an enormous glass skybridge. Enter on the south side of Pike Avenue, and ride up the multiple escalators to check out the ever-changing local art exhibits. If it's raining, you can hang out in the underground concourse, which starts at the convention center, winds under the Seattle Hilton and past shops, cafes, and historical exhibits, and comes out at 5th Avenue Theatre and the Rainier Square Shopping Center. ⏱ *15 min. 800 Convention Place.* ☎ *206/447-5000. www.wsctc.com. Daily 6am–10pm.*

② kids GameWorks. This 30,000-square-foot (2,787-sq. m) virtual-entertainment center is a bit too loud for my ears, but for kids (including many of the grown-up variety) it's a paradise of futuristic fun and games. You can stay all day if you like: There's a cafe, sports bar, and pool room upstairs. But if you're over 30, bring earplugs. On Thursdays, you can play from 7 to10pm for $10. ⏱ *15 min. 1511 7th Ave.* ☎ *206/521-0952. Mon–Thurs 11am–midnight, Fri 11am–1am, Sat 10am–1am, Sun 10am–midnight.*

③ ★ Pacific Place. You can gaze at all four floors of this upscale, contemporary mall as you wind your

Get your one-stop shopping done at Pacific Place.

The nationwide Nordstrom chain got its start in Seattle.

to choose from, including **Il Fornaio,** which serves fresh Italian fare in three locations, depending on your budget and time constraints: an atrium kiosk, a cafe, and a full-service restaurant. No matter where I'm going downtown, I always park at Pacific Place. It's centrally located, owned by the city, and one of the best deals in a town where parking is at a premium. At night, there's a special 4-hour rate of $6. ⏲ *1 hr. 6th Ave. & Pine St.* ☎ *206/405-2655. www.pacificplaceseattle.com. Mon–Sat 10am–8pm, Sun 11am–7pm.*

④ ★★ **Nordstrom.** Nordstrom, one of Seattle's oldest families, moved their flagship store in 1998 from its cramped quarters to an empty 1918 building that was the former home of the iconic Frederick & Nelson department store. Nordstrom has come a long way since Swedish immigrant John Nordstrom opened his first shoe store in 1901, using Gold Rush money he brought back from Alaska. My favorite story about the chain's legendary customer service is about a businessman who called the store from the airport, in a panic because he didn't have a tie for a business meeting. A salesperson was dispatched to the

way up the escalator up to the 11-screen theater. The shops along the way are a who's who of retail: Barneys New York, Eddie Bauer, Williams-Sonoma, Barnes & Noble, Cartier, J. Crew, Tiffany & Co., Restoration Hardware. If you find yourself at Pacific Place at lunch or dinner time, you'll find several restaurants

Shop Savvy

Shopping at Pacific Place can be a full-day experience. But if you'd rather skip the national chain stores and focus on the local highlights, stop by **Twist,** a Northwest boutique that's as colorful as it is fun. The glassware and home decor items will lure you in; the unusual jewelry by artists around the world will keep you browsing. Then there's **Top Ten Toys,** where you won't find Barbies, but you will find quality old-fashioned toys and mind-challenging games. And don't miss the chic **Sixth Avenue Wine Seller,** where owner Beverly Shimada pours wines from around the world for $5 a glass during happy hour, from 3 to 6pm weekdays. You can also grab a bite from the yummy menu of shareable plates.

Dot-com Delirium

Seattle has always been a boom-or-bust town, starting with the Gold Rush, and continuing much later with a series of massive hirings and devastating layoffs by Boeing. Then in the 1990s, strange things began happening in the once aviation-dependent economy. First, grunge rock grabbed the limelight for Seattle. Then a little company named Microsoft, started by hometown boys Bill Gates and Paul Allen, mushroomed into a billion-dollar-a-year-plus business by 1990, helping to spawn an entire industry of dot-com startups. By the late '90s, Seattle's economy was flying high from the glorious infusion of dot-com dollars. World-class restaurants, theater, and other cultural activities sprang up or expanded, eager to fill the after-hours entertainment needs of the newly moneyed. Though the dot-com bubble burst in Seattle, and throughout the country, just a couple of years later, Seattle's now-diversified economy quickly revived. While Seattle has struggled during the recent economic downturn, its downtown remains vibrant and its night scene lively.

airport with a selection of ties. Considering Seattle's tangled traffic, I wouldn't count on the ties arriving in time these days, but the store's service is still hard to beat. And, though today's Nordstrom is a full-service department store, the shoes are still exquisite. But before I try on a pair, I usually walk three blocks west to check out **Nordstrom Rack** (1601 2nd Ave.), where you can save up to 75% on clothing and shoes. ⏱ *30 min. 500 Pine St.* ☎ *206/628-2111. Mon–Sat 9:30am–9pm, Sun 11am–7pm.*

⑤ ★★ Westlake Center. This is a chic mall, but with a comfy Seattle feel. I especially love browsing in the Seattle-based shops, such as Romy Boutique, a hip home-grown apparel shop; Fireworks, an incredibly fun store crammed with playful art; and Made in Washington, which sells souvenirs your friends will actually like. Seattle's mile-long monorail, built for the 1962 World's Fair, runs between Seattle Center

and the top floor of Westlake Center. If your kids can't take any more shopping, treat them to a quick ride for a break. ⏱ *1 hr. 400 Pine St.* ☎ *206/467-1600. www.westlake center.com. Mon–Sat 10am–8pm; Sun 11am–6pm.*

⑥ ★ kids Food court at Westlake. This is a food court like none other I've seen. There's something to please every palate, from quesadillas to sushi, all amazingly fresh and tasty. It's easy on the family budget, and wiggle worms have plenty of room to stretch when they're done eating. A few highlights: Bobachine bubble tea & baguettes, Bombay Wala, Salena Mexicana, Noodle Zone, Sarku-Japanese Sushi, Mediterranean Avenue, and Emerald City Smoothie. *400 Pine St. $.*

⑦ ★ Macy's. The famous high-end department store is ironically housed in the former Bon Marche

Head to the escalators to check out the bronze plates on display in Macy's.

department store, which for over 100 years catered to Seattle's working class. But look closely and you'll find traces of the old Bon. Check beside the escalators for the intricate 1929 bronze panels depicting industries of the Northwest, from fisheries to technology. Look also for good clothing buys on the sales racks. ⏱ *15 min. 1601 3rd Ave.* ☎ *206/506-6000. www.macys.com.*

8 City Centre. This mixed-use building is a prestigious downtown office address, but it also houses some great little upscale shops, including American Eagle Outfitters, Aldo (leather goods), Grace Diamonds, and Facèrè (antique and art jewelry). You can grab a veggie sub at Jimmy John's, a wrap at Sandella's Flat Bread Café, or something Japanese at Sushi Kudasai. On the top retail floor, you'll find an excellent full-service restaurant (Palomino—with both a cafe and fine-dining room). But what I like best about City Centre is its dazzling glass collection by the famed Pilchuck Glass School. Kids go nuts for the life-size glass dinosaur skeleton. ⏱ *15 min. 1420 5th Ave.* ☎ *206/624-8800. Store hours vary. Most open at 10am Mon–Sat & noon Sun; and close daily btw. 5pm & 9pm (Palomino stays open later).*

☕ **Soups!** A bowl of soup is just the thing for a drizzly Seattle day. I can never decide between the chicken basil chili and the lobster bisque. Usually I ask for a sample of one, and buy a bowl of the other. This is just a small stand on the first floor of City Centre, but the taste is big, and there's plenty of room to sit and enjoy your soup. *1420 5th Ave. $.*

The schockingly chartreuse escalators at the Seattle Central Public Library.

Cai Guo-Qiang's massive work greets visitors to the Seattle Art Museum.

⑩ ★★★ Benaroya Hall. Home to the Seattle Symphony, Benaroya is a modernist dream. I highly recommend catching a concert here, but even if you're not in the mood, the hall is worth a peek. Check out the colossal glass chandeliers by world-famous Seattle glass artist Dale Chihuly. ⊕ *30 min. 200 University St.* ☎ *206/215-4800. www. seattlesymphony.org. Ticket prices vary; free admission to see the chandeliers. See p 27.*

⑪ ★★★ Seattle Art Museum. Seattleites take their art seriously, and SAM is a reflection of that. The museum is home to an outstanding array of works from all over the world, but be sure to check out the Northwest Native American collection, which is one of the finest you'll find anywhere. ⊕ *90 min.* ☎ *206/654-3100. www.seattleart museum.org. Admission $15 adults, $12 seniors over 62, $9 students & kids 13–17, free for kids 12 & under. 1300 1st Ave. Wed–Sun 10am–5pm, Thurs–Fri 10am–9pm. See p 27.*

⑫ ★★★ kids Seattle Central Public Library. It's hard to say which is more fun, admiring the building or browsing its well-stocked shelves. One thing is for sure: You'll have to drag the kids out of the children's section. And of course, you can get a latte. *1000 4th Ave.* ☎ *206/386-4636. www.spl.org. Mon–Thurs 10am–8pm, Fri–Sat 10am–6pm, Sun noon–6pm.*

Kids love the life-size glass dinosaur skeleton at City Centre.

Capitol Hill

```
0          1/5 mi
0       0.2 km
```

Lake View Cemetery

Volunteer Park
Conservatory

VOLUNTEER
PARK
1

Seattle
Asian Art
Museum

Reservoir

Water
Tower

E. Highland Dr.

Lakeview Blvd. E.

Volunteer Park Rd

Volunteer Pkwy.

E. Prospect St.

HARVARD
BELMONT
LANDMARK
DISTRICT
2

E. Aloha St.

E. Prospect St.

E. Aloha St.

E. Roy St.

E. Roy St.

E. Mercer St.

Tashkent
Park

E. Republican St.

E. Harrison St.
3

4

7

CAPITOL HILL

E. Thomas St.

Thomas
Street
Park

E. John St.

5

E. Denny Way

E. Howell St.

E. Olive Way

SEATTLE
CENTRAL
COMMUNITY
COLLEGE

Cal
Anderson
Park

E. Olive St.

E. Pine St.

6

E. Pike St.

E. Union St.

Summit Ave. E.
Bellevue Ave. E.
Belmont Ave. E.
Bellevue Pl. E.
Belmont Pl. E.
Boylston Ave. E.
Harvard Ave. E.
Broadway
10th Ave. E.
Federal Ave. E.
11th Ave. E.
12th Ave. E.
13th Ave. E.
14th Ave. E.
15th Ave. E.
Malden Ave. E.
Nagle Pl.

SEATTLE

Puget Sound

Lake Washington

Area of
detail

```
0     5 mi
0    5 km
```

1 Volunteer Park
2 Harvard-Belmont
Landmark District
3 Consignment Apparel
Shops
4 Espresso Vivace
5 Dance Footsteps
6 Elliott Bay
Book Company
7 Charlie's Bar & Grill
8 Museum of History
& Industry

Remnants of the grunge era live on in this eclectic neighborhood, which is also the center of gay life in Seattle. In addition to jet-black attire and gratuitous piercings, expect to see the occasional neon-blue Mohawk, cross-dressing shoppers, and panhandlers who may at times be a bit unsteady on their feet. The housing is also diverse, with seedy apartments sharing blocks with spectacular mansions. Likewise, the shops along Broadway range from retro-consignment to ultra trendy fashion. It's safe to bring young children here, but there's not much of interest for them, except for Volunteer Park—far removed from the Broadway street scene. **START: Bus 10 to Volunteer Park.**

① ★★ **kids** **Volunteer Park.**
Flush with Gold Rush money, Seattle hired the Olmsted family (of New York City's Central Park fame) in 1903 to design an elaborate series of parks, including this one. There's lots of room to run and many trails to explore in this urban oasis. If you climb the 106 indoor steps to the top of the Water Tower at the south end of the park, you'll be rewarded with one of the best views in town. But if you're out of breath by the time you climb the two flights to the entrance, don't even bother! Just west of the tower is the **Seattle Asian Art Museum** Farther west is the **Volunteer Park Conservatory,** bursting with colorful exotic plants, including a large

An exotic bloom at Volunteer Park Conservatory.

orchid collection. You'd hardly be surprised if a parrot landed on your shoulder. ⏱ *1 hr. 1400 E. Galer St.* ☎ *206/684-4743. www.seattle.gov/ parks. Free admission. Tues–Sun 10am–4pm. See p 67.*

The greenhouse at Volunteer Park.

2 Harvard-Belmont Landmark District. Seattle has more than its share of millionaires—both dot-com and otherwise—and quite a few live in this tree-shaded neighborhood, ensconced in graceful, sprawling mansions built in the early 20th century. The best walk is along the northern end of Broadway, between East Highland and East Roy. You can also drive, but walking allows for better peeking through the hedges. 🕙 *30 min. Bounded roughly by Harvard Ave., Broadway, Bellevue Place & Boylston.*

3 Consignment Apparel Shops. With two colleges nearby (Seattle University and Seattle Central Community College), previously worn—and retro—clothing is highly sought after. There aren't as many vintage apparel shops as there once were along Broadway, but the ones that remain are excellent. **Crossroads Trading Co.** (325 Broadway Ave. E; ☎ 206/328-5867) focuses on contemporary styles. Some items are new, but the only way to tell is by their blue tags. This is not the cheapest consignment shop in town, but the merchandise is topflight. There's also a men's section.

Pick up some funky footwear at Metro Clothing Co. in Capitol Hill.

Take a moment to add a little dance to your day.

At the **Metro Clothing Co.** (231 Broadway E; ☎ 206/726-7978), only the hip—or wannabes—need enter this delightfully eccentric shop. 🕙 *1 hr. Broadway E.*

4 ★★ Espresso Vivace. This is a no-frills stand, but the coffee drinks are sublime, right down to the Rosetta pattern the barista "draws" in the foam. Sidewalk seating is available. My favorite: the rich, creamy caffe caramel. *321 Broadway Ave. E. $.*

5 Dance Footsteps. One of the most unusual displays of public art you'll find is embedded in the sidewalks along Broadway. *Dancers' Series: Steps* consists of bronze shoeprints of dancers performing various steps. There are eight sets along the avenue, from the tango to the foxtrot, and a couple of steps that artist Jack Mackie made up just for fun. Go ahead and try them out! No need to feel self-conscious: It takes a lot to turn heads on Capitol Hill. 🕙 *15 min. Along Broadway.*

6 ★★★ kids Elliott Bay Book Company. Seattleites love

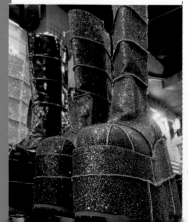

Bigfoot

The most popular legend in the Northwest, without a doubt, is that of Sasquatch, more fondly dubbed Bigfoot. Believers swear that Sasquatches roam the forests and mountains of the Pacific Northwest. Reports of an enormous hairy beast in the region have been circulating since the early 1800s. Some, but not all, of the stories have been proven fraudulent. In 1969, a man in northern Washington reported finding Sasquatch footprints in a ghost town called Bossburg. Bigfoot hunters rushed to the scene and found additional tracks nearby—more than 1,000 in all. One of them was measured at more than 17 inches long. At least one British anthropologist was impressed with the find. Sasquatch-spotters often report an awful, skunklike smell just before they see the beast or its tracks. But with no scientifically confirmed hard proof, the mystery—and perhaps the ape-man—lives on.

their books, and this is the city's favorite bookstore. In its new location—a 20,000-square-foot historic 1917 building on quirky Capitol Hill—Elliott Bay still feels like Seattle's comfy living room. Peruse the shelves at your leisure in this old Ford truck service center with its fir floors and massive ceiling beams. Your challenge: not to bring home more than you can fit in your carry-on! ⏱ *30 min. 1521 10th Ave.* ☎ *206/624-6600. www.elliottbaybook.com. Mon–Thurs 10am–10pm; Fri–Sat 10am–11pm; Sun 11am–9pm.*

7 Charlie's Bar & Grill. This cozy spot has been serving up comfort food for about as long as Microsoft has been around. Even a hefty hunger will be tamed by the Monte Cristo sandwich, but if you're in the mood for something lighter, Charlie's is famous for its pepper pot soup. *217 Broadway E.* ☎ *206/323-2535. broadwaycharlies.com. $.*

8 ★★ kids Museum of History & Industry (MOHAI). This gem of a museum, which opened in 1952, is operated by the Seattle Historical Association and its fascinating collection will give you an excellent overview of the Northwest's history. The core exhibit focuses on Seattle and tells the city's story through pictures, artifacts, and oral histories. It is slated to move in 2012 to a refurbished military building on the shores of South Lake Union. ⏱ *1 hr. 2700 24th Ave. E.* ☎ *206/324-1126. www.seattlehistory.org. $7 adults, $5 ages 5–17 & seniors, free 4 & under. Also, free first Thurs. Daily 10am–5pm, first Thurs 10am–8pm. See p 24.*

Chinatown/International District

← To Pioneer Square

Yesler Way

S. Washington St.

Kobe Terrace Park

S. Main St.

❸

❹

S. Jackson St.

Union Station

Hing Hay Park

❷

Alley

Alley

❺ S. King St.

S. King St.

❽ finish here

❼

❻

Canton

Manard

S. Weller St.

7th Ave. S.

8th Ave. S.

Uwajimaya

❶

start here

Maynard Ave. S.

International Children's Park

S. Lane St.

4th Ave. S.

5th Ave. S.

6th Ave. S.

S. Dearborn St.

Airport Way S.

S. Charles St.

S. Plummer St.

SEATTLE

Puget Sound

Lake Washington

Area of detail

0   5 mi
0   5 km

6th Ave. S.

S. Royal Brougham Way

0   100 yds
0   100 m

❶ Uwajimaya
❷ Hing Hay Park
❸ Panama Hotel Tea & Coffee
❹ Kobo at Higo
❺ A Piece of Cake
❻ Wing Luke Asian Museum
❼ Ambrosia Cafe
❽ Chinese Gate

Though not as large as San Francisco's Chinatown, this Asian neighborhood is lively—and about as diverse as they come, with a flood of Southeast Asian immigrants joining the mix in recent years. Its name has morphed from Chinatown to International District to the current compromise. When I feel like globe-trotting but can't spare the time, I'll spend an afternoon here, strolling past rows of whole barbecued ducks hanging by their feet, riotously colorful vegetable markets spilling out into the streets, window displays of exotic herbs and medicines, and pastry shops hawking some of the tastiest wares in town. It's all about the smells, the colors, and the single-minded shoppers tracking down bargains. **START: Bus 3 or 4 to 5th Avenue & James Street.**

1 ★★ **kids** **Uwajimaya.** Yes, it's a grocery store, but this is also a bona fide tourist destination. Built by a Japanese patriarch whose family was interned during World War II, this enormous supermarket—now run by his children—is stocked with exotic Asian produce, meats, baked goods, and other products. You can check its website for recipes from eight Asian countries, then do some shopping! There is also an Asian bookstore, gift shop, and a large dine-in area that gives an entirely new meaning to the term "food court." It's easy to lose track of time in here. 🕐 *1 hr. 600 5th Ave. S.* ☎ *206/624-6248.*

www.uwajimaya.com. *Mon–Sat 8am–10pm, Sun 9am–9pm.*

2 **kids** **Hing Hay Park.** This small but unusual park is situated on a red-bricked square. The colorful pagoda, crafted in Taipei, Taiwan, is the genuine article, as is the spectacular dragon artwork. If you have time, settle in at one of the chess tables for a leisurely game. The city is in the process of doubling the size of the park, a popular gathering spot that often hosts the Lunar New Year Lion Dances in February. 🕐 *15 min. 423 Maynard Ave. S. (at King St.).*

Hing Hay Park reflects the influence of Chinese culture on the neighborhood.

At the Panama Hotel, trunks left behind by Japanese families sent to internment camps are a reminder of a painful past.

❸ ★ Historic Panama Hotel Bed & Breakfast Tea & Coffee House.

You can sip Italian Lavazza coffee or choose from a global tea menu at this elegant shop in the historic Panama Hotel, which housed Japanese workingmen in the early 20th century. When owner Jan Johnson bought the hotel, she discovered trunks full of personal items left behind and never reclaimed by Japanese families sent off to internment camps. You can view one of these trunks through a glass window in the tea shop's wooden floor. Many other items are on display as a history lesson and a reminder of a regrettable moment in time. 🕐 *30 min. 607 S. Main St.* ☎ *206/515-4000. www.panama hotelseattle.com.*

❹ ★ Kobo at Higo.

History stands still at this shop, housed in the former Higo Variety Store, a Japanese five-and-dime that stood in this spot for 75 years. The Murakami family

had to board it up while they were sent to an internment camp, but reopened when they returned. Sadly, Mr. Murakami died very shortly afterward, but his widow and children kept it going until 2003, when the youngest daughter retired. Happily, the new owners, John Bisbee and Binko Chiong-Bisbee, have preserved much of the past, including pre-war merchandise and family mementos. Be sure to check out the display wall devoted to the old Higo. But the Bisbees have brought stylish new treasures to the shop, which they have turned into a Japanese and Northwest fine-art and craft gallery. 🕐 *30 min. 604 S. Jackson St.* ☎ *206/381-3000. koboseattle.com. Mon–Sat 11am–6pm, Sun noon–5pm.*

Take a Break

❺ ★★ A Piece of Cake.

This is my favorite bakery in Seattle. The cakes are feather-light, the frosting flavorful but not too sweet, and the fillings creative. My favorite, in season, is the melon ball-filled cake. Yum! The cakes here are works of art, perfect for a very special occasion. Other times, I order a cup of tea and a pineapple bun. 🕐 *30 min. 514 S. King St.* ☎ *206/381-3000. $.*

❻ ★★ 𝗸𝗶𝗱𝘀 Wing Luke Asian Museum.

This Smithsonian Institution–affiliated museum, one of the best of its kind in the nation, is a great community resource in the midst of a diverse neighborhood. Its library, which is open to the public during

Desserts at A Piece of Cake taste as good as they look.

Chinatown/International District

Kobo at Higo is more than a shop—it offers a glimpse into the area's past.

Take a Break

7 Ambrosia Cafe. This was the first shop in the International District to specialize in pearl tea, a craze that started in Taiwan. Now available all over town—more often called "bubble tea"—the icy drink consists of brewed tea mixed with sweetened milk and syrups, poured into a tall cup filled with gumball-size tapioca balls. You drink it through a straw wide enough to suck up the "bubbles." It's an odd sensation the first time or two, but then you get hooked. Try the mango and green tea flavors. *619 S. King St.* ☎ *206/623-9028.* **$.**

museum hours, includes a wealth of oral and video histories, photos, and books about the experiences of Asian-Pacific Americans in the Northwest. ⏱ *1 hr. 719 S. King St. at 8th Ave. S.* ☎ *206/623-5124. www.wingluke.org. $12.95 adults, $9.95 seniors & students, $.95 ages 5–12. Price includes tour of historic building/former hotel. Tues–Sun 10am–5pm, 1st Thurs of month & 2nd Sat of month 10am–8pm. See p 23.*

8 Chinese Gate. After a half-century of grassroots efforts, Seattle's Chinatown has its own traditional entrance gate, just like other major cities with large Chinese populations, such as San Francisco and Los Angeles. The eye-catching, 45-foot archway was unveiled in 2008. The $500,000 gate, according to tradition, should bring luck and strength. It also greets visitors and makes it easier to spot the district. There are hopes of building a second gate on the other end of the neighborhood. *S. King St., just east of 5th Ave. S.*

Bathhouse Tour

When early Japanese immigrants came to the United States, they built hundreds of community bathhouses, just like they had at home. The bathhouses, or *sentos*, were culturally important places to socialize, relax in the hot water, and clean off after a hard day's work. Only one remains intact in its original location, and that is the marble bath in the basement of the **Historic Panama Hotel Bed & Breakfast in Seattle.** It officially closed in 1950, but is still open for historic tours. To schedule one, call Jan Johnson at ☎ **206/223-9242.**

Wallingford

7th Ave. NE

5

finish here 12

4th Ave. NE

Latona Ave. NE

Thackery Pl. NE

2nd Ave. NE

1st Ave. NE

NE 43rd St.

NE 42nd St.

1st Ave. NE

NE 40th St.

NE Pacific St.

Eastern Ave. N.

Sunnyside Ave. N.

Corliss Ave. N.

Bagley Ave. N.

N. 42nd St.

N. 41st St.

10

9

N. 45th St.

8

N. 44th St.

N. 43rd St.

Meridian Ave. N.

Burke Ave. N.

N. 40th St.

11

5 6

Wallingford Ave. N.

4

Densmore Ave. N.

7

3

Woodlawn Ave. N.

Wallingford Playfield

Ashworth Ave. N.

N. 46th St.

2

Interlake Ave. N.

Interlake Ave. N.

1

start here

N. 45th St.

Stone Way N.

Midvale Ave. N.

Area of detail

Lake Washington

SEATTLE

Puget Sound

5 mi

5 km

200 yds

200 m

① Archie McPhee
② Alphabet Soup
③ Molly Moon's Ice Cream
④ Fuel Coffee
⑤ Bad Woman Yarn
⑥ Izilla Toys
⑦ Wallingford Playfield
⑧ Not a Number
⑨ Guild 45th
⑩ The Erotic Bakery
⑪ Irwin's Neighborhood Bakery and Cafe
⑫ Wine World Warehouse

One of Seattle's most charming residential neighborhoods, Wallingford's leafy streets are lined with lovingly restored Craftsman bungalows. Some of the city's finest ethnic restaurants—and a few of its most eclectic shops—can be found in Wallingford's lively business district. There are parks galore for the kids to romp in, and a great little 1920s-era Art Deco movie house—it's an ideal spot to catch a blockbuster or, especially, an indie film. If you're here in early July, check the neighborhood website (www.wallingford.org) for the date of the annual Seafair Kiddies Parade & Fair. It's a day full of pirates, clowns, and general merrymaking for all ages. START: **Bus 16 or 44 to Stone Way North & N. 45th Street.**

1 ★★ kids Archie McPhee.
From rubber chickens to avenging narwhals to underpants for your hands, if it's weird, wacky, and fun, this is where you'll find it. For a quarter-century, Seattleites have flocked to Archie McPhee for sensory overload—or just a giggle. And yes, there really was an Archie McPhee, a fun-loving guy. ⏲ *30 min. 1300 N. 45th St. ☎ 206/297-0240. www.archiemcpheeseattle.com. Mon–Sat 10am–7 pm, Sun 11am–6pm.*

2 ★ kids Alphabet Soup.
This is a magical place for kids, well-stocked with new, used, and vintage

If it's wacky, you'll find it at Archie McPhee.

children's books—and even a small used section for Mom and Dad. The picture books are wonderful, and the prices are low enough that you'll leave with an armful. ⏲ *15 min. 1406 N. 45th St. ☎ 206/547-4555. Thurs–Sun 10am–8pm.*

3 ★★ kids Molly Moon's Ice Cream. Sure, you can find an ice-cream shop just about anywhere. But you can only find Molly Moon's Ice Cream in two locations on the planet, and this is one of them. The ingredients are locally made, but the flavors are celestial. Try maple bacon, blood orange sorbet, or balsamic strawberry. Of course, you can get vanilla, but don't. ⏲ *15 min. 1622 N. 45th St. ☎ 206/547-5105. Daily noon–11pm.*

4 Fuel Coffee. Friendly baristas and comfy chairs make this a great spot for refueling. You might need the caffeine to keep you moving post-Molly Moon's. And if you need to catch up on e-mail, you'll find lighted tables in the back, and free Wi-Fi. *1705 N. 45th St. ☎ 206/634-2700. $.*

5 Bad Woman Yarn. Tucked into the Wallingford Center—a historic schoolhouse-turned-shopping-destination—is this gem of a shop,

Try the maple bacon at Molly Moon's Ice Cream, where the ingredients are local and the flavors are out of this world.

overflowing with colorful, fluffy balls and a staff that will help you find the right yarn to bring that perfect pattern to life. If you have an open afternoon or evening, join the locals for a free knitting group or sign up for a class ($17 and up). Check the schedule on the website. ⏱ *15 min. 1815 N. 45th St.* ☎ *206/547-5384. www.badwomanyarn.com. Mon–Fri 10am–8pm, Sat 10am–6pm, Sun 11am–5pm.*

❻ ★ **Izilla Toys.** Whether you're in the market for a child-size accordion or a basic set of wooden blocks, you'll probably find it here among the rows of quality toys from around the world. The self-serve gift-wrapping table is a nice touch. Even better, Izilla offers free music classes and storytimes for the little ones. Check the website for dates and times. ⏱ *15 min. 1815 N. 45th St.* ☎ *206/547-5204. www.izillatoys. com. Mon–Fri 10am–8pm, Sat 10am–6pm, Sun 10am–5pm.*

❼ **kids Wallingford Playfield.** After a morning of shopping, the kids will be ready to burn off some energy. A great place to do that is at Wallingford Park, where you'll find lots of equipment for climbing, a water play area for splashing—and a huge grassy area. ⏱ *30 min. 4219 Wallingford Ave. N.* ☎ *206/ 684-4075. www.seattle.gov/parks. Daily 4am–11:30pm.*

❽ ★ **Not a Number.** This is one of my favorite shops to poke around in, especially if I have a friend's birthday coming up—and a good sense of humor. You can buy cat-butt refrigerator magnets, clever cards, and fun jewelry and T-shirts by local artists. There are also loads of (left-leaning) buttons with attitude. ⏱ *15 min. 1907½ N. 45th St.* ☎ *206/784-0965. notanumbergifts. com. Tues–Fri 11am–7pm, Sat 11am–8pm, Sun noon–5pm.*

❾ **Guild 45th.** This Art Deco–style theater has screens in two separate buildings. The first one opened in 1919; the second in the 1980s. The Guild specializes in running edgy and foreign films. *2115 N. 45th St.* ☎ *206/781-5755. www.landmark theatres.com/Market/Seattle/ Guild45thTheatre.htm.*

❿ **The Erotic Bakery.** Oh, my! These baked goods—cookies and cakes with suggestive decorations—are for adults only. They're in demand for bachelor's and bachelorette's parties, and the staff is

Gasworks Park

Seattle's favorite place to go fly a kite, this former gas-manu-facturing-plant-turned-park also boasts one of the most spectacular views in town. If you don't happen to have a kite, stop at the **Gasworks Park Kite Shop** (3420 Stone Way; ☎ 206/633-4780; www.gasworksparkkiteshop.com), where you'll find an assortment ranging from box to stunt kites to windsocks. Take along a blanket and throw a picnic at the top of the hill, overlooking Lake Union, the Space Needle and—on a clear day—Mount Rainier. It doesn't get better than this. Years ago, the city—making lemonade out of the proverbial lemon—turned the abandoned boiler house into a picnic shelter and the old compressor building into a play area where kids can explore the now brightly painted machinery. From the parking lot, you can also access the popular **Burke-Gilman Trail,** a 12.5-mile route following the old path of the Burlington-Northern Railroad. Walkers, joggers, cyclists, and skaters share the fresh air.

happy to ship for you. ⏱ *15 min. 2323 N. 45th St.* ☎ *206/545-6969. www.theeroticbakery.com. Mon–Sat 10am–7pm.*

Flying a kite at Gasworks Park.

⑪ Irwin's Neighborhood Bakery and Cafe. Right about now, a homemade pizza, soup, or chicken potpie should hit the spot. Real men—and women—will love the quiche Diablo, chock-full of hot peppers. Go ahead, finish up with a slice of pie. *2123 N. 40th St.* ☎ *206/675-1484. $.*

⑫ Wine World Warehouse. The latest addition to Wallingford's shopping menu is this 23,000-square-foot superstore, the largest wine shop in the Northwest. It's packed with gleaming bottles from around the world—including at least 500 wines from Washington State, whose wineries have made a major global splash in recent years. Step up to the elegant tasting bar for daily wine samplings (Mon–Fri 6–8pm, Sat–Sun 2–5pm) from up to 10 wineries. ⏱ *30 min. 400 NE 45th St.* ☎ *206/402 6086. www. wineworldwarehouse.com. Daily 11am–9pm.*

Fremont

1 Fremont Troll
2 Statue of Lenin
3 Royal Grinders
4 Fremont Rocket
5 PCC Natural Markets
6 *Waiting for the Interurban* Statue

The self-proclaimed center of the universe (with a sign to prove it), this funky north-end neighborhood has a quirkiness that several years of gentrification have failed to destroy. Tech firms Adobe Systems and Getty have built their headquarters here, and high-end condos followed. Though some of the cottage-industry art studios have given way to higher-rent tenants, this is still an artsy kind of place. One of my favorite things about Fremont is the eccentric public art scattered about the neighborhood. When I'm not in the mood for the urban pace of shopping downtown, I head for friendly, relaxed Fremont. **START: Under the north end of the Aurora Avenue Bridge, at N. 36th St.**

---

1 ★★ kids Fremont Troll. If you drive over the Aurora Avenue Bridge, better hope your car doesn't suffer the same fate as the Volkswagen Bug plucked off the road by the nasty-tempered troll lurking below. At least, that's how the story goes. The 18-foot-high troll, which reflects

the neighborhood's Scandinavian roots, is much friendlier if you visit him in person. You can climb on him all you want, and he's okay with family pictures, too. Back in 1989, when the Fremont Arts Council held a nationwide search for a piece of public art to go under the bridge,

Yes, that rocket was once property of the U.S. Army.

Fremont residents overwhelming voted for the troll—and the VW held in his clutches. 🕐 *15 min. N. 36th St., under the Aurora Ave. Bridge, also known as the George Washington Memorial Bridge.*

2 ★ Statue of Lenin. We're talking Vladimir. The sculpture of the former Russian revolutionary ended up in Fremont on a fluke, and

Stop by and say hi to VI Lenin.

here it has stayed, despite controversy. It was brought back from Slovakia by a Seattle-area bronze artist who was considering selling it for scrap when he met with an untimely death. His family had the statue moved near a brass foundry In Fremont, and no one has figured out what to do with it since. Now it's become a part of this eccentric neighborhood where hardly anything seems out of place. If you're here during a holiday season, expect to see Lenin decked out in appropriate garb. 🕐 *15 min. 36th St. & Evanston Ave. N.*

Take a Break

3 Royal Grinders. Tucked behind Lenin's statue is a great little spot where you can cool off with a tasty gelato. The challenge is choosing from the eclectic menu of flavors—a couple of dozen, ranging from lavender to cappuccino chip. Feeling droopy? Try one "drowned" in espresso. If you're hungry, the freshly made, toasted subs come piled high with veggies and meats. *3526 Fremont Place N.* ☎ *206/545-7560. $.*

Commuters everywhere can relate to Waiting for the Interurban.

❹ ★ Fremont Rocket. It's an odd twist of fate that the statue of Lenin ended up just down the block from a 55-foot for-real Cold War-era rocket, taken from an Army surplus store, mounted on a building in Fremont and—voila!—turned into art. Stop by in the evening to see the rocket's onboard lights ablaze. ⏱ *15 min. 35th St. & Evanston Ave. N.*

❺ PCC Natural Markets. Fruits and veggies have never been so much fun, and these are bursting with flavor, much of it from local farms. PCC is an all-organic store with a produce section so irresistible, I'll go out of my way to shop here. Kids get free fruit, so be sure to ask. This is a full-service grocery store, and all the cosmetic and fragrance products are animal cruelty-free. It's technically a co-op, but non-members can shop here, too. I can never pass by the bakery, which features such unusual items as Paris balsamic pear tarts—a personal favorite—and vegan carrot cake. *600 N. 34th St.* ☎ *206/632-6811.*

❻ ★ *Waiting for the Interurban.* Six passengers and a dog wait endlessly for their train in this cast-aluminum sculpture memorializing the era of the electric rail line. It also memorializes a squabble between the sculptor, John Bayer, and Fremont political leader Armen Stepanian: the dog, as you'll notice, has a human face. Rumor has it that it's Stepanian's. Unless you look closely, you might mistake the riders for real people, as locals like to dress them up to mark everything from national holidays to weddings. It's such a tradition that the neighborhood's website (www.fremont.com) has a list of rules for decorating the statue. ⏱ *15 min. South side of N. 34th St.* ●

Shopping **Best Bets**

Best **Art Jewelry**
★★★ Twist, *600 Pine St. (p 92)*

Best **Bookstore** (New books)
★★★ Elliott Bay Book Company, *1521 10th Ave. (p 87)*

Best **Bookstore** (Used)
★★ Twice Sold Tales, *1833 Harvard Ave. (p 88)*

Best **Gifts**
★★★ Millstream, *112 1st. Ave. S. (p 92)*

Best **Glass**
★★★ Glasshouse Studio, *311 Occidental Ave. S. (p 93)*

Best **Hand-Crafted Wood Furniture**
★★ Northwest Fine Woodworking, *101 S. Jackson St. (p 91)*

Best **Pirates' Booty**
Pirates Plunder Gift Shop, *1301 Alaskan Way, Pier 57 (p 92)*

Best Place to Find an **Out-of-Town Newspaper**
★ First and Pike News, *93 Pike St. (p 88)*

Best **Rugs**
★ Palace Rug Gallery, *323 1st Ave. S. (p 96)*

Best **Fashion Bargains**
★★★ Nordstrom Rack, *1601 2nd Ave. (p 89)*

Best Place to Find **a Manly Skirt**
★ Utilikilts, *620 1st Ave. (p 91)*

Best **Shoes**
★★★ Nordstrom, *500 Pine St. (p 89)*

Best **Souvenirs**
★★ Made in Washington, *400 Pine St. (p 92)*

Best Place to Buy a **Gown for the Opera**
★★ Mario's, *1513 6th Ave. (p 90)*

Best **Toys**
★★ Magic Mouse Toys, *603 1st Ave. (p 96)*

Glass as works of art at Glasshouse Studios.

Downtown Shopping

See "Pike Place Market Shopping" map

See "Pioneer Square Shopping" map

Area of detail

SEATTLE

City Centre **14**	Facèré **14**	Nordstrom **6**	See's Candies **11**
City Kitchens **10**	Fireworks **7**	Nordstrom Rack **9**	Silver Platters **1**
Driscoll Robbins Fine Carpets **17**	Jeffrey Moose Gallery **15**	Pacific Place **5**	Twist **5**
Easy Street Records & CDs **3**	LUSH **7**	Pelindaba Lavender Gallery **14**	Watson Kennedy Fine Home **18**
Eddie Bauer **5**	Macy's **8**	Pirates Plunder **16**	Westlake Center **7**
E.E. Robbins **4**	Mario's **12**	Seattle Glassblowing Studio **2**	Young Flowers **19**
	Niketown **13**		

Pioneer Square Shopping

85

Pike Place Market Shopping

Shopping Best Bets

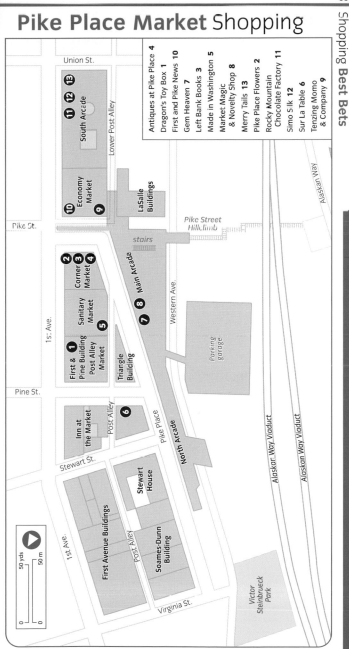

Antiques at Pike Place 4
Dragon's Toy Box 1
First and Pike News 10
Gem Heaven 7
Left Bank Books 3
Made in Washington 5
Market Magic
& Novelty Shop 8
Merry Tails 13
Pike Place Flowers 2
Rocky Mountain
Chocolate Factory 11
Simo Silk 12
Sur La Table 6
Tenzing Momo
& Company 9

Capitol Hill Shopping

Crossroads Trading Co. **3**
Dilettante Mocha Café **2**
Elliott Bay Book Company **9**
Kobo Shop and Gallery **1**
Metro Clothing Co. **5**

Mud Bay Granary **4**
Panache **6**
Trendy Wendy **7**
Twice Sold Tales **8**
Wall of Sound **10**

Seattle Shopping **A to Z**

Antiques
Antiques at Pike Place PIKE PLACE MARKET   This is a wonderful shop to poke around in, and you'll likely find something you can't live without, whether it's a Mickey Mantle baseball card, a toy from your past, or a gorgeous estate ring. *92 Stewart St.* ☎ *206/441-9643. www. antiquesatpikeplace.com. AE, DISC, MC, V. Bus: 10 or 99. Map p. 85.*

The Cutty Sark PIONEER SQUARE Nautical antiques— from compasses to ship's wheels—are sold here, making it the perfect place to grab gifts for all the old salts on your list. *320 1st Ave. S.* ☎ *206/262-1265. www.cutty antiques.com. AE, DISC, MC, V. Bus: 85 or 99. Map p 84.*

Flanagan & Lane Antiques features fine china and glassware, among other items.

★ Flanagan & Lane Antiques PIONEER SQUARE   The French furniture is exquisite; so are the Chinese fans and dishes. Don't miss the interesting assortment of antique clocks. *165 S. Jackson St.* ☎ *206/682-0098. AE, DISC, MC, V. Map p 84. Bus: 13, 85, or 99.*

Art
Akanyi African & Tribal Art Gallery PIONEER SQUARE   African and tribal art are showcased at this unique shop, which features a large collection of musical instruments, masks and furniture from the various regions of Africa. *155 S. Main St.* ☎ *206/381-3133. www.akanyiafrican art.com. AE, DISC, MC, V. Bus: 1, 2, 4, 13, 43, 49, 85, or 99. Map p 84.*

G. Gibson Gallery PIONEER SQUARE   The focus here is on fine art photography. You'll also find contemporary sculptures and paintings by locally and internationally important artists. *300 S. Washington St.* ☎ *206/587-4033. www.ggibson gallery.com. MC, V. Bus: 1, 2, 4, 13, 43, or 49. Map p 84.*

★★ Jeffrey Moose Gallery DOWNTOWN   This eclectic shop specializes in indigenous art, including Australian aboriginal works, Native-American masks and carvings. *1333 5th Ave., Ste. 511.* ☎ *206/467-6951. www.jeffreymoosegallery.com. AE, MC, V. Bus: 85, 106, 150, 255, 545, or 577. Map p 83.*

Books and Magazines
★★★ kids Elliott Bay Book Company CAPITOL HILL   Seattle's

Jeffrey Moose Gallery specializes in indigenous art.

premier bookstore is a must-do for any bibliophile. *1521 10th Ave. ☎ 206/624-6600. www.elliottbay book.com. AE, DISC, MC, V. Bus: 10, 11, 43, 49, 60, or 84. Map p 86.*

★ **First and Pike News** PIKE PLACE MARKET   With more than 1,000 magazine titles and over 200 newspapers from around the world, this is my favorite place to go to read all about it. *93 Pike St. ☎ 206/624-0140. www.firstandpikenews. com. AE, DISC, MC, V. Bus: 10, 99, 113, 121, or 122. Map p 85.*

★ **Globe Bookstore** PIONEER SQUARE   Be forewarned: It's easy to spend more time than you planned in this terrific little bookshop, packed with new and used mysteries, history books, children's books, and cookbooks. *218 1st Ave. S. ☎ 206/682-6882. AE, DISC, MC, V. Bus: 16, 66, 86, or 99. Map p 84.*

★ **Left Bank Books** PIKE PLACE MARKET   For nearly 4 decades, this employee-owned collective has reflected Seattle's labor-movement roots. Its collections include an anarchy section, LGBT literature, short stories, an amazing collection of magazines, and lots of clever, left-leaning T-shirts. *92 Pike St. ☎ 206/622-0195. www.leftbank books.com. AE, DISC, MC, V. Bus: 10, 99, 113, 121, or 122. Map p. 85.*

★ **Seattle Mystery Bookshop** PIONEER SQUARE   Skullduggery reigns supreme here. Word of warning to mystery-lovers: This will not be a quick stop for you. And good luck stumping the well-informed staff. *117 Cherry St. ☎ 206/587-5737. www.seattlemystery.com. MC, V. Bus: 16, 66, 99, 554, or 594. Map p 84.*

★★ **Twice Sold Tales** CAPITOL HILL   You'd be hard-pressed to find a deeper inventory of used books. Plan on plenty of time to browse.

Mystery buffs will want to set aside plenty of time for the Seattle Mystery Bookshop.

And if you're a cat-lover, make time to play with the kitties that roam the shop as well. Locations include: *1833 Harvard Ave. ☎ 206/324-2421. 4501 University Way NE. ☎ 206/545-4226. www.twicesoldtales.info. MC, V. Bus: 8, 43, 49, or 60. Map p 86.*

Candy

★★ **Dilettante Mocha Café** CAPITOL HILL   Don't pass up the hand-dipped truffles, made with recipes passed down from the owners' great uncle, who prepared them for the Imperial Court of Austria. If you fall in love, you can join their chocolate club and get treats delivered to your door every month. Locations include: *538 Broadway E. ☎ 206/329-6463. www.dilettante.com. AE, MC, V. Bus: 49 or 60. Map p 86.*

Rocky Mountain Chocolate Factory PIKE PLACE MARKET   The colorful rows of apples dipped in rich chocolates and caramel, then rolled in a variety of toppings, are almost irresistible. And once you're inside, may as well sample a piece of creamy homemade fudge. *1419 1st Ave.* ☎ *206/262-9581. www.rmcf.com. AE, DISC, MC, V. Bus: 10, 99, 113, 121, or 122. Map p 85.*

★★ **See's Candies** DOWNTOWN See's offers scrumptious gourmet candies at a good value. The company has been around for about 90 years, and it has come up with a variety of new tastes in addition to its tried-and-true favorites. Downtown location: *1518 4th Ave.* ☎ *206/682-7122. www.sees.com. AE, DISC, MC, V. Bus: 10, 11, 14, 43, or 81. Map p 83.*

Department Stores

★★ **Macy's** DOWNTOWN High-end clothing, jewelry, housewares and cosmetics are beautifully displayed in a historic Seattle building. Check out the sales racks. *1601 3rd Ave.* ☎ *206/506-6000. www.macys.com. AE, DISC, MC, V. Bus: 1, 11, 13, 14, or 43. Map p 83.*

★★★ **Nordstrom** DOWNTOWN The shoes! Nordstrom got its start over a century ago as a humble Seattle shoe store and, while it's hardly humble anymore, it's still those fabulous shoes that lure me in. Of course, there's much, much more, and it's high quality, with high price tags to match. Watch for Nordstrom's legendary Half Yearly sales. *500 Pine St.* ☎ *206/628-2111. www.nordstrom.com. AE, DISC, MC, V. Bus: 10, 11, 14, 43, or 83. Map p 83.*

Discount/Consignment Shopping
Crossroads Trading Co. CAPITOL HILL Not all the clothes here are used, but the only way to tell is by the tags, because everything looks new and hip. This is not the cheapest consignment shop, but you'll find great stuff here, especially since its new expansion doubled the fun. *325 Broadway E.* ☎ *206/328-5847. www.crossroadstrading.com. DISC, MC, V. Bus: 8, 43, 49, or 60. Map p 86.*

★★★ **Nordstrom Rack** DOWNTOWN You'll have to do some hunting, but that's part of the fun. Among the racks and racks of designer clothes, housewares, and—yes!—shoes, quite a few treasures are usually waiting to be discovered. *1601 2nd Ave.* ☎ *206/448-8522. www.nordstrom.com. AE, DISC, MC, V. Bus: 10, 11, 14, 99, or 554. Map p 83.*

Fashion
Eddie Bauer DOWNTOWN This Northwest-based company specializes, fittingly, in sportswear and

Stock up on fabulous fashions at Trendy Wendy.

Polka dots are all the rage at funky Capitol Hill boutiques.

outdoor gear. You can also find business casual attire and bedding. *600 Pine St., Ste. 230.* ☎ *206/622-2766. www.eddiebauer.com. AE, DISC, MC, V. Bus: 10, 11, 14, 43, or 49. Map p 83.*

★★ **Mario's** DOWNTOWN   For that perfect evening gown, if money is no object, you're sure to find a jaw-dropper here. The men's clothing is also exceptional. Everything is beautifully tailored, and the service equally impeccable. *1513 6th Ave.* ☎ *206/223-1461. www.marios.com. AE, DISC, MC, V. Bus: 10, 11, 14, 43, or 49. Map p 83.*

The Metro Clothing Co. CAPITOL HILL   This shop is for the painfully hip only (except at Halloween!), or just the curious. If you're looking for leather and lace, or thigh-high red boots, this is your destination. *231 Broadway E.* ☎ *206/726-7978. MC, V. Bus: 8, 9, 43, 49, or 60. Map p 86.*

Panache CAPITOL HILL   The name fits this quirky little shop perfectly. The clothing here is trendy but elegant, and there are plenty of options for accessorizing. They have misses' and junior sizes, plus

a separate men's section. *225 Broadway E.* ☎ *206/726-3300. MC, V. Bus: 9, 49, or 60. Map p 86.*

★ **Ragazzi's Flying Shuttle** PIONEER SQUARE   The art is wearable at this shop, which offers hand-woven apparel and accessories, and a fun collection of original contemporary jewelry. *607 1st Ave.* ☎ *206/343-9762. www.ragazzisflyingshuttle.com. AE, MC, V. Bus: 10, 11, 16, 66, or 99. Map p 84.*

★ **Simo Silk** PIKE PLACE MARKET   Named for the owner's sons, Simeon and Moses, this shop offers a large selection of buttery soft, mostly washable, silk shirts, scarves, jackets, and bedding from Asia. There's now a second shop in Pioneer Square. *1411 1st Ave. #108.* ☎ *206/521-8816. www.simosilk.com. AE, DISC, MC, V. Bus: 10, 99, 113, 121, or 122. Map p 85.*

Trendy Wendy CAPITOL HILL   You'll get the red-carpet welcome here, literally. Very hip clothes and accessories. And there's even a plus-size section. *211 Broadway E.* ☎ *206/322-6642. AE, DISC, MC, V. Bus: 8, 9, 43, 49, or 60. Map p 86.*

Artisan woodworkers craft stunning furniture at Northwest Fine Woodworking.

★ **Utilikilts** PIONEER SQUARE If the slogan "Free Your Balls and Free Yourself" appeals, you'll want to check out these liberating kilts for men. There are eight basic styles, all handmade; custom orders cost extra. *620 1st Ave.* ☎ *206/282-4226. www.utilikilts.com. AE, DISC, MC, V. Bus: 10, 11, 16, 66, or 99. Map p 84.*

Flowers

★ **Pike Place Flowers** PIKE PLACE MARKET This charming little corner shop, near the entrance to Pike Place Market, has been the focus of many photos of the Market. The arrangements are unique. *1501 1st Ave.* ☎ *206/682-9797. www. pikeplaceflowers.com. AE, DISC, MC, V. Bus: 10, 99, 113, 121, or 122. Map p 85.*

★ **Young Flowers** DOWNTOWN If you're looking for something sophisticated and different, you can't do better than this little shop, small in size but very big in creativity. *1111 3rd Ave.* ☎ *206/628-3077. AE, MC, V. Bus: 11, 15, 18, 121, or 122. Map p. 83.*

Furniture

★ **Northwest Fine Woodworking** PIONEER SQUARE The one-of-a-kind furniture and decor items you'll find at this 30-year-old cooperative are crafted by artisan woodworkers. They feature stunning blends of woods. The price tags are high, but the quality is superb. *101 S. Jackson.* ☎ *206/625-0542. www. nwfinewoodworking.com. AE, DISC, MC, V. Bus: 10, 11, 85, or 99. Map p 84.*

Gems

★ **kids Agate Designs** PIONEER SQUARE A 300-pound amethyst geode might be a bit large for your house, but a pair of bookends or a small fountain might be just right. The items sold here are made from

Rock collectors rejoice! Even non-collectors will enjoy checking out Agate Designs' cool offerings.

dazzling gems, minerals, and fossils. There's something for every budget, and the owner is happy to share his wealth of knowledge. *120 1st Ave S.* ☎ *206/621-3063. www.agatedesigns. com. AE, DISC, MC, V. Map p 84.*

kids Gem Heaven PIKE PLACE MARKET You'll feast your eyes on gorgeous gemstones, crystals, minerals, and jewelry at this great little shop "Down Under" in the Market. *1501 Pike Place #408.* ☎ *206/381-9302. www.gemheaven.net. AE, MC, V. Bus: 10, 99, 113, 121, or 122. Map p 85.*

Gifts

★★★ **kids Fireworks** DOWNTOWN There are two themes at Fireworks: whimsy and inspiration, and often a combination of the two. Check out the revolving shadow lanterns, handmade by Northwest artists. *400 Pine St.* ☎ *206/-682-6462. www.fireworksgallery.net. AE, DISC, MC, V. Bus: 10, 14, 41, 71, or 72. Map p 83.*

★ **Kobo Shop and Gallery** CAPITOL HILL Beautiful and sophisticated Northwest and Asian

Fireworks offers one-stop shopping for all of those items you don't really need but really, really want.

products are the focus here: pottery, teas, unusual gifts, and travel items. *814 E. Roy St.* ☎ *206/726-0704. www.koboseattle.com. MC, V. Bus: 9 or 49. Map p 86.*

★★ **Made in Washington** PIKE PLACE MARKET This is no tacky souvenir shop. Take something home to your friends from Made in Washington and it's guaranteed not to end up at their garage sale. *1530 Post Alley.* ☎ *206/467-0788. Downtown location: 400 Pine St.* ☎ *206/623-9753. www.madeinwashington.com. AE, DISC, MC, V. Bus: 10, 99, 113, 121, or 122. Map p 85.*

★ **Merry Tails** PIKE PLACE MARKET This is a great place to find a souvenir for Fido, or for any pet lover on your list. You'll find lots of breed-specific items and unusual gifts. *1409 1st Ave.* ☎ *206/623-4142. AE, DISC, MC, V. Bus: 12, 99, or 125. Map p. 85.*

★★★ **Millstream** PIONEER SQUARE I always feel like I'm stepping into a mountain cabin when I enter this woodsy-themed shop. Inside you'll find the talents of many serious Pacific Northwest artists—jewelry crafted from British Columbia jade and wood carvings. Millstream is back in its original location after spending a decade at Westlake Center. *112 1st*

Ave. S. ☎ *206/233-9719. www.millstreamseattle.com. AE, DISC, MC, V. Bus: 10, 11, 16, 66, or 99. Map p 84.*

★ **Noble Horse Gallery** PIONEER SQUARE True to its name, this unusual shop is filled with every horse item imaginable—and quite a few you'd never think of. You can buy equestrian-themed art, clothes, books, and home decor, including horse-shaped shower hooks. And yes, you can buy a saddle here. *216 1st Ave. S.* ☎ *206/382-8566. www.noblehorsegallery.com. AE, DISC, MC, V. Bus: 10, 11, 16, 66, or 99. Map p 84.*

kids **Pirates Plunder** WATERFRONT Here's where to go for everything pirate! Seriously, this shop specializes in pirate-related booty ranging from T-shirts to artwork. *1301 Alaskan Way.* ☎ *206/624-5673. www.piratesplunder.com. AE, DISC, MC, V. Bus: 10, 11, 12, 99, or 113. Map p 83.*

★★★ **Twist** DOWNTOWN This exuberant Northwest store, located in Pacific Place shopping mall, features whimsical hand-carved furniture, avant garde art, jewelry, and beautiful glassware. *600 Pine St., Ste. 130.* ☎ *206/315-8080. www.twistonline.com. AE, DISC, MC, V. Bus: 10, 11, 14, 43, or 49. Map p 83.*

Millstream showcases the work of local talent.

Ahoy, matey! A wooden pirate keeps an eye on Pirates Plunder.

fanciful work by a variety of artists. Be sure to check out the unique glass-art sinks. The studio is open to the public, so you can watch the artists at work. *2227 5th Ave.* ☎ *206/448-2181. www.seattleglassblowing. com. AE, DISC, MC, V. Bus: 56, 82, or 202. Map p 83.*

Housewares

★ **City Kitchens** DOWNTOWN Think kitchen stores are boring? You haven't seen this one. The shelves are filled with every gadget imaginable, plus an array of products for the serious cook, ranging from Cuisinart cookware to fine knives. Don't miss the close-out room. *1527 4th Ave.* ☎ *206/382-1138. www.city kitchensseattle.com. AE, DISC, MC, V. Bus: 81, 202, 215, 550, or 554. Map p 83.*

★ **Sur La Table** PIKE PLACE MARKET Everything at this store inspires even a mediocre cook like myself to go home and put on an apron. Better yet, pick one from the beautiful selection of kitchen and dining linens. My favorite section is the exotic oils and spices. *84 Pine St.* ☎ *206/448-2244. www.surla table.com. AE, DISC, MC, V. Bus: 99, 113, 121, or 122. Map p 85.*

★ **Watson Kennedy Fine Home** DOWNTOWN You'll feel like you're shopping along the Left Bank in this charmingly eclectic store, stocked with French teas and soaps, antiques, housewares, and bath products. I bought a decorative map of the Paris metro here. *1022 1st Ave.* ☎ *206/652-8350. www.watsonkennedy.com. AE, MC, V. Bus: 12, 16, 66, or 99. Map p 83.*

Glass

★★★ **Foster/White** PIONEER SQUARE This gallery, housed in a century-old building, is more than glass; you'll also find contemporary paintings and sculptures by premier artists. But its claim to fame is representing world-famous glass artist Dale Chihuly. Check the website for upcoming exhibitions. *220 3rd Ave. S.* ☎ *206/622-2833. www.foster white.com. AE, MC, V. Bus: 1, 2, 13, or 14. Map p 84.*

★★★ **kids Glasshouse Studio** PIONEER SQUARE In addition to being a working artists' studio, Glasshouse sells the wares of many local glass artists. The colors are exquisite, and you can buy everything from a simple vase to a huge chandelier shaped like an explosion of peppers. *311 Occidental Ave. S.* ☎ *206/682-9939. www.glasshouse-studio.com. AE, DISC, MC, V. Bus: 10, 85, or 99. Map p 84.*

★★★ **kids Seattle Glassblowing Studio** DOWNTOWN The studio offers classes in glassblowing, and the gallery features elegant and

Jewelry

★ **E.E. Robbins** DOWNTOWN Seattle's romantic place, and if you decide to pop the question while you're here, head to E.E. Robbins, where the owner is a third-generation diamond expert. The staff is friendly, never pushy, and they'll offer you a glass of wine while you shop. *2200 1st Ave.* ☎ *206/826-7464. www.eerobbins. com. AE, DISC, MC, V. Bus: 81 or 99. Map p 83.*

★ **Facèré** DOWNTOWN   This small store at City Centre is chock-full of stylish, unique art jewelry by Northwest, national, and international artists. You'll also find just the right antique or vintage piece to make your party dress sparkle. *1420 5th Ave. #108.* ☎ *206/624-6768. www.facerejewelryart.com. AE, MC, V. Bus: 306, 312, or 522. Map p 83.*

Malls

City Centre DOWNTOWN
Despite a limited number of stores, City Centre features some interesting clothing, leather goods, and jewelry shops; several excellent fast-food restaurants, and Palomino, a beautiful sit-down restaurant that happens to be among my

One of the unique displays at Twist (p. 82).

favorite lunch spots. *1420 5th Ave.* ☎ *206/624-8800. Store hours vary. Most open at 10am Mon–Sat and noon Sun; and close daily btw. 5pm & 9pm (Palomino stays open later). Bus: 306, 312, or 522. Map p. 83.*

★ **Pacific Place** DOWNTOWN
This elegant upscale mall is a great place for shopping, if your budget allows, but I also love just browsing its many unusual and artsy shops. *6th Ave. & Pine St.* ☎ *206/405-2655. www.pacificplaceseattle.com. Bus: 10, 11, 14, 43, or 49. Map p 83.*

★★ **Westlake Center** DOWN-TOWN   This is usually where I go when I actually want to buy something at a mall. You'll find lots of clothing and gift stores, with merchandise in every price range. *400 Pine St.* ☎ *206/467-1600. www. westlakecenter.com. Link Light Rail Westlake Station or bus 41, 71, 72, 301, or 316. Map p 83.*

Music/CDs

★★ **Easy Street Records and CDs** QUEEN ANNE   This roomy store is a music-lover's nirvana, offering a vast inventory of CDs and vinyl, and even in-store concerts. Private listening stations are scattered throughout the store. *20 Mercer St.* ☎ *206/691-3279. www. easystreetonline.com. AE, DISC, MC, V. Bus: 1, 8, 13, 15, or 18. Map p 83.*

★★ **Silver Platters** QUEEN ANNE
Odds are you'll be able to find that obscure CD at this spacious independent music shop, whether you're into punk or jazz. The staff is very knowledgeable. They also have a great movie selection on DVD. Check online for in-store performances and signings. *701 5th Ave. N.* ☎ *206/283-3472. www.silverplatters.com. MC, V. Bus: 3, 16, or 82. Map p 83.*

★★ **Wall of Sound** CAPITOL HILL
This eclectic shop specializes in

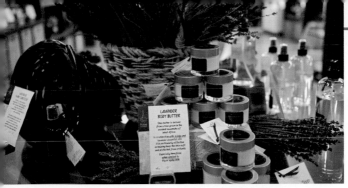

If you don't have time to visit the San Juan Islands, at least stock up on the area's finest lavender at Pelindaba Lavender Gallery.

international, avant-garde, electronic and experimental music, and you'll also find a great selection of mainstream CDs. Check the website for visiting artists and indie movie screenings. *315 E. Pine St.* ☎ *206/441-9880. www.wosound. com. AE, DISC, MC, V. Bus: 10, 11, 14, 43, or 49. Map p 86.*

Perfume/Skincare/Herbal Products

LUSH DOWNTOWN Who would have thought soap could be so much fun? You can suds yourself in just about any scent your heart desires. If you like, pick a sparkly bar, with glitter that lasts as long as the soap. *400 Pine St., Ste. 100.* ☎ *206/624-5874. www.lush.com. AE, DISC, MC, V. Link Light Rail Westlake Station or bus 41, 71, 72, 301, or 316. Map p 83.*

Pelindaba Lavender Gallery DOWNTOWN The home decor, personal care, and culinary items in this beautiful little shop are made from flowers grown on the organic Pelindaba Lavender farm on San Juan Island, northwest of Seattle. *400 Pine St.* ☎ *206/624-3236. www. pelindabalavender.com. AE, DISC, MC, V. Link Light Rail Westlake Station or bus 41, 71, 72, 301, or 316. Map p 83.*

Tenzing Momo & Company PIKE PLACE MARKET This little shop will meet all your New Age needs: aromatherapy oils and books, incense, herbs, and tarot cards. *93 Pike St., Ste. 203.* ☎ *206/ 623-9837. www.tenzingmomo.com. AE, DISC, MC, V. Bus: 10, 99, 113, 121, or 122. Map p 85.*

Pets

Mud Bay Granary CAPITOL HILL The pet food is natural and healthy, and you'll find every accessory a well heeled doggy—or feline—could dream of. *321 E. Pine St.* ☎ *206/322-6177. www.mudbay. us. AE, DISC, MC, V. Bus: 8, 43, 49, or 60. Map p 86.*

Rugs

★ **Driscoll Robbins Fine Carpets** DOWNTOWN Yes, there is a Driscoll Robbins, and he travels around the world in search of eye-catching hand-woven rugs—from traditional to contemporary designs—then displays them in an equally beautiful showroom. Warning: They are hard to resist. *1002 Western Ave.* ☎ *206/292-1115. www.driscollrobbins.com. AE, MC, V. Bus: 12, 16, or 66. Map p 83.*

★ **Palace Rug Gallery** PIONEER SQUARE   Colorful wool and silk rugs from Afghanistan, Pakistan, and China are stacked high in this large space. They are all handmade, and some take up to 16 months to complete. If you're local, you can take several home and try them out. *323 1st Ave. S. ☎ 206/382-7401. www.palacerug.com. AE, MC, V. Bus: 10, 85, or 99. Map p 84.*

Shoes

★ **The Clog Factory** PIONEER SQUARE   Talk about a niche! If you're in the market for clogs, this is definitely the place to go. Even if you're not, you might change your mind. They've got high-quality clogs in all colors, shapes, and sizes, from Mary Janes to slippers. *217 1st Ave. S. ☎ 206/682-2564. www.clog heaven.com. AE, DISC, MC, V. Bus: 10, 85, or 99. Map p 84.*

kids **Niketown** DOWNTOWN You'll find all the latest Nike shoes here, and lots of tributes to the top athletes who endorse them. *1500 6th Ave. ☎ 206/447-6453. AE, DISC, MC, V. Bus: 10, 11, 14, or 81. Map p 83.*

Nordstrom DOWNTOWN   No footwear listing is complete without the name that's synonymous with shoes in Seattle. *Map p 83.*

The Clog Factory specializes in—what else?—clogs.

Toys and Novelties

★ **kids** **Dragon's Toy Box** PIKE PLACE MARKET   From bath toys to puppets to chemistry sets, the shelves here are filled with top-quality toys designed to stimulate the imagination. The very helpful owners are a mother-and-daughter team. *1525 1st Ave., Ste. 2A. ☎ 206/652-2333. www.dragonstoybox.com. AE, DISC, MC, V. Bus: 10, 99, 113, 121, or 122. Map p 85.*

★★ **kids** **Izilla Toys** CAPITOL HILL   You'll find a world of fun here—literally. The shop features quality games and unusual toys from places like Vienna and Germany, plus a unique selection of arts & crafts projects. There's something for every kid here, from a Sock Monkey Jack-in-the-Box to medieval castle blocks. *1429 12th Ave., Ste. D. ☎ 206/322-8697. www.izillatoys.com. AE, DISC, MC, V. Bus: 2 or 12.*

★★ **kids** **Magic Mouse Toys** PIONEER SQUARE   Grown-ups have just as much trouble as kids in tearing themselves away from this wonderful, multi-level toy store. These are real toys, the kind built to last. Wander through rooms filled with learning-focused books, games, and kits—there's an entire room dedicated to puzzles. And of course, everyone is encouraged to play. *603 1st Ave. ☎ 206/682-8097. AE, DISC, MC, V. Bus: 10, 99, 157, or 158. Map p 84.*

★★ **kids** **Market Magic & Novelty Shop** PIKE PLACE MARKET   Making magic for 30 years, this store buried deep in the Market has been visited by a number of well-known magicians over the years. There's usually some sleight-of-hand in progress; just look for the row of gawking kids. *1501 Pike Place #427. ☎ 206/624-4271. AE, DISC, MC, V. Bus: 10, 99, 113, 121, or 122. Map p 85.* ●

98

The Seattle **Waterfront**

8th Ave.

Vine St.
Wall St.
BATTERY ST.
TUNNEL
BELLTOWN
MONORAIL
6th Ave.
Westlake Ave.

Western Ave.
Battery St.
Bell St.
Blanchard St.
3rd Ave.
4th Ave.
5th Ave.
Olive Way
7th Ave.

Elliott Ave.
1st Ave.
2nd Ave.
Lenora St.
Virginia St.
Stewart St.
Monorail Terminal

Pier 67
99
Alaskan Way
Victor Steinbrueck Park
Pine St.
5th Ave.
6th Ave.

Pier 66
(Bell Street Pier)
PIKE PLACE MARKET
Pike St.
4th Ave.
3rd Ave.
Union St.

DOWNTOWN
Benaroya Hall
University St.

Pier 63
Pier 62
Seattle Aquarium
Pike Street Hillclimb
Seattle Art Museum
2nd Ave.
Seneca St.

Pier 59
Waterfront Park
Harbor Steps
Spring St.

Pier 57
Pier 56
Western Ave.
Madison St.

Pier 55
Post Alley
Marion St.

To Bainbridge Island
Pier 54
Alaskan Way Viaduct
Columbia St.

To Bremerton
Pier 53
Alaskan Way
Pioneer Square
Yesler Way
PIONEER SQUARE

To Vashon Island
Pier 52
Pier 50
Occidental Park
S. Main St.

Elliott Bay
Pier 48

99
Alaskan Way S.
1st Ave. S.

Pier 46
Railroad Way S.

SEATTLE
Area of detail
Puget Sound
Lake Washington
0   1/4 mi
0   0.25 km
0   5 mi
0   5 km

1 Victor Steinbrueck Park
2 Cruise Terminals
3 Seattle Aquarium
4 Waterfront Park
5 Bay Pavilion
6 Argosy Cruises
7 Ivar's Seafood Bar
8 Ye Olde Curiosity Shop
9 Washington State Ferry Terminal

If there's one thing that rivals mountains in the hearts of Pacific Northwesterners, it's water. At the Seattle waterfront—on a clear day—you get both. The Olympics form a jaggedly endearing backdrop to the sparkling Elliott Bay. Add a few gleaming white ferryboats crisscrossing their way over the Puget Sound, and your souvenir snapshot is waiting. This is a lively place to spend the day—though noisy, because of traffic rushing along an elevated highway across from the waterfront. The city has plans to replace it, but not for a few years. START: **Bus 99, 113, 121, or 122 to 1st Avenue, walk to Western Avenue.**

❶ Victor Steinbrueck Park. Just north of Pike Place Market, toward the bay, lies a waterfront park named for a local architect who helped spearhead the efforts to save Pike Place Market. It's a great place for a picnic or people-watching. If the weather gods are with you, you'll be treated to a panorama of mountains—the Cascades (starring Mt. Rainier) curving around to the east and the Olympics to the west. Just be aware that panhandlers are frequent guests here, too. *2001 Western Ave. Daily 6am–10pm.*

❷ Cruise Terminals. Seattle is a great hopping-off point for cruises to Alaska, and that's where most of the luxury cruise ships you'll see here are headed. Six major cruise lines come and go from Seattle, which recently added a new terminal north of the old one. The cruise schedule is available on the Port of Seattle's website. I always get a kick out of watching the enormous floating hotels come and go. *2225 Alaskan Way S., Pier 66; 2001 W. Garfield St., Pier 91. ☎ 206/615-3900. www.portseattle.org/seaport/cruise/.*

❸ ★★ kids Seattle Aquarium. Be sure to grab a schedule of animal feeding times when you buy your tickets. It's not every day you'll get to see a gentle, giant octopus dine! At each mealtime "show," a naturalist gives a short talk. *1483 Alaskan*

Way on Pier 59. ☎ 206/386-4300. www.seattleaquarium.org. Admission: $17 adults, $11 ages 4–13. Daily 9:30am– pm (exhibits close at 6pm). See p 35.

❹ Waterfront Park. Stretching between Piers 57 and 59, this concrete park is my favorite spot for watching all the action out in Elliott Bay. It's not a green oasis, but you can't beat the location. With the *Waterfront Fountain* sculpture splashing merrily in the background, you can peer at your leisure at the working boats, cruise ships, and the occasional seal. Coin-operated

A statue of Christopher Columbus graces Waterfront Park.

Rides on the vintage carousel at Bay Pavilion cost $1.50 per person.

telescopes bring it all into focus. *1301 Alaskan Way.*

5 **kids** **Bay Pavilion.** On a drizzly day, this is a good place to duck out of the rain, browse the fun shops, and let the kids play the arcade games or take a spin on the merry-go-round. It's on Pier 57.

6 ★★★ **Argosy Cruises.** In addition to its tours of Tillicum Village and Elliott Bay, Argosy offers brunch, lunch, and dinner cruises; a tour of lakes Washington and Union (including the famous Seattle houseboats); and a cruise through the Hiram M. Chittenden Locks. There are themed cruises, holiday cruises, musical cruises—you name it, they've got a cruise. 🕐 *1–2½ hours. Pier 55, Seattle Waterfront.* ☎ *206/622-8687. www.argosycruises.com.*

7 ★ **Ivar's Seafood Bar.** The best bowl of clam chowder in Seattle, for my money, is right here at Ivar's, which has been dishing out local seafood since 1938. You can also get clams 'n chips, oysters 'n chips and a variety of other fresh, locally caught treats for munching as you wander the waterfront. Or take a break and relax at one of the outdoor tables set up beside the bar. *Pier 54, 1001 Alaskan Way.* ☎ *206/624-6852. $.*

Stop into Ivar's and try the excellent clam chowder.

Seattle Celebrates Summer

When the winters are as long and gray as they are in Seattle, who can blame the locals for going a little nuts when summer shows up, with its picture-perfect days that stretch until 10 at night? Getting a jump on the season is the **Northwest Folklife Festival,** which is held at Seattle Center in May and showcases the region's cultures. In June, the **Seattle Pride Festival** celebrates the gay community. At **Bite of Seattle** in July, crowds elbow their way into Seattle Center to hear live bands and sample gourmet treats and wine from local restaurants. Summer is officially kicked off by the **Fourth of July** fireworks over Lake Union, one of the finest displays in the nation. **Seafair** is a month of parades, competitions, and hydroplane races celebrating pirates and everything aquatic. The mother of all festivals, **Bumbershoot,** marks the end of summer and the return of drizzle. Fine arts, crafts, acrobats, big-name bands, and general zaniness rule supreme at Seattle Center over the Labor Day weekend.

8 Ye Olde Curiosity Shop. A century-old Seattle landmark, this is as much quirky museum as it is souvenir shop. The owner's great-grandfather gathered oddities from around the world and hired local Native Americans to carve totem poles. Shrunken heads and mummies share the shelves with Seattle T-shirts and homemade fudge. You'll never find another store like this! *Pier 54, 1001 Alaskan Way.* ☎ *206/682-5844. www.yeolde curiosityshop.com.*

9 Washington State Ferry Terminal. From here, you can glide your way to Bainbridge Island, Bremerton, or Vashon Island. There is passenger-only service to Vashon

from this spot, and if you're headed to Bainbridge Island or Bremerton you can walk on or take your car. The latter is pricier, and the lines can be much longer. If you just want to walk on a ferry, go for a ride and poke around town, Bainbridge (35 min.) is your best option. If you'd like a long, leisurely ride, take the hour-long Bremerton run. And if you want to go exploring the Kitsap or Olympic peninsulas (the latter takes you through the rainforest to the northwestern edge of the state), drive onto the Bremerton ferry and leave from the western side of Puget Sound. *801 Alaskan Way, Pier 52.*

Lake Union

N. 40th St.

Ship Canal

Bridge

University Bridge

Fuhrman Ave. E.

N. 39th St.

Fremont Ave. N.

Aurora Ave. N.

Stone Way N.

Wallingford Ave. N.

N. Pacific St.

FREMONT

WALLINGFORD

N. 35th St.

N. 34th St.

Eastlake Ave. E.

5

Fremont Bridge

G. Washington Mem. Bridge

Gasworks Park

Queen Anne Dr.

4th Ave. N.

Westlake Ave. N.

8th Ave. N.

E. Roanoke St.

520

EASTLAKE

Eastlake Ave. E.

Boylston Ave. E.

10th Ave. E.

Boston St.

5th Ave. N.

Newton St. N.

Lake Union

WESTLAKE

QUEEN ANNE

99

Garfield St.

Bigelow Ave.

Westlake Ave. N.

Aurora Ave. N.

Dexter Ave. N.

❶ Kayaking Lake Union

❷❹❻❼

Fairview Ave. N.

SEATTLE

Area of detail

Lake Washington

Aloha St.

Taylor Ave. N.

6th Ave. N.

❺

Valley St.

❸ Valley St.

Puget Sound

0   5 mi
0   5 km

LOWER QUEEN ANNE

Roy St.

Broad St.

Mercer St.

5

Melrose Ave. E.

SEATTLE CENTER

5th Ave.

8th Ave. N.

9th Ave. N.

SOUTH LAKE UNION

Republican St.

Westlake Ave. N.

Terry Ave. N.

Boren Ave. N.

Minor Ave. N.

Pontius Ave. N.

Yale Ave. N.

Eastlake Ave. N.

Harrison St.

Thomas St.

Taylor Ave. N.

6th Ave. N.

John St.

Denny Park

Fairview Ave.

Denny Way

❶ Kayaking Lake Union

❷ Center for Wooden Boats

❸ Tin Cup Espresso

❹ Sunday Ice Cream Cruise

❺ Kenmore Seaplanes

❻ The Farm Boat

❼ Queen of Seattle Paddlewheel

Broad St.

Clay St.

Cedar St.

Vine St.

7th Ave.

Terry Ave.

Westlake Ave.

Stewart St.

Howell St.

Olive Way

Pine St.

BELLTOWN

MONORAIL

DOWNTOWN

0   1/4 mi
0   0.25 km

D espite its prime waterfront location, this nei
north of downtown has been somewhat und
Seattleites. That's all changing now; apartments, shop
rants are popping up along the shore. This is an enterta
borhood, with seaplanes gracefully ascending and landi
gliding dreamily along the lake, and neighborhoods of h
dwellers going about their daily lives. START: **South Lake Union** Streetcar 98, or Bus 17, 70, 71, 72, or 73 to Lake Union.

The Seattle Streetcar runs along Lake Union.

❶ ★★ Kayaking Lake Union.

There's nothing quite like paddling a boat right in the heart of a city, especially one as picturesque as Seattle. Seaplanes buzz overhead and splash down nearby as you explore the houseboat "neighborhoods" and soak in the dramatic view of the Space Needle and Seattle's distinctive skyline. If you want to pay for the extra rental time, you can paddle up to the dock at one of the waterfront restaurants and enjoy a scenic lunch. Stay out for an hour or an entire day. You probably won't need lessons to kayak Lake Union, as it's usually calm, but they're available at the rental sites if you'd like a little training. *Boats may be rented at Moss Bay (1001 Fairview Ave. N., #1900, ☎ 206/682-2031. Kayak rentals June 1–Sept 15 $13/hr. single, $18/hr. double;*

guided lake tours available for small to large groups year-round, weather pending). Or head a bit farther west along the lake and rent a kayak year-round from Northwest Outdoor Center (2100 Westlake Ave. N., Ste. 1; ☎ 206/281-9694. Kayak rentals $13/hr. single, $19/hr. double, or $20/hr. triple). You can try out as many styles as you like before you choose which one to rent.

❷ ★ Center for Wooden Boats.

This unusual spot is basically an outdoor museum, where you can walk along the dock and enjoy a fascinating collection of historic and replica human- and wind-powered boats. You can also rent a sailboat or rowboat and take sailing lessons, and old salts will love the maritime library. *1010 Valley St. ☎ 206/382-2628. www.cwb.org. Rowboats and sailboats from*

The Center for Wooden Boats has an extensive collection of historic boats, both human- and wind-powered.

$20/hr. No admission fee. The Center offers a free sailboat ride at 2pm Sun. Come as early as 10am to sign up—these are popular events.

3 ★ **Tin Cup Espresso.** All that paddling around the lake really makes you work up an appetite, so grab a mocha and a sandwich (try the almond chicken salad) or a muffin. *900 Broad St.* ☎ *206/464-7296.*

4 ★ **Sunday Ice Cream Cruise.** Capt. Larry (Kezner) is your congenial host for a 45-minute cruise of Lake Union on his charming ferry boat. The captain knows everything there is to know about Lake Union, its houseboat communities, and environs—and provides a lively, entertaining narrative while passengers down their chocolate ice-cream floats. Other treats are also available. The boat—the *m/v Fremont*—leaves on the hour from 11am to 4pm year-round. *Valley Street & Terry Ave. N.* ☎ *206/713-8446. www.seattleferryservice.com. The cruise costs $11 adults, $10 seniors, $7 ages 5–13, $2 4 & under.*

5 ★ **Seaplane Flights.** What better way to see Seattle than from the air, and what more fitting take-off and landing than the water? Seaplanes have been leaving from Lake Union since 1916, and Kenmore Air has been flying floatplanes in the Pacific Northwest for more than half a century. Its Lake Union facility is

Don't miss getting an up-close view of Lake Union's charming houseboats.

Mega-Makeover

South Lake Union is undergoing a major transformation, thanks in large part to Microsoft co-founder/real estate magnate Paul Allen's vision of the area as a biotech hub and urban center. It's easy to get there via trolley—the new, bright red South Lake Union Streetcar—which runs between this neighborhood and downtown every 15 minutes. In addition to the biotechs, online bookseller Amazon.com is building a huge campus in South Lake Union, and the old Navy armory building is slated to become the new home of Seattle's much-loved Museum of History & Industry by 2012. In the meantime, visitors can enjoy the wide variety of boating and other waterfront activities along South Lake Union. If you work up a hunger, grab a burger or taco—or choose to dine at one of the stylish lakeside restaurants. Try **Daniels' Broiler** (809 Fairview Pl. N.), or watch the boats from the outdoor deck at **Joey Lake Union** (901 Fairview Ave. N.) or at **McCormick & Schmick's** (1200 Westlake Ave. N.).

the busiest commercial seaplane terminal in the country. You can take the popular 20-minute City Explorer flightseeing excursion, or opt for a longer flight to a private beach and a gourmet catered picnic, a day trip to the San Juan Islands, or even a getaway to Victoria (don't forget your passport). *950 Westlake Ave. N.* ☎ *425/486-1257. www.kenmoreair.com. 20-min. City Explorer tour: $89 per person; prices vary for longer tours.*

6 The Farm Boat. A floating farmers market is the newest attraction at South Lake Union. You can buy fresh-picked produce, right from the boat, and listen to local musicians from noon to 7pm Wednesdays in the summer and fall. The farmers' cooperative that runs the market is restoring a large fishing schooner that will become the permanent farm boat. As the smaller, interim Farm Boat makes its way to the lake on market days, it stops at a nearby island and coastal farms along the way, gathering produce as it goes. ☎ *206/355-0133.*

7 Queen of Seattle Paddlewheel Cruises. Steam along the water the old-fashioned way—just as the Gold Rushers traveled up the Yukon River in Alaska, toward the fabled fields of gold. This 2-hour trip cruises through Lake Union and under the Lake Washington Ship Canal drawbridges in funky Fremont and Ballard, where you'll see the Fisherman's Terminal (home of more than 500 commercial fishing boats) and the Hiram M. Chittenden Locks, which allow ships to make the transition from sea to lake level. As if the backdrop of the Space Needle and Olympic Mountains (on a clear day) weren't enough entertainment, you'll be treated to a Klondike Cabaret Show on the way back. *Lake Union Park dock (Terry Ave. N. & Valley St.).* ☎ *425/898-2701. www.queenofseattle.com. Mid-May to mid-Sept 11am and 2pm; mid-Sept to mid-Oct 1pm. $29 adults, $15 ages 5–12.*

Hiram M. Chittenden Locks

1. Visitors Center
2. Carl S. English, Jr. Botanical Garden
3. Fish Ladder
4. Hiram J. Chittenden Locks
5. Lockspot Café

NW Market St.

32nd Ave. NW

BALLARD

NW 54th St.

Carl S. English, Jr. Botanical Garden

Lake Washington Ship Canal

Commodore Park

W. Commodore Way

MAGNOLIA

Area of detail

Puget Sound

SEATTLE

Lake Washington

0   5 mi
0   5 km

0   100 yds
0   100 m

Watching the boats navigate the locks is a fascinating enough way to spend an afternoon, but at Hiram M. Chittenden, there's much more: those amazing climbing fish, the painstakingly tended botanical gardens, and the best grassy hills in town for kids to roll down. (Do keep an eye out for goose droppings.) You'll find lots of prime picnic spots where you can munch as you watch the boats go by. START: **Bus 44 to Northwest 54th Street & 30th Ave. NW.**

1 Visitors Center. Stop here first for free brochures on the locks and garden, and watch the informational video shown every half-hour. Free hour-long guided tours of both the locks and the garden are offered from March 1–November 30 (call for tour times). *3015 NW 54th St.* ☎ *206/783-7059. May 1–Sept 30 daily 10am–6pm; Oct 1–Apr 30 Thurs–Mon 10am–4pm, Tues–Wed closed.*

2 Carl S. English, Jr. Botanical Garden. Building and dredging

Come watch the salmon head upstream with little help from human technology at the Fish Ladder.

The Botanical Garden is one of Seattle's hidden gems.

the locks produced a vast amount of empty space. Botanist Carl S. English, Jr., came to the rescue, transforming the grounds into a splendid English-style garden with plants from around the globe. This fragrant, blooming quilt is a little-known Seattle secret. *3015 NW 54th St.* ☎ *206/783-7059. Daily 7am–9pm.*

③ ★ kids Fish Ladder. Salmon have got to be the most inspirational fish in the sea. They hatch in streams, swim out to the ocean, then years later manage to swim upstream, against the odds, back to their exact birthplace to start the cycle again. Here, they swim from the ocean into the Puget Sound, climb a 21-"step" ladder to get up to freshwater Lake Washington level, then head home. It takes a lot of energy for a salmon to swim and flop its way up the ladder, but persistence pays. At different times during the summer you might see sockeye, Chinook, Coho, and steelhead salmon. Watch them climbing the ladders outdoors, then head down to an underwater viewing room for a different perspective. Though it's open year-round, you won't find much but water from October

through May. Call ahead to see what's running. *3015 NW 54th St.* ☎ *206/783-7059. Daily 7am–9pm.*

④ kids Hiram M. Chittenden Locks. I never tire of watching the boats of all shapes and sizes make their ascent from the salty Puget Sound up into the fresh waters of Lake Washington. Some pretty magnificent boats come through here. If you're lucky, you might spot one of billionaire Paul Allen's mega-yachts. You might also spot a sea lion or harbor seal, hoping for a tasty salmon lunch. *3015 NW 54th St.* ☎ *206/783-7059. Daily 7am–9pm.*

⑤ Lockspot Café. You can't miss this eatery at the entrance to the locks: Just look for the undersea mural, complete with mermaid and orca. Grab some fish and chips at the outside counter and have a picnic at the locks. You can also dine inside in a publike atmosphere, but if it's a nice day, I'd opt for the picnic. *3005 NW 54th St.* ☎ *206/789-4865. $.*

The Lockspot Café is a perfect place for a seafood break.

Green Lake Park

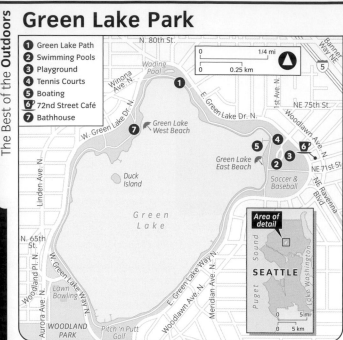

1 Green Lake Path
2 Swimming Pools
3 Playground
4 Tennis Courts
5 Boating
6 72nd Street Café
7 Bathhouse

Rain or shine, the locals grab their babies and dogs and head here for their daily dose of fresh air. The path, nearly 3 miles long, winds around a beautiful glacier-carved lake, ringed by spectacular trees and Northwest plants. Cars zoom past on busy State Road 99, but the highway is just far enough away from this green oasis that you barely notice. START: **Bus 16 or 316 to Woodlawn Avenue & NE 71st St., walk to East Green Lake Drive North.**

1 ★★ **Green Lake Path.** This 2.8-mile trail around the lake has a crushed granite inner lane for walkers, joggers, and strollers; and an outer asphalt lane for bicyclists and skaters. The bird-watching is great! *7201 E. Green Lake Dr. N.*

2 **kids Swimming Pools.** In addition to the outdoor wading pool and indoor heated pool, there is a beach on the lakefront with lifeguards and diving boards in the summertime. *Note:* Green Lake has frequent

algae blooms when the weather turns warm, which means the lake is closed to swimmers, so check for informational signs before you go for a dip. *See p 37, bullet* 10.

3 ★ **kids Playground.** Parents and kids alike can take a break at this terrific play area, which offers some cool features not found in other parks. My daughter's favorite was always the sand pit with the sand-digging machine and canoe for imaginary trips. If the weather turns nasty, the

Strolling the Green Lake Path affords excellent views of the surrounding area.

park's nearby community center has an indoor playroom for the younger set. *E. Green Lake Way and Latona Ave. NE (near the main entrance).*

4 Tennis Courts. You'll find some just inside the main entrance, at 7201 E. Green Lake Dr. N., and also at W. Greenlake Way & Stone Ave. N. To reserve a court, call ☎ **206/684-4075.** Fees to rent the tennis courts are $32 for singles and $40 for doubles, for a 1¼-hour reservation.

5 Boating. Take a canoe out on the lake—or a kayak or paddle boat. Or try out one of the new stand-up paddle boards. You can rent them north of the main entrance, from **Green Lake Rentals,** and launch from there or the boat launch on the southwest side of the lake. *7351 E. Green Lake Dr. N.* ☎ *206/527-0171. Rentals start at $15/hr.*

6 72nd Street Café. Genial baristas, rich Zoka coffee beans—what more could you ask for? Maybe some tasty pastries, or a grilled panini from Mike's East Coast Sandwiches. The kids can chomp on PBJs while you sit back and smell the coffee. *308 NE 72nd St.* ☎ *206/523-5623. $.*

7 ★ Seattle Public Theater at the Bathhouse. This 1920s-era bathhouse has been converted into a popular playhouse on the west side of the lake. Here, tucked away in the middle of Green Lake Park, Seattle Public Theatre presents shows that are sometimes controversial and usually worth watching. *7312 W. Greenlake Dr. N.* ☎ *206/524-1300. www.seattlepublictheater.org.*

Take a boat out on the lake, just like the locals do.

Washington Park Arboretum

E. Roanoke St.

E. Louisa St.

E. Miller St.

E. Calhoun St.

E. McGraw St.

E. Lynn St.

E. Newton St.

24th Ave. E.

To 520

from Hwy 520 Westbound

to Hwy 520 Eastbound

Lake Washington Blvd. E.

The Lagoons

Foster Island

Duck Bay

E. Foster Island Rd

5P

200 yds

200 m

0

0

Walking trail

1

Meadow

2

Lower Trail

Honeysuckle Hill

3

Azalea Way

Upper Trail

Arboretum Dr. E.

Broadmoor Golf Club

Parkside Dr. E.

24th Ave. E.

25th Ave. E.

26th Ave. E.

Boyer Ave. E.

Lake Washington Blvd. E.

Interlaken Blvd

Interlaken Pl. E.

E. Galer St.

E. Interlaken Blvd

E. Lee St.

23rd Ave. E.

25th Ave. E.

26th Ave. E.

Rhododendron Glen

Lookout Gazebo

Japanese Garden

4

Upper Trail

Lake Washington Blvd. E.

Area of detail

Lake Washington

5 mi

5 km

0

0

Puget Sound

SEATTLE

1 Graham Visitors Center

2 Nature Trails

3 Azalea Way

4 Japanese Garden

5P Montlake Ale House

This is Seattle's garden, sprawled along 200 acres of lush property, with Lake Washington winding its way around the northern edge. Breathtaking any time of year, the arboretum is especially stunning in the spring and early summer. Thousands of exotic plants have been gathered from every corner of the world. START: **2300 Arboretum Dr.**

Get lost in a sea of color along Azalea Way.

① **Graham Visitors Center.** Stop here for a map of the trails, then wander among the trees, ponds, and shrubs of the Arboretum (open daily dawn–dusk) at your leisure. *2300 Arboretum Dr.* ☎ *206/543-8800. www.depts.washington.edu/uwbg/gardens/wpa.shtml. Daily 10am–4pm.*

② ★★ **kids** **Nature Trails.** Pick a trail on your map and start hiking! It's a good idea to bring along a light backpack for snacks and water. These trails are all easy walks with no hills to scale. My favorite is the 3.5-mile Foster Island trail, which winds along a boardwalk through an emerald-green wetland area, and leads to two islands. You'll be rewarded with spectacular views of Lake Washington. *2300 Arboretum Dr.*

③ **Azalea Way.** This garden near Graham Visitors Center comes alive in the springtime, when it is transformed into a riotous ¾-mile promenade of azaleas and cherry blossoms. *2300 Arboretum Dr.*

④ ★★★ **Japanese Garden.** The centerpiece of the Arboretum, this exquisite garden is where I come to unwind. It's the perfect place to sit and contemplate life. World-famous garden artist Juki Iida designed it with nearly divine beauty. Formal tea ceremonies cost $10 per person and are held at the Shoseian Teahouse inside the garden, from April to October (check dates on the Urasenke Foundation's website: www.urasenkeseattle.org). *1075 Lake Washington Blvd. E.* ☎ *206/684-4725. $5 adults, $3 seniors & ages 6–17. Open mid-Feb to mid-Nov. Daily 10am–dusk.*

5⃣ **Montlake Ale House.** You can bring the kids along to this friendly pub, where a dining bar surrounds a sunken play area filled with toys. It's nice to be able to relax with a pint and a plate of tortilla chips and guacamole with the kiddies safely confined. *2307 24th Ave. E.* ☎ *206/726-5968. $.*

The best time to visit is in the spring, when everything is in bloom, but the arboretum is gorgeous year-round.

Woodland Park

1. Woodland Park Zoo
2. Woodland Park Rose Garden
3. ZooTunes
4. Woodland Park

The focal point, of course, is the Woodland Park Zoo, a **must-see stop for families with kids.** It's surrounded by grassy hills that are perfect for picnics and afternoons of fun. The part west of S.R. 99 (Aurora Ave.) is occupied mainly by the zoo; to the east of the highway stretch the parklands, which adjoin Green Lake Park. **START: Bus 5 or 82 to Phinney Ave. N. & N. 50th Street, walk to 750 N. 50th St.**

① ★★★ kids **Woodland Park Zoo.** There's never a dull moment at the Woodland Park Zoo, where the tenants range from red pandas to Komodo dragons. Though a zoo of some sort has occupied Woodland Park since the 1890s, the animal habitats at the present-day facility are on the cutting edge of zoo technology. Its Humboldt penguin exhibit, which opened in 2009, won the national zoo association's best-exhibit award. The next year, the zoo added eight playful meerkats to its menagerie. *750 N. 50th St.* ☎ *206/684-4800. www.zoo.org. Admission May–Sept: $17.50 ages 13-64, $15.50 ages 65 & older, $11.50 ages 3–12; Oct–Apr: $11.50 ages 13–64, $9.50 ages 65 & older, $8.50 ages 3–12. May–Sept daily 9:30am–6pm; Oct–Apr daily 9:30am–4pm. See p 37.*

② ★★ **Woodland Park Rose Garden.** Roses love the Pacific Northwest, and even non-flower-lovers will be captivated by the beauty and diversity packed into this 2½-acre

Come visit the local fauna, along with more exotic species, at the Woodland Park Zoo.

garden. One of only 24 All-America Rose Selections test sites in the country, the Woodland Park Rose Garden displays the very latest varieties. It's no wonder the garden is always in great demand for weddings. You'll find it east of the zoo's south entrance gate, but in the summertime your nose will lead you there. *700 N. 50th St. Free. Daily 7am–dusk.*

❸ ★★ **kids** **ZooTunes.** Summertime means outdoor concert season at Woodland Park Zoo, and they're always great fun. I've seen acts as time-honored as Art Garfunkel and as hip as Pink Martini. Bring a blanket or a low beach chair—yours might actually be measured if it looks too tall—and settle in on the meadow, just inside the zoo's north entrance. Kids are welcome and dancing is encouraged! If you plan to visit Seattle from mid-June through August, check the schedule (www.zoo.org/zootunes) in early May. If you see a concert you like, book early because they sell out fast. The website explains how to buy tickets online. The prices are quite reasonable compared to most venues, averaging around $21 a ticket, plus service fee for web sales. *N. 59th & Evanston Ave.* ☎ *206/615-0076.*

❹ **kids** **Woodland Park.** This large urban park is a favorite picnic spot. Sheltered areas hold from 50 to 300 people, and these may be rented starting at $90 per day from April 1 to September 30 (other times they're free and first-come, first-served). You'll also find tennis courts, horseshoes, a ball field, playground, and an off-leash dog area. *Aurora Ave. N. & N. 59th St.* ☎ *206/684-4081.*

The Woodland Park Rose Garden.

Seattle Center

1 Seattle Center House
2 Space Needle
3 Movies at the Mural
4 Seattle Children's Museum
5 Winterfest
6 Experience Music Project
7 International Fountain
8 Pacific Science Center
9 Seattle Fudge
10 Seattle Children's Theatre

This is where Seattle comes to party. From the spectacular fountain—where Northwesterners "cool off" as soon as it hits the 60s—to the myriad of festivals that mark summertime in Seattle, there's always fun to be had here. Even in the winter, the grounds are a lovely place to enjoy a book on a sunny day. If it gets too chilly, I usually pop into the Center House for hot chocolate. START: **Monorail or bus 3, 4, 8, 16, or 30 to Seattle Center.**

1 ★ kids **Seattle Center House.** This huge building is a focal point of Seattle Center, offering indoor activities that go hand-in-hand with the festivities outside. Even during the rare times when there's no festival in progress, Seattle Center often hosts art shows and cultural activities, and frequently has musical performances on stage. The inside perimeter is lined with restaurants, cafes, and a candy shop. There are indoor tables, but on a nice day, it's much more fun to take your food outside and people-watch while you eat! See p 36.

2 ★★★ kids **Space Needle.** Take a ride to the observation deck. On a clear day, you'll see all of Seattle (and Mt. Rainier) at your feet. See p 48, bullet **14**.

3 kids **Movies at the Mural.** Every August weekend, families bring their blankets and low folding chairs to the Mural Amphitheatre, to lounge on the lawn and watch a free movie projected onto a giant screen. Outdoor cinema on a perfect Seattle evening with the Space Needle as a backdrop—what could be better? Check the website for the schedule (www.seattlecenter.com), click on "Events & Programs," then "Film and Movies."

4 ★ kids **Seattle Children's Museum.** Crafts and exhibits for the younger set transform education into playtime. See p 36, bullet **4**.

5 ★ kids **Winterfest.** From Thanksgiving weekend through December, this celebration puts a little magic into the cold season. An antique carousel is set up outside the Center House, and rides are just $1. There are also bonfires, choirs, ice sculpting, and storytelling. Chilly? Duck inside and admire the huge train set, complete with an oversized turn-of-the-20th-century village, set up in the Center House. Outside, Fisher Pavilion becomes an ice rink (Sun–Thurs 11am–8pm; Fri–Sat 11am–10pm; $5 adults, $3 ages 6–12), open through the first weekend of January. *305 Harrison St.* ☎ *206/684-7200. www.seattlecenter.com.*

6 ★ **Experience Music Project.** Microsoft co-founder Paul

Yes, it's indoors, but the Experience Music Project shouldn't be missed.

The Pacific Science Center.

through the glorious spray, while sunbathers arrange themselves around the fountain to soak up the rays. At night, the waters dance to rainbow colors.

8 ★★ kids **Pacific Science Center.** Spend some time with the cool outdoor exhibits before you go inside. Walk through a giant water wheel, spin a 2-ton granite ball, or ride a high-rail bicycle (weather permitting). This hands-on approach to science is fun for everyone. *See p 36, bullet* **5**.

9 ★ **Seattle Fudge.** Don't even pretend to look for a healthy snack here (unless popcorn counts?). Just go ahead and indulge in the rich, creamy fudge. The kids can watch taffy being pulled—hey, consider it an educational experience! *Center House.* ☎ 206/441-0524. $.

Allen's museum is fascinating for music-lovers of all ages and tastes. *See p 47, bullet* **13**.

7 ★ kids **International Fountain.** It's hard to match Seattle on a summer day for sheer joy, and you'll see plenty of it on the faces of kids, grown-ups and a dog or two at this colossal fountain just north of the Center House. Water-lovers charge down the concrete ramp to splash

10 ★★★ kids **Seattle Children's Theatre.** The shows at this first-rate playhouse are based on beloved classic and contemporary books and movies. *201 Thomas St. at Seattle Center.* ☎ 206/441-3322. www.sct.org. Ticket prices vary. *See p 35, bullet* **2**. ●

The International Fountain is the perfect place to cool down on a hot summer day—go ahead and splash away.

Dining **Best Bets**

Best **French**
★★★ Rover's $$$–$$$$$ 2808 E. Madison St. (p 131)

Best **Brunch**
★★ Salty's on Alki Beach $$$ 1936 Harbor Ave. SW (p 131)

Best **Special Occasion**
★★★ Canlis $$$$–$$$$$ 2576 Aurora Ave N. (p 124)

Best **Steak**
★★★ Metropolitan $$$$ 820 2nd Ave. (p 129)

Most Exciting **Fusion Cuisine**
★★★ Joule $$–$$$ 1913 N. 45th St. (p 128)

Best **Waterfront Dining**
★★ Waterfront Seafood Grill $$$–$$$$$ 2801 Alaskan Way, Pier 70 (p 134)

Best for **Vegetarians**
★★ Wild Ginger $$–$$$ 1401 3rd Ave. (p. 134)

Best **Dim Sum**
★ Jade Garden $–$$ 424 7th Ave. S (p 127)

Best **Hotel Fine Dining**
★★★ Hunt Club $$$ 900 Madison St. (p 127)

Best **Pre-Theater**
★★ Tulio $$$ 1100 5th Ave. (p 134)

Best **Sushi**
★★ Shiro's $$ 2401 2nd Ave. (p 132)

Best **Tapas**
★★ Taberna del Alabardero $$–$$$ 2328 1st Ave. (p 133)

Best **Italian**
★★ Assaggio $$–$$$ 2010 4th Ave. (p 123)

Best **Late-Night**
★★ Ten Mercer $$–$$$ 10 Mercer St. (p 133)

Best **Fine Dining with Kids**
★★ Cutters Bayhouse $$$ 2001 Western Ave. (p 124)

Hottest New **Seafood Spot**
★★ Blueacre $$–$$$ 1700 7th Ave., Ste. 100 (p 123)

Most Fun **Near the Market**
★★ Steelhead Diner $$–$$$ 95 Pine St. (p 132)

Best **Italian Menu**
★★ Il Fornaio $$–$$$ 600 Pine St., Ste. 132 (p 127)

Best **Organic**
★★★ Tilth $$–$$$ 1411 N. 45th St. (p 133)

Best **Pizza**
★★ Pagliacci Pizza $–$$ 426 Broadway Ave. E. (p 130)

Most Likely to **Delight the Whole Crowd**
★★ Mistral Kitchen $$$–$$$$ 2020 Westlake Ave. (p 130)

Best Marriage of **Tuscany & the Northwest**
★★ Volterra $$–$$$ 5411 Ballard Ave. NW (p 134)

Salty's is a shellfish lover's dream come true.

Pike Place Market Dining

Café Campagne **4**
Carr pagne **5**
Cutters Bayhouse **1**
Etta's Seafood **2**
Le Pichet **3**
Matt's in the Market **7**
Maximilien **8**
Place Pigalle **9**
Steelhead Diner **6**

Union St.

South Arcade

Lower Post Alley

Economy Market

LaSalle Buildings **8 9**

Pike St.

Pike Street Hillclimb

Corner Market **7**

Sanitary Market

First & Pine Building Post Alley Market **6**

Triangle Building

1st Ave.

Main Arcade

Western Ave.

Parking garage

Pine St.

Post Alley

Inn at the Market **4 5**

Pike Place

North Arcade

Alaskan Way

Stewart St.

Stewart House

1st Ave.

First Avenue Buildings **3**

Post Alley

Soames-Dunn Building

Alaskan Way Viaduct

Alaskan Way Viaduct

Virginia St.

Victor Steinbrueck Park

2

1

50 yds
50 m

Downtown/Pioneer Square

Map labels:
Roy St.
2nd Ave. W.
Mercer St.
Seattle Repertory Theatre
McCaw Hall
LOWER QUEEN ANNE
Republican St.
SEATTLE CENTER
Memorial Stadium
W. Harrison St.
Key Arena
Seattle Center House
Experience Music Project
Space Needle
Thomas St.
John St.
Pacific Science Center
Denny Way
Myrtle Edwards Park
Olympic Sculpture Park
Broad St.
Clay St.
Cedar St.
1st Ave.
Vine St.
Western Ave.
Wall St.
Battery St.
BATTERY STREET TUNNEL
MONORAIL
BELLTOWN
Elliott Ave.
Pier 70
Pier 69
Bell St.
Blanchard St.
Pier 67
Alaskan Way
99
Pier 66 (Bell Street Pier)
See "Pike Place Market Dining" map
Elliott Bay
Post Alley
Pine St.
PIKE PLACE MARKET
Pike St.
Pier 63
Pier 62
Seattle Aquarium
Pike Street Hillclimb
Western Ave.
Harbor Steps
Pier 59
Waterfront Park
Pier 57
Pier 56
Pier 55
Pier 54
29
30
Pier 52
Stewart St.
Virginia St.
3rd Ave.
4th Ave.
5th Ave.
6th Ave.
7th Ave.
Lenora St.
Republican St.
8th Ave. N.
9th Ave. N.
Westlake Ave. N.
Aurora Ave. N.
Dexter Ave. N.
Denny Park
Taylor Ave. N.
6th Ave. N.
5th Ave. N.
Broad St.
99
Queen Ave. N.
1st Ave. W.
1st Ave. N.
2nd Ave. N.

0 1 mi
0 1 km
QUEEN ANNE
CAPITOL HILL
Area of main map
DOWNTOWN
33
WEST SEATTLE
99
5
99
Pier 48

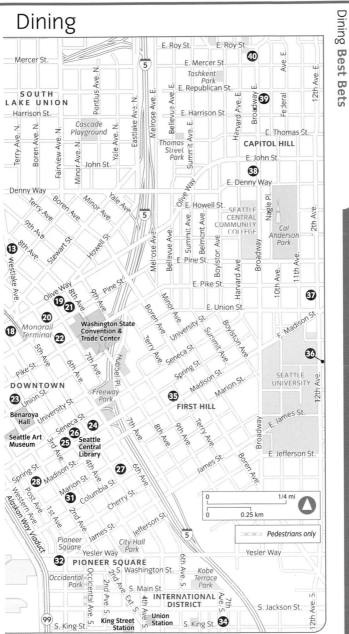

Dining

North Seattle Dining

40th Ave. NE

NE 55th St.

25th Ave. NE

Ravenna Park

UNIVERSITY DISTRICT

NE 41st St.

Union Bay

Evergreen Point Floating Bridge

520

Washington Park Arboretum

MADISON PARK

E Madison St.

Lake Washington Blvd. E

M.L. King Jr. Wy.

9

24th Ave E

MONTLAKE

Boyer Ave. E

Interlaken Park

E Aloha St.

15th Ave. E

CAPITOL HILL

NE 45th St.

UNIVERSITY OF WASHINGTON

NE Pacific St.

University Bridge

Portage Bay

Boren Ave. E

Lake View Cemetery

Volunteer Park

E John St. E Thomas St.

Broadway E

11th Ave. NE

Roosevelt Wy. NE

Fuhrman Ave. E

10th Ave. E

5

Ship Canal Bridge

Eastlake Ave. E

5

Eastlake Ave. N

GREEN LAKE

N 50th St.

N 45th St

3 WALLINGFORD **4 5**

N 40th St.

Wallingford Ave. N

Gasworks Park

Lake Union

SOUTH LAKE UNION

Green Lake

Wood-land Park

3

Stone Way N

Westlake Ave. N

7

99

Wood-land Park Zoo

Phinney Ave. N.

N 46th St.

Aurora Ave. N

G. Washington Mem. Bridge

6

Aurora Ave. N

Taylor Ave. N

Mercer St.

Denny Way

FREMONT

N 36th St.

Fremont Bridge

Boston St.

QUEEN ANNE

SEATTLE CENTER

NW Market St.

3rd Ave. NW

Queen Anne Ave. N

W McGraw St.

LOWER QUEEN ANNE

8th Ave. NW

Leary Wy. NW

Ship Canal

W Nickerson St.

10th Ave. W

Elliott Ave. W

BALLARD

15th Ave. NW

NW 46th St.

Ballard Bridge

W Dravus St.

15th Ave. W

2

24th Ave. NW

Ballard Ave. NW

20th Ave. W

W Garfield St.

Gilman Ave. W

Thorndyke Ave. W

W Galer St.

8

32nd Ave. NW

Hiram Chittenden Locks

28th Ave. W

MAGNOLIA

Magnolia Park

34th St.

Ave. W

W Emerson St.

Magnolia Blvd. W

1

Seaview Ave. NW

Lake Washington

Discovery Park

1 mi

1 km

0

0

Canlis **6**
Joule **4**
Kabul **5**
McCormick & Schmick's **7**
Palisade **8**
Ray's Boathouse **1**
Rover's **9**
Tilth **3**
Volterra **2**

Seattle Restaurants **A to Z**

★★ **Andaluca** DOWNTOWN *MEDI-TERRANEAN* Spain meets the Northwest in perfectly spiced paellas and other Mediterranean-influenced choices. The romantic Andaluca is at the Mayflower Park Hotel. *407 Olive Way.* ☎ *206/382-6999. www.andaluca.com. Entrees $21–$37. AE, DC, DISC, MC, V. Breakfast daily, lunch Mon–Fri, dinner Tues–Sun. Bus: 25, 79,123, or 202. Map p 120.*

★★ **Assaggio** DOWNTOWN *ITALIAN* From the Michelangelo-inspired art (look up!) to the personal welcome by gregarious owner/chef Mauro Golmarvi to the melt-in-your-mouth veal dishes, there's no doubt you've entered a world where food is a passion. The boisterous back room is a fun place to meet friends; the front room has more private spaces. Everything from the simple Margarita pizza to the sophisticated osso buco is fresh and memorable. Don't pass on dessert. *2010 4th Ave.* ☎ *206/441-1399. www.assaggioseattle.com. Entrees $16–$26. AE, MC, V. Lunch Mon–Fri, dinner Mon–Sat. Bus: 1, 13, 15, 16, or 17. Map p 120.*

★★ **Blueacre** DOWNTOWN *SEA-FOOD* Northwest cuisine shines at this friendly but elegant new spot, where the oyster bar serves up a variety of tender, buttery local offerings. The dinner menu offers inventively prepared, sustainably caught seafood. My favorite is the lemon-crusted salmon with horseradish brown butter. When available, don't miss the lightly battered local chanterelle mushrooms in hot-sweet mustard vinaigrette. *1700 7th Ave., Ste. 100.* ☎ *206/659-0737. www.blueacreseafood.com. Entrees $16–$29. AE, MC, V. Lunch & dinner daily. Bus: 25, 66, 70, 73, or 123. Map p 120.*

★★ **BOKA Kitchen + Bar** DOWNTOWN *NEW AMERICAN* Food is art, and art is food for the soul at this stylish cafe in the ultra-hip Hotel 1000. It's hard to decide whether to take a bite or a picture—take a bite! The flavorful, inventive menu shifts with the season. The petrale sole is fabulous. *1010 1st Ave.* ☎ *206/357-9000. www.bokaseattle.com. Entrees $14–$31. AE, MC, V. Breakfast daily, lunch Mon–Fri, dinner daily. Bus: 12, 16, 66, or 99. Map p 120.*

The art on the walls is as inventive as the cuisine at Assaggio.

★★ **Café Campagne** PIKE PLACE MARKET *FRENCH* Sister restaurant to the upscale Campagne, the Café Campagne offers a casual, oh-so-French bistro experience. You won't find a better *Croque-monsieur* outside Paris. *1600 Post Alley.* ☎ *206/728-2233. www.campagne restaurant.com. Entrees $15–$23. AE, DISC, MC, V. Lunch Mon–Fri, brunch Sat–Sun, dinner daily. Bus: 10, 99, 113, 121, or 122. Map p 119.*

★ **Café Paloma** PIONEER SQUARE *MEDITERRANEAN* At this intimate Turkish cafe, you'll find the Mediterranean standards, plus some creative choices—think gorgonzola panini. *93 Yesler Way.* ☎ *206/405-1920. www.cafepaloma.com. Entrees $6–$12. MC, V. Lunch Mon–Sat, dinner Tues–Sat. Bus: 99, 143, 157, or 158. Map p 120.*

★★ **Campagne** PIKE PLACE MARKET *FRENCH* This is classic French country cooking—sunny southern France, to be precise—at its flavorful best. The seafood and game meats are fresh and local, as is the produce. From *foie gras* to *steak frites* to roast duck, the presentations are beautiful and the sauces outstanding. In the

The wine list is seemingly endless at Campagne.

summertime, you can dine in a charming courtyard. *86 Pine St.* ☎ *206/728-2800. www.campagne restaurant.com. Entrees $25–$48. AE, DISC, MC, V. Dinner Tues–Sun. Bus: 10, 99, 113, 121, or 122. Map p 119.*

★★★ **Canlis** DOWNTOWN *NORTHWEST* Dining here is more an experience than a meal. The food is fabulous—fresh and inventive—and the wine list outstanding. The seasonal salad features creative pairings—mango with prawns; beets with pears—and the lamb chops with couscous are among my favorites. But it's the service, impeccable without being stuffy, that makes Canlis perfect for a special occasion. Plan to spend longer than usual for dinner, because you won't want the pampering—or the view of Lake Union—to end. *2576 Aurora Ave. N.* ☎ *206/283-3313. www.canlis.com. Entrees $36–$68. AE, DISC, MC, V. Dinner Mon–Sat. Bus: 5, 16, or 28. Map p 122.*

★★ **Coldwater Bar and Grill** DOWNTOWN *SEAFOOD/NORTHWEST* This contemporary bistro in the Westin Seattle serves up fresh Northwest seafood, prepared with panache. The crab cakes are among the standouts on an imaginative regional menu. The raw bar offers a tasty sample of succulent Pacific Northwest oysters. *1900 5th Ave.* ☎ *206/256-7697. Entrees $15–$28. AE, DISC, MC, V. Lunch & dinner Mon–Sat. S. Lake Union Street Car 98 or Bus: 25, 79, 123, or 355. Map p 120.*

★★ 🄺🄸🄳🅂 **Cutters Bayhouse** PIKE PLACE MARKET *NORTHWEST* This lovely restaurant is just steps from Pike Place Market. With sweeping views of Elliott Bay and friendly service, it's the perfect place to relax after shopping—and you won't feel uncomfortable bringing the kids. (There's a children's menu.) The seafood shines; try the tasty crab cakes. *2001 Western Ave.* ☎ *206/448-4884. www.cuttersbayhouse.com. Entrees $15–$49. AE, DISC, MC, V. Lunch & dinner daily. Bus: 99, 113, 121, or 122. Map p 119.*

★★★ **Dahlia Lounge** BELLTOWN *NORTHWEST* The menu at this quintessential Seattle restaurant never fails to enchant with unique flavor combinations. Think five-spice Peking duck with curry fried rice and orange chili dip. Beautiful and classy, the Dahlia is owned by legendary chef Tom Douglas, who runs a steadily growing number of Seattle establishments, including a bakery. Leave room for dessert. *2001 4th Ave.* ☎ *206/682-4142. www.tomdouglas.com/restaurants/dahlia-lounge. Entrees $27–$38. AE, DISC, MC, V. Lunch Mon–Fri, brunch Sat–Sun, dinner daily. Bus: 1, 13, 15, 26, or 202. Map p 120.*

kids **Dick's Drive-In** CAPITOL HILL *BURGERS* Seattle's iconic burger joint still has the orange awnings from the '50s, though the drive-up service has ended. Many locals won't eat burgers anywhere else. *115 Broadway Ave. E.* ☎ *206/323-1300. www.dicksdrivein.com. Entrees $1.20–$2.50. Lunch & dinner daily. Bus: 8, 43, 49, or 60. Map p 120.*

★★ **Earth & Ocean** DOWNTOWN *NEW AMERICAN* Showcasing the best of the region from land and

Be sure to leave room for the desserts at Canlis.

sea, this hip restaurant in the stylish W Hotel cures its own meats and offers a great chef's tasting menu, including an outstanding vegetarian option. At lunchtime, don't miss the truffle fries. *1112 4th Ave.* ☎ *206/264-6060. Entrees $13–$25. AE, DC, DISC, MC, V. Breakfast & lunch Mon–Fri, dinner Tues–Sat, brunch Sat–Sun. Bus: 7, 39, 85, 106, or 202. Map p 120.*

★★ **El Gaucho** BELLTOWN *STEAK* The steaks are perfection, the service attentive at this upscale, supper-club-style steakhouse. For a special occasion, order the chateaubriand for two. *2505 1st Ave.* ☎ *206/728-1337. www.elgaucho.com. Entrees $17–$75. AE, DISC, MC, V. Dinner daily. Bus: 19, 24, 81, or 99. Map p 120.*

The decor is nearly as big a draw as the food at Dahlia Lounge.

Seattle: A Locavore's Dream

Washington state's temperate climate is ideal for growing every-thing from apples to zucchinis. Small farms grow such a wide variety of fresh produce throughout the year that the locavore movement (eating locally as much as possible) has rapidly gained ground among chefs at top restaurants like Tilth (see photo).

Seafood Silvery salmon, hefty Dungeness crabs, clams, mussels, and dozens of varieties of oysters are the seafood stars in this city on the shores of Puget Sound. Salmon, although not always local, is a Northwest icon that shows up both fresh and smoked on Seattle menus. Wish you could take some home? Not a problem. Pike Place Market fishmongers will pack fresh salmon for you to take home on the plane, and some vacuum-packed smoked salmon doesn't even need to be refrigerated.

Chocolate Seattle's **Theo Chocolate** (☎ 206/632-5100; www.theochocolate.com), a company that gives tours of its chocolate factory, roasts its own organic and fair-trade cocoa beans. Finally, guilt-free chocolate!

Coffee Of course, as nearly everyone on the planet knows, Star-bucks got its start in Seattle, and espresso here has been raised to an art form. Even espresso stands around town have jumped on the wagon, serving organic, fair-trade, and shade-grown coffees.

Wine & Beer Many of Washington state's best and biggest wineries are in the town of Woodinville, just a 30-minute drive north of Seattle. Washington wineries are best known for their cabernet sauvignon and merlot, but you should also keep an eye out for excellent syrahs and semillons. Seattle is also home to quite a few craft breweries. Check out **Big Time Brewery & Alehouse** (☎ 206/545-4509; www.bigtimebrewery.com) and the **Elysian Brewing Company** (p 140).

—Karl Samson

★★ kids Elliott's Oyster House

WATERFRONT *SEAFOOD* This is an oyster-lover's nirvana, with a huge selection of local oysters, raw, steamed or pan-fried. The seafood is fresh and local, with standouts including the salmon (always non-farmed) and the Dungeness crab with chili-lime sauce. If it's a nice day, dine outside on the deck over-hanging Elliott Bay. *1201 Alaskan Way, Pier 56.* ☎ *206/623-4340. www.elliotsoysterhouse.com. Entrees $18–$38. AE, DISC, MC, V. Lunch & dinner daily. Bus: 12, 99, 113, or 121. Map p 120.*

★★ Etta's Seafood PIKE PLACE

MARKET *SEAFOOD* Casual but classy, Etta's caters to the tourist crowd (you can even get a burger) but also has a loyal local following. Owned by chef Tom Douglas, Etta's is my favorite destination for salmon. Another sure bet is Tom's famous Dungeness crab cakes. *2020 Western Ave.* ☎ *206/443-6000. www.tom douglas.com. Entrees $16–$36. AE, DISC, MC, V. Lunch Mon–Fri, brunch/breakfast Sat–Sun, dinner daily. Bus: 19, 21, 99, or 113. Map p 119.*

Galerias CAPITOL HILL *MEXICAN*

This is a lovely spot to linger after a movie. I'm partial to the vegetarian tamales, made of spinach corn dough and stuffed with feta and Poblano chiles. *611 Broadway E.* ☎ *206/322-5757. www.galerias gourmet.com. Entrees $11–$16.50. AE, DC, DISC, MC, V. Lunch & dinner daily, brunch Sat–Sun. Bus: 9 or 49. Map p 120.*

★★★ Hunt Club FIRST HILL

NORTHWEST/MEDITERRANEAN Inside the elegant Sorrento Hotel, this warm, sophisticated restaurant delivers classic cuisine with imaginative touches, especially in its sauces. The duck with huckleberry sauce is a standout, and the black truffle mashed potatoes are not to be missed. (Even worse would be missing the croissant bread pudding for dessert.) *900 Madison St.* ☎ *206/ 343-6156. www.hotelsorrento.com/ food-drink. Entrees $21.50–$38.50. AE, DISC, MC, V. Breakfast, lunch & dinner daily, brunch Sat–Sun. Bus: 12 or 60. Map p 120.*

★★ Il Fornaio DOWNTOWN *ITAL-*

IAN By featuring a different region of Italy each month, this stylish eatery keeps things fresh. The breads, baked on site, are divine; the sauces scrumptious; and many of the wines come from Il Fornaio's own vineyard in Tuscany. My favorite: the ravioli stuffed with butternut squash and walnuts. The bakery and cafe are downstairs; climb up the spiral staircase to the classy dining room. *600 Pine St., Ste. 132.* ☎ *206/264-0994. www.ilfornaio.com. Entrees $13– $35. AE, MC, V. Breakfast, lunch & dinner daily. Bus: 10, 11, 14, 43, or 49. Map p 120.*

★★ kids Ivar's Acres of Clams

WATERFRONT *SEAFOOD* This iconic Seattle establishment, perched on Pier 54, has been in business in various forms for 70 years. The clam chowder is arguably the best in the universe. It's a charming place to eat fresh seafood and watch the ferries cross the sound. *1001 Alaskan Way.* ☎ *206/ 624-6852. www.ivars.com. Entrees $16–$34. AE, DISC, MC, V. Lunch Mon–Sat, brunch Sun, dinner daily. Bus: 16, 66, or 99. Map p 120.*

★ kids Jade Garden INTERNA-

TIONAL *ASIAN* In a town blessed with a number of good dim sum spots, this is one of the best for variety, freshness and ambience. If you're new to dim sum, start with some basics like *humbow* (steamed buns stuffed with sweet barbecued pork), *ha gao* (shrimp dumpling), and sticky rice wrapped in lotus leaves. *424 7th Ave. S.* ☎ *206/622-8181. Entrees*

Dining Out of Town

Located in Woodinville, about 30 miles north of Seattle, **The Herb-farm** (☎ **425/485-5300**; www.theherbfarm.com) is known for its lavish, themed meals that change with the seasons. Wild gathered vegetables, Northwest seafood and meats, organic produce, wild mushrooms, and, of course, fresh herbs from the Herbfarm gardens are the ingredients from which the restaurant creates its culinary extravaganzas. Dinners are paired with complementary Northwest wines.

The restaurant is in a reproduction country inn beside a contemporary Northwest-style lodge. Dinner highlights might include paddlefish caviar on crisp salmon skin; rosemary-mussel skewers with cucumber kimchi; oysters with sorrel sauce; Dungeness crab and wild mushroom "handkerchiefs"; salmon in a squash blossom with lemon thyme; perch on salsify puree with parsley-lovage sauce; lamb served three ways; truffled cheese; and, for dessert, muscat-poached peaches with anise hyssop ice. If you're a foodie, you need to have a dinner like this at least once in your life.

—Karl Samson

$5–$13. MC, V. Lunch & dinner daily. Bus: 7, 14, 36, or 99. Map p 120.

★★★ **Joule** WALLINGFORD *KOREAN/FRENCH FUSION* Though Asian influence is common in the Seattle culinary world, there is nothing common about the cuisine at Joule. The young owners blend French, Korean, and American flavors in delightful ways. The names are exotic—black bean and squid pancake, Kabocha rice grits, octopus and smoked pork belly salad—the tastes divine. On a chilly day, don't miss the roasted apple bisque with curry. *1913 N. 45th St. ☎ 206/632-1913. www.joulerestaurant.com. Entrees $16–$24. AE, DC, DISC, MC, V. Dinner Tues–Sun. Bus: 16 or 44. Map p 122.*

★ **Kabul** NORTH SEATTLE *AFGHAN* Kabul transforms the humble eggplant into a dish so flavorful, I come back here again and again. Finish the night with a cup of cardamom tea.

2301 N. 45th St. ☎ 206/545-9000. www.kabulrestaurant.com. Entrees $16–$28. AE, DISC, MC, V. Dinner daily. Bus: 16 or 44. Map p 122.

★★ **La Spiga** CAPITOL HILL *ITALIAN* Lovingly prepared Northern Italian cuisine takes the spotlight at this contemporary, inviting spot. The delicate handmade gnocchi is a standout, in a cream and truffle sauce spiced with Italian sausage that transforms the dumplings into comfort food at its best. *1429 12th Ave. ☎ 206/323-8881. www.laspiga.com. Entrees $13–$24. AE, DC, DISC, MC, V. Dinner daily. Bus: 2 or 12. Map p 120.*

★★ **Lark** CAPITOL HILL *INTERNATIONAL* This trendy bistro has earned a name for service and quality. The eclectic menu ranges from scrambled eggs with truffles to caviar with potatoes and cream, served on small to medium plates for sharing. *926 12th Ave. ☎ 206/323-5275. www.larkseattle.com. Entrees*

$11–$20. MC, V. Dinner Tues–Sun. Bus: 2, 9, or 12. Map p 120.

★★ **Le Pichet** PIKE PLACE MARKET *FRENCH* This casual bistro serves a classic French menu that would make a Parisian feel right at home. The ingredients are simple and fresh; the sauces superb. *1933 1st Ave.* ☎ *206/256-1499. Entrees $17–$19. DISC, MC, V. Casse-croute (pastry/ snacks) daily, lunch & dinner daily. Bus: 10, 99, 113, or 121. Map p 119.*

★ **Marco's Supperclub** BELL-TOWN *INTERNATIONAL* Diners can travel the world without leaving Belltown. Don't miss the light, crispy fried sage leaves with dipping sauces. *2510 1st Ave.* ☎ *206/441-7801. www.marcossupperclub.com. Entrees $18–$23. AE, MC, V. Lunch Tues–Sat, dinner daily. Bus: 19, 24, or 99. Map p 120.*

★ **Marrakesh Moroccan Restaurant** BELLTOWN *MOROCCAN* This cozy spot has the exotic feel of an Arabian tent. Diners sit on cushions or benches at round tables as tantalizing aromas and belly dancers (Wed–Sun) drift through the room. *2334 2nd Ave.* ☎ *206/ 956-0500. Entrees $18.50–$30. MC, V. Dinner daily. Bus: 1, 13, 15, 19, or 24. Map p 120.*

★★ **Matt's in the Market** PIKE PLACE MARKET *NORTHWEST* Chef Chester Gerl doesn't have far to go to get market-fresh produce and seafood. Matt's expanded location is right above Pike Place Market. *94 Pike St., Ste. 32.* ☎ *206/467-7909. www.mattsinthemarket.com. AE, MC, V. Entrees $28–$39. Lunch & dinner Mon–Sat. Bus: 99, 113, 121, or 122. Map p 119.*

★★ **Maximilien** PIKE PLACE MARKET *FRENCH* Watch the sun set over Elliott Bay through panoramic windows as you dine on classic French fare. *81A Pike St.*

☎ *206/682-7270. AE, DISC, MC, V. Entrees $27–$47. Lunch & dinner daily, brunch Sun. Bus: 99, 113, 121, or 122. Map p 119.*

★ **McCormick & Schmick's** LAKE UNION *SEAFOOD* With a spectacular view of Lake Union and an outside deck, this elegant restaurant is a great spot for dinner. But it's also popular at lunchtime, when you can watch the seaplanes take off. Seafood is the star, and the "fresh list" is impressively long. Don't miss the bay shrimp cake appetizers. *1200 Westlake Ave. N.* ☎ *206/270-9052. www.mccormick andschmicks.com. Entrees $16–$45. AE, DISC, MC, V. Lunch Mon–Fri, dinner daily, brunch Sat–Sun. Bus: 17 or 30. Map p 122.*

★★★ **Metropolitan Grill** DOWN-TOWN *STEAKS* This historic Seattle restaurant could make a beef-eater out of anyone. If you're in the mood for extravagance, order the prized wagyu beef. But the steak on the regular menu is so flavorful, and cooked to such perfection, there's

Metropolitan Grill.

no need to look further. At lunchtime, it's very popular with the business crowd. *820 2nd Ave.* ☎ *206/624-3287. www.the metropolitangrill.com. Entrees $20–$74. AE, MC, V. Lunch Mon–Fri, dinner daily. Bus: 143, 157, 158, or 159. Map p 120.*

★★ MistralKitchen DOWNTOWN

CONTEMPORARY AMERICAN/ GLOBAL They say you can't please everyone, but chef/ owner William Belickis does his best, mingling influences from Africa, France, Spain, Japan, and the U.S. Food is prepared at four stations: a wood-fired/ tandoor oven; traditional kitchen; pastry kitchen; and a high-tech kitchen. Don't miss the heavenly *foie gras* and the tropical *baba* dessert. Excellent wine and cocktail list. *2020 Westlake Ave.* ☎ *206/623-1922. www.mistral-kitchen.com. Entrees $21–$36. AE, DISC, MC, V. Lunch Mon–Fri, brunch Sat–Sun, dinner & happy hour daily. Bus: 25, 98, 250, 252, or 257. Map p 120.*

The pizza at Pagliacci is some of the best in town.

★★ Morton's The Steakhouse

DOWNTOWN *STEAKS* This classic steakhouse is reminiscent of a glamorous era of crisp, white linens; rich cherrywood; and tuxedoed waiters. The service is excellent without being obtrusive; the steaks divine. My favorite? The melt-in-your-mouth filet mignon. The lengthy wine list includes an unusually interesting by-the-glass selection. *1511 6th Ave.* ☎ *206/223-0550. www.mortons. com. Entrees $33–$64. AE, DC, DISC, MC, V. Dinner daily. Bus: 10, 11, 14, 306, or 312. Map p 120.*

★ O'Asian Kitchen DOWNTOWN

CHINESE The best thing at this

stylish restaurant is the dim sum, popular with the office lunch crowd, which comes delicious and steaming-hot from the kitchen on traditional carts. *800 5th Ave.* ☎ *206/264-1789. Entrees $8–$19. AE, MC, V. Lunch, dinner & dim sum daily. Bus: 250, 252, 257, or 260. Map p 120.*

★★ kids Pagliacci Pizza CAPI-

TOL HILL *PIZZA* The pies here come with thin, crunchy crusts and bold, tasty toppings. Try a slice of pesto primo with garlic sauce, topped with fontina, mozzarella, and ricotta. *426 Broadway Ave. E.* ☎ *206/726-1717. www. pagliacci.com. Entrees $10–$24. AE, MC, V. Lunch & dinner daily. Bus: 9 or 49. Map p120.*

★★ Palisade NORTH SEATTLE

NORTHWEST/POLYNESIAN This landmark Seattle restaurant has a Polynesian influence. The panoramic views of Elliott Bay, Mt. Rainier, and the city are stunning; the seafood fresh and expertly prepared. Start with the lemon-grass calamari; finish with a clever bento box dessert, packed with goodies such as jasmine rice and mango tapioca "sushi." *2601 W. Marina Place.* ☎ *206/285-1000. www.palisade restaurant.com. Entrees $19–$59. AE, DC, DISC, MC, V. Lunch Mon–Fri, dinner daily, brunch Sun. Bus: 19, 24, or 33. Map p 122.*

★★ Place Pigalle PIKE PLACE

MARKET *FRENCH* You can't beat the mussels at this romantic spot perched above the sound. Dine to the strains of Edith Piaf. *81 Pike St.* ☎ *206/624-1756. www.placepigalle-seattle.com. Entrees $19–$36. AE, DISC, MC, V. Lunch daily, dinner Mon–Sat, brunch Sat–Sun. Bus: 99, 113, 121, or 122. Map p 119.*

★★ **Racha Noodles & Thai Cuisine** QUEEN ANN *ASIAN* Sure, you can get a delicious pad Thai at this elegant spot, but with so many more inventive items on the menu, why not branch out? The catfish Panang and Golden Duck with ginger sauce are real standouts. *23 Mercer St.* ☎ *206/281-8883. Entrees $10–$31. AE, MC, V. Lunch & dinner daily. Bus: 1, 8, 13, 15, or 18. Map p 120.*

★★ **Ray's Boathouse** NORTH SEATTLE *SEAFOOD* An iconic seafood restaurant in the Ballard neighborhood, Ray's menu is as fresh and delicious as ever. The view, looking out over the Puget Sound, is jaw-dropping. Families with kids may opt for the more casual cafe. *6049 Seaview Ave. NW.* ☎ *206/789-3770. www.rays.com. Entrees $24–$39. AE, DISC, MC, V. Dinner daily. Map p 122.*

★★★ **Rover's** DOWNTOWN *FRENCH* Famed Chef Thierry Rautureau serves up a creative new menu every day in his warm, inviting rooms. The dishes are bursting with flavor, built around fresh local ingredients, and prepared with French élan. Plates are small, so try several. Don't miss the scrambled egg with lime crème fraiche and caviar, one of the chef's signature dishes. And if venison medallions are on the menu, you won't want to miss these. *2808 E. Madison St.* ☎ *206/ 325-7442. www.thechefinthehat.com/ rovers. Entrees (tasting-size) $14–$24. Five-course tasting menu $99 (veggie version $85). Or try the smaller prix fixe for $59. The wine pairings are a must; you'll likely find a new favorite. AE, MC, V. Lunch Fri, dinner Tues–Sat. Bus: 8 or 11. Map p 122.*

★★ kids **Salty's on Alki** WEST SEATTLE *SEAFOOD* The panoramic view looking across the bay at Seattle is an eye-popper—but so is the brunch buffet, laden with fresh

seafood (basics along with inventive dishes like Vietnamese catfish with red pepper sauce), pasta, and omelets to order (try the lobster-filled pasta), meats and more. The gingerbread pancakes are addictive! But save room for the dessert buffet, starring a chocolate fountain. Or come for a sunset dinner. *1936 Harbor Ave. SW.* ☎ *206/937-1600. www.saltys.com/seattle. Entrees $14–$56. AE, DC, DISC, MC, V. Lunch Mon–Fri, dinner daily, brunch Sat–Sun. Bus: 37. Map p 120.*

★★ **Sazerac** DOWNTOWN *AMERICAN/SOUTHERN* The focus at this New Orleans-influenced restaurant in the beautiful Monaco Hotel is as much on fun as it is on food, and it gets them both right. You can't get better catfish this side of the Mississippi. And order whatever bread pudding is on the menu. *1101 4th Ave.* ☎ *206/624-7755. www.sazerac restaurant.com. Entrees (small and big plates) $11–$26. AE, DISC, MC, V. Breakfast & lunch Mon–Fri, dinner Mon–Sat (lounge service Sun), brunch*

Ray's Boathouse is a Seattle institution, thanks to its superb seafood.

Six Seven offers the best of both worlds: excellent food and excellent views.

Sat–Sun. Bus: 7, 39, 124, 202, or
554. Map p 120.

★★ **Serious Pie** DOWNTOWN
PIZZA   Chef Tom Douglas is serious
about food, and that includes pizza.
His applewood-burning oven turns
out artisan-quality pies. My mouth
waters for the Yukon gold potato
pizza with rosemary and pecorino.
Of course, you can order a gourmet
appetizer and wine. *316 Virginia St.*
☎ *206/838-7388. www.tomdouglas.
com. Entrees $15–$17. AE, DISC, MC,
V. Lunch & dinner daily. Bus: 1, 13,
15, 16, or 17. Map p 120.*

★★ **Shiro's** BELLTOWN *SUSHI*
Try to get a seat at the sushi bar,
where you can watch legendary
sushi Chef Shiro Kashiba work his
genial magic. *2401 2nd Ave.* ☎ *206/
443-9844. www.shiros.com. Entrees
$4.50–$17; assortments $15 & up.
AE, DISC, MC, V. Dinner daily. Bus:
19, 24, 116, or 118. Map p 120.*

★★ **Six Seven** WATERFRONT *SEA-
FOOD*   Located in the historic
Edgewater Hotel (where the Beatles
once stayed), Six Seven feels like a
cozy lodge. It showcases the best of
the region's seafood. My favorite
entree is the sea bass, cooked to
juicy perfection with a crispy skin.
Holiday brunches are spectacular.

The view of Elliott Bay is dramatic;
in the summertime, you can eat outside. *2411 Alaskan Way.* ☎ *206/
269-4575. www.edgewaterhotel.
com/edgewater_dining. Entrees $26–
$48. AE, DISC, MC, V. Breakfast &
dinner daily, lunch Mon–Sat,
brunch Sun. Bus: 19, 24, or 99.
Map p 120.*

★ **SkyCity at the Needle**
DOWNTOWN *NORTHWEST*   The
menu features well-prepared local
seafood, berries, and other produce, but the main attraction is the
view. You'll see Seattle from every
angle as you rotate around the
Space Needle. Don't forget: Dinner
includes observation deck admission. *400 Broad St.* ☎ *206/905-
2100. www.spaceneedle.com/
restaurant. Entrees $34–$59. AE,
DISC, MC, V. Monorail or Bus: 3, 4, 8,
16, or 30. Map p 120.*

★★ **Steelhead Diner** PIKE PLACE
MARKET *SEAFOOD/NEW AMERI-
CAN*   This lively new spot features
the cooking of Kevin Davis, who
brings together influences of New
Orleans, France, California, and the
Northwest, making for a unique and
exciting dining experience. Don't
miss the fried cheese curds with
mustard vinaigrette, using cheese

from the market, or the caviar pie, a creamy concoction topped with a variety of roe. Other standouts: Oregon petrale sole, and a fabulous veggie "meatloaf." *95 Pine St.* ☎ *206/625-0129. www.steelhead diner.com. Entrees $15–$29. AE, DISC, MC, V. Lunch & dinner daily, brunch Sat–Sun. Bus: 10, 99, 113, 121, or 122. Map p 119.*

★★ Taberna del Alabardero

BELLTOWN *SPANISH* A relative newcomer, this is Taberna's second restaurant in the U.S. The original one opened in Madrid 35 years ago, near the Royal Palace. Pungent, savory paellas showcase ingredients like saffron, squid, and asparagus. Or take your pick from the tapas menu—don't miss the Madrid-style fried potatoes or the perfectly spiced Basque sausage. *2328 1st Ave.* ☎ *206/448-8884. www.alabardero. com. Entrees $18.50–$28.50. Dinner daily. Bus: 1, 13, 15, 24, or 99. Map p 120.*

★★ Tavolata BELLTOWN *ITALIAN*

This hip new urban space serves up mouthwatering Italian dishes, always with more than a dash of ingenuity. The menu changes daily,

The Steelhead Diner offers one of the most creative menus in Seattle.

so one day you'll find linguine with mussels; the next, it may come with chili and prosciutto. The mozzarella is homemade, as are the succulent pastas. *2323 2nd Ave.* ☎ *206/838-8008. www.tavolata.com. Entrees $17–$38. AE, DISC, MC, V. Dinner daily. Bus: 1, 15, 27, 19, or 24. Map p 120.*

★★ Ten Mercer QUEEN ANNE *CONTEMPORARY AMERICAN*

Upstairs is elegantly formal; downstairs is more casual. Either way, it's a great spot for dinner before or after the opera or a play at Seattle Center—they're open 'til midnight! You can't beat the Washington chicken, juicy and tender with a perfect, crisp skin. *10 Mercer St.* ☎ *206/691-3723. www.tenmercer.com. Entrees $13–$28. AE, DISC, MC, V. Dinner daily. Bus: 1, 8, 13, 15, or 18. Map p 120.*

★★★ Tilth NORTH SEATTLE *ORGANIC/NEW AMERICAN* This cozy restaurant in a Craftsman house showcases the organic bounty of the region. Renowned chef Maria Hines whips up a mouthwatering menu of seasonal delicacies. If the pumpkin soup with cinnamon and crème fraiche is available, don't miss it. *1411 N. 45th St.* ☎ *206/633-0801. www.tilthrestaurant.com.*

Cozy Tilth, located in a Craftsmen house, shows off the region's organic bounty.

Entrees $12–$29. AE, MC, V. Dinner Tues–Sun, brunch Sat–Sun. Bus: 16 or 44. Map p 122.

★★ **Tulio Ristorante** DOWN-TOWN *ITALIAN*   The pasta is painstakingly handmade at this warm, inviting spot, which I love to visit before a show at the 5th Avenue Theatre. Chef Walter Pisano is a maestro at Italian cooking with contemporary flair. One customer comes from Canada just for the sweet potato gnocchi, and when you taste it you'll know why. *1100 5th Ave. (at the Hotel Vintage Park).* ☎ 206/624-5500. www.tulio.com. Entrees $14–$35. AE, DISC, MC, V. Breakfast & lunch Mon–Fri, dinner daily, brunch Sat–Sun. Bus: 12, 143, 157, 158, or 545. Map p 120.

★★ **Urbane** DOWNTOWN *NORTH-WEST*   Blue lighting accents this chic new bistro at the Hyatt at Olive 8, which manages to be both ultra-modern and warmly inviting. The menu features sustainable Northwest bounty, and the chef is not afraid to mix up the flavors. Beets with melted goat cheese and pistachios? Steamed clams with bacon, mint, and jalapeño? Scrumptious! *1639 8th Ave.* ☎ 206/676-4600. www.urbaneseattle.com. Entrees $18–$27. AE, MC, V. Breakfast & lunch Mon–Fri, dinner daily, brunch Sat–Sun. Bus: 10, 11, 14, or 49. Map p 120.

★★ **Volterra** NORTH SEATTLE *ITALIAN*   The rich flavors of a Tuscan village meld with the bounty of the Northwest on Don Curtiss's inventive menu. The signature dish, wild boar tenderloin with gorgonzola sauce, is rich and creamy. The polenta with wild mushrooms is a standout appetizer. Don't pass on

the chocolate orange cake. (Trust me.) *5411 Ballard Ave. NW.* ☎ 206/789-5100. www.volterrarestaurant. com. Entrees $15–$29. AE, DC, DISC, MC, V. Dinner daily, brunch Sat–Sun. Bus: 17, 18, or 44. Map p 122.

★★ **Waterfront Seafood Grill** WATERFRONT *SEAFOOD*   From a seasonal variety of local oysters to crispy-skinned salmon to king crab legs in truffle aioli, Chef Peter Levine's seafood is always fresh and delicious. And, being the sister restaurant to El Gaucho steakhouse, this is one seafood spot where landlubbers are just as happy. Nightly piano music adds a touch of elegance. If you have room—and even if you don't—order the baked Alaska. It's a show in itself. *2801 Alaskan Way, Pier 70.* ☎ 206/956-9171. www. waterfrontpier70.com. Entrees $28–$79. Dinner daily. Bus: 99. Map p 120.

★★ **Wild Ginger** DOWNTOWN *PAN-ASIAN*   This wildly popular restaurant is sophisticated, glamorous, and boasts a very tempting menu. You can't go wrong with the Wild Ginger fragrant duck. There's a terrific separate vegetarian menu. *1401 3rd Ave.* ☎ 206/623-4450. www. wildginger.net. Entrees $7–$30. AE, DC, DISC, MC, V. Lunch & dinner daily. Bus: 1, 13, 14, 16, or 17. Map p 120.

★★ **kids Zeek's** DOWNTOWN *PIZZA*   The crust is to die for; the toppings unconventional. Try the Tree-Hugger, with mozzarella, sun-dried tomato, spinach, mushroom, artichoke hearts, broccoli, tomato, garlic, and olives. *419 Denny Way.* ☎ 206/285-8646. Entrees $14–$24. AE, MC, V. Lunch & dinner daily. Bus: 8 or 30. Map p 120. ●

7

Nightlife Best Bets

Best Fine-Dining Wine Bar
★★ Purple Café and Wine Bar
1225 4th Ave. (p 141)

Best Place to Dance with the
Beautiful People
★★ Baltic Room *1207 Pine St.*
(p 142)

Hippest Wine Bar
★★ The Local Vine *1410 12th Ave.*
(p 141)

Best Bartenders
★★ ZigZag Café *1501 Western Ave.*
(p 142)

Best Date Spot
★★ BOKA Kitchen + Bar *1010 1st*
Ave. (p 139)

Best Brewpub
★★ Elysian Brewing Company
1221 E. Pike St. (p 140); and ★ The
Pike Pub & Brewery *1415 1st Ave.*
(p 141)

Best Mariners Game-Day
Hangout
★ Pyramid Alehouse *1201 1st*
Ave. S. (p 141)

Best Jazz Club
★★★ Dimitriou's Jazz Alley *2033*
6th Ave. (p 143)

Best Happy Hour
★ Contour *807 1st Ave. (p 142)*

Best Hotel Bar
★★ Oliver's Lounge *405 Olive Way*
(p 141)

Best Bar Burger
Two Bells *2313 4th Ave. (p 142)*

Best Bar to Run Into Your
Roommate from Harvard
★★ Bookstore Bar *1009 1st Ave.*
(p 139)

Best Bar to Combine Spirits
from Two Worlds
★★ Chapel *1600 Melrose Ave.*
(p 140)

Best Place to Drink Tequila
Del Rey *2332 1st Ave. (p 140)*

Best (and Only) Lesbian Bar
Wild Rose *1021 E. Pike St. (p 143)*

Best Place to Dance in
Pioneer Square
★ Last Supper Club *124 S.*
Washington St. (p 142)

Best Place to See and Be Seen
★★ Vessel *1312 5th Ave. (p 142)*

Best Martinis
★ Karma Martini Lounge & Bistro
2318 2nd Ave. (p 140)

Best Gay-Friendly Bar
★ Neighbours *1509 Broadway*
(p 143)

Try the cocktails at Chapel.

Pioneer Square

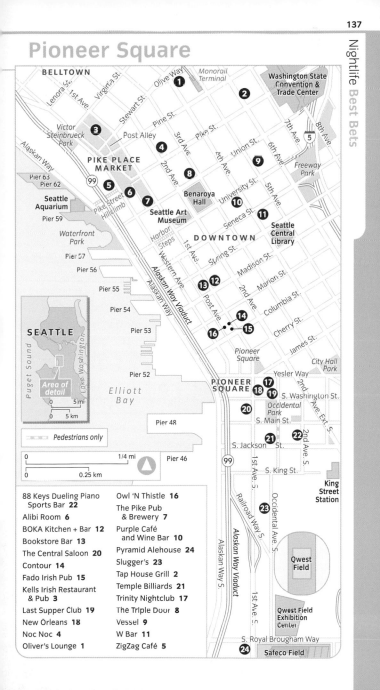

88 Keys Dueling Piano Sports Bar **22**	Owl 'N Thistle **16**
Alibi Room **6**	The Pike Pub & Brewery **7**
BOKA Kitchen + Bar **12**	Purple Café and Wine Bar **10**
Bookstore Bar **13**	Pyramid Alehouse **24**
The Central Saloon **20**	Slugger's **23**
Contour **14**	Tap House Grill **2**
Fado Irish Pub **15**	Temple Billiards **21**
Kells Irish Restaurant & Pub **3**	Trinity Nightclub **17**
Last Supper Club **19**	The Triple Door **8**
New Orleans **18**	Vessel **9**
Noc Noc **4**	W Bar **11**
Oliver's Lounge **1**	ZigZag Café **5**

Downtown

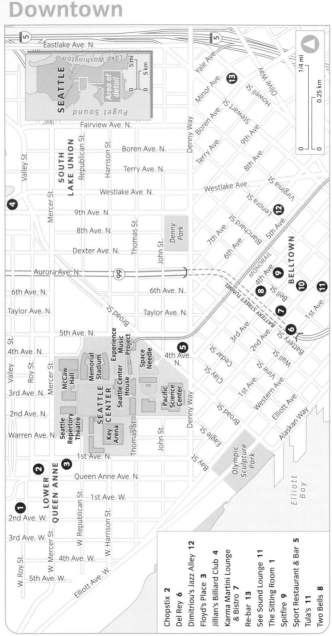

Chopstix **2**

Del Rey **6**

Dimitriou's Jazz Alley **12**

Floyd's Place **3**

Jillian's Billiard Club **4**

Karma Martini Lounge & Bistro **7**

Re-bar **13**

See Sound Lounge **11**

The Sitting Room **1**

Spitfire **9**

Sport Restaurant & Bar **5**

Tula's **11**

Two Bells **8**

Capitol Hill

Baltic Room 2
Cha Cha Lounge 5
Chapel 3
Chop Suey 9
The Cuff Complex 7

Elysian Brewing Company 8
Fireside Room 1
Licorous 12
The Local Vine 11

Madison Pub 10
Neighbours 4
The Wild Rose 6

Seattle Nightlife A to Z

Bars/Lounges

★ **Alibi Room** PIKE PLACE MARKET Tucked away underneath the market, this hip pub serves up potent drinks and very good food. Club nights with dance DJs are Fridays and Saturdays, in the downstairs room. *85 Pike St., Ste. 410.* ☎ *206/623-3180. www.seattlealibi.com. Bus: 19, 21, 99, 113, or 157. Map p 137.*

★★ **BOKA Kitchen + Bar** DOWNTOWN This contemporary bar is a beautiful place to relax and enjoy gourmet bar food—the pear and blue cheese bruschetta, perhaps, or the sugar cane-skewered crab cakes. The seasonal cocktails are fun and delicious. *1010 1st Ave.* ☎ *206/357-9000. www.bokaseattle.com. Bus: 12, 16, 66, or 99. Map p 137.*

★★ **Bookstore Bar** DOWNTOWN This elegant bar at the Alexis Hotel makes you feel like you're enjoying drinks in a well-heeled friend's private library. *1009 1st Ave.* ☎ *206/624-3646. www.librarybistro.com. Bus: 12, 16, 66, or 99. Map p 137.*

The Central Saloon PIONEER SQUARE The oldest saloon in Seattle, the Central is a favorite neighborhood hangout. The food is good, and the live rock can be fabulous.

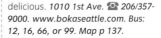

The Central Saloon is a Seattle institution.

Kells is one of Seattle best Irish pubs and the perfect place for a pint.

207 1st Ave. S. ☎ 206/622-0209. www.centralsaloon.com. Cover $5–$10 (or joint Pioneer Square cover $12 Fri–Sat, check www.seattlejointcover.com). Bus: 85, 99, 143, 157, or 158. Map p 137.

Cha Cha Lounge CAPITOL HILL Red lighting, kitschy velvet paintings, piñatas hanging from the ceiling. Punk and heavy metal shake the rafters. Get your nachos upstairs at Bimbo's Cantina. 1013 E. Pike St. ☎ 206/322-0703. www.chachalounge.com. Bus: 2, 10, or 11. Map p 139.

★ Chapel CAPITOL HILL This stylish bar is housed in a former funeral home, but it's anything but morbid. Chapel makes good use of its building's history; even the bar is made from a mausoleum. 1600 Melrose Ave. ☎ 206/447-4180. www.chapelseattle.com. Bus: 10, 11, 14, 43, or 49. Map p 139.

Del Rey BELLTOWN A great place to see and be seen, this Art Deco lounge serves great food and an amazing variety of tequilas. And you get two happy hours—one from 4 to 7pm; one from 11pm to 1am. 2332 1st Ave. ☎ 206/770-3228. www.delreyseattle.com. Bus: 1, 13, 19, 24, or 99. Map p 138.

★★ Elysian Brewing Company CAPITOL HILL This award-winning microbrewery offers great beer and great food. A customer favorite is the Avatar Jasmine, an Indian pale ale brewed with jasmine flowers. 1221 E. Pike St. ☎ 206/860-1920. www.elysianbrewing.com. Bus: 2, 10, or 11. Map p 139.

★ Fado Irish Pub DOWNTOWN Throw back a pint of Irish ale with the regulars at this popular after-work tavern. They also serve up a mean corned beef and cabbage. Irish bands play frequently. 801 1st Ave. ☎ 206/264-2700. www.fadoirishpub.com/seattle. Bus: 99, 143, 157, or 158. Map p 137.

★★ Fireside Room FIRST HILL This elegant lounge at the Sorrento Hotel is a romantic spot to stop for a drink, especially on Friday and Saturday nights, when you can hear live music, often jazz. 900 Madison St. ☎ 206/622-6400. Bus: 12. Map p 139.

★ Karma Martini Lounge & Bistro BELLTOWN You've never had martinis like they make them at Karma. Think cucumber. Think Washington apple. Think delicious. 2318 2nd Ave. ☎ 206/838-6018. www.karmamartinilounge.com. Bus: 1, 13, 17, 19, or 24. Map p 138.

★ **Kells Irish Restaurant & Pub**
PIKE PLACE MARKET   If it's a nice day, settle in on the patio with a shepherd's pie and a pint, and enjoy the lively mixed crowd of tourists and students. Live Irish music. *1916 Post Alley.* ☎ *206/728-1916.www. kellsirish.com. Cover $0–$5. Bus: 10, 99, 113, 121, or 122. Map p 137.*

Licorous CAPITOL HILL   This elegant tavern mixes up yummy specialty cocktails, and has a terrific menu prepared by the wonderful chef at sister restaurant Lark. *928 12th Ave.* ☎ *206/325-6947. Bus 2 or 12. Map p 139.*

★★ **The Local Vine** CAPITOL HILL
A great alternative to the neighborhood coffee shop, this cozy, hip spot boasts more than 100 wines—hailing from Washington and the far corners of the world—starting at $5 a glass. Sea-salted kale chips? Yes, you want some! *1410 12th Ave.* ☎ *206/257-5653. Bus: 2, 10, 11, or 12. Map p 139.*

★★ **Oliver's Lounge** DOWNTOWN   This relaxing bar at the elegant Mayflower Park Hotel serves award-winning martinis and upscale bar food. *405 Olive Way.* ☎ *206/ 623-8700. Bus: 25, 79, 123, or 355. Map p 137.*

★ **Owl 'N Thistle** DOWNTOWN
A popular Irish bar, the Owl 'N Thistle offers an eclectic variety of bands, including its own house Irish folk band, and a dance area. *808 Post Ave.* ☎ *206/621-7777. Cover $0–$5 (occasionally more for special bands). Bus: 12, 16, 66, or 99. Map p 137.*

★ **The Pike Pub & Brewery**
PIKE PLACE MARKET   One of the largest breweries in the state, Pike keeps customers coming back for labels like the Scotch Style Pike Kilt Lifter and Naughty Nellie. *1415 1st Ave.* ☎ *206/622-6044. Bus: 99, 113, 121, 143, or 157. Map p 137.*

★★ **kids** **Purple Café and Wine Bar** DOWNTOWN   Boasting an amazing focal point—a soaring wine tower with wraparound spiral staircase—Purple has an impressive selection of vino. If you're hungry, order a cheese and wine flight, or try several small plates. Though it's a sophisticated space, children are welcome to dine. *1225 4th Ave.* ☎ *206/829-2280. Bus: 14, 21, 22, 202, or 210. Map p 137.*

★ **Pyramid Alehouse** PIONEER SQUARE   There are two big draws here: the location (across the street from Safeco Field) and the beer (including the award-winning

Local Vine boasts more than 100 wines and a casual, relaxed ambience.

Pyramid Hefenweizen). On Mariners game days, it fills up fast. *1201 1st Ave. S.* ☎ *206/682-3377. Bus: 12, 21, 54, 56, or 99. Map p 137.*

See Sound Lounge BELLTOWN Trendy and lively, See Sound's crowd tends toward the younger side. A smaller club, See Sound has DJs from around the world, and cool visual projections on the walls. *115 Blanchard St.* ☎ *206/374-3733. Bus: 19, 24, or 99. Map p 138.*

★★ The Sitting Room QUEEN ANNE A cozy spot with more than a dash of Euro-style, the Sitting Room serves yummy specialty cocktails and gourmet eats at intimate candle-lit tables. *108 West Roy.* ☎ *206/285-2830. Bus: 1, 2, 8, 13, or 15. Map p 138.*

★ Tap House Grill DOWNTOWN With more than 150 beers on tap and an excellent menu (includes steaks and sushi), this upscale spot is a fun place to watch a game. *1506 6th Ave.* ☎ *206/816-3314. Bus: 10, 11, 14, 43, or 545. Map p 137.*

Two Bells DOWNTOWN A favorite neighborhood hangout, Two Bells serves beer, wine, and some of the best burgers in Seattle. *2313 4th Ave.* ☎ *206/441-3050. Bus: 1, 13, 15, 16, or 17. Map p 138.*

★★ Vessel DOWNTOWN This ultra-hip bar is the place to see and be seen. The atmosphere is more L.A. than Seattle, but the coolness is just in the decor. *1312 5th Ave.* ☎ *206/652-0521. Bus: 250, 252, 257, 260, or 261. Map p 137.*

★ W Bar DOWNTOWN With a classy decor, great happy hour, and gourmet bar food, the W is a favorite after-work gathering spot. *1112 4th Ave.* ☎ *206/264-6000. Bus: 202, 210, 214, 215, or 554. Map p 137.*

★★ ZigZag Café PIKE PLACE MARKET The bartenders at this friendly, comfortable lounge are

practically magicians (say hi to Murray!), and more than happy to fill you in on all their amazing cocktails, many made with fresh-squeezed juices. The food's great, too—try the Sangrita pork, flamed in tequila. *1501 Western Ave.* ☎ *206/625-1146. Bus: 12, 99, 113, 121, or 122. Map p 137.*

Dance Clubs

★★ Baltic Room CAPITOL HILL This classy, romantic club plays themed music from around the globe. A fun clientele of various ethnicities and sexual persuasions packs the small dance floor. *1207 Pine St.* ☎ *206/625-4444. www.thebaltic room.net. Cover $0–$10. Bus: 10, 11, 14, 43, or 49. Map p 139.*

Chop Suey CAPITOL HILL The dance floor is usually packed at this eclectic bar. Bands and DJs range from punk to techno. *1325 E. Madison.* ☎ *206/324-8005. www.chop suey.com. Cover $0–$30. Bus: 2, 10, 11, or 12. Map p 139.*

★ Contour DOWNTOWN This is where serious partiers dance till dawn to DJs and live bands. Happy hour on Friday lasts 6 hours, ending at 9pm. *807 1st Ave.* ☎ *206/447-7704. www.clubcontour.com. Cover $0–$10. Bus: 12, 16, or 66. Map p 137.*

★ Last Supper Club PIONEER SQUARE This fashionable club spreads out over three floors, including a laser-lit dance floor. House and headliner DJs keep a dressy crowd hopping. *124 S. Washington St.* ☎ *206/748-9975. www. lastsupperclub.com. Cover $0–$10. (or joint Pioneer Square cover $10 Fri–Sat). Map p 137.*

Noc Noc DOWNTOWN Known for its happy hour ($3 beer and the world's best Tater Tots!) from 5 to 9pm weekdays, this friendly club packs 'em in. *1516 2nd Ave.* ☎ *206/223-1333. www.clubnocnoc.com. Cover*

$0–$5 (occasionally $10). Bus: 143, 157, 158, 161, or 162. Map p 137.

★ **Trinity Nightclub** PIONEER SQUARE   A young clientele dances its way through three areas, each with a different type of music, at this multi-level dance club. The floor is one of the largest in town. *111 Yesler Way.* ☎ *206/447-4140. Cover $0–$15. Bus: 99, 143, 157, 158, or 161. Map p 137.*

Disco balls light up the room at Trinity.

Gay & Lesbian-Friendly
The Cuff Complex CAPITOL HILL   This very popular gay bar draws mostly men. It has pool tables, pinball, a small dance floor, and nice outdoor deck in the back. *1533 13th Ave.* ☎ *206/323-1525. Bus: 2, 10, 11, or 12. Map p 139.*

Madison Pub CAPITOL HILL   The crowd at this low-key pub is mixed, but mostly gay and male. It's a down-to-earth place with welcoming bartenders. *1315 E. Madison St.* ☎ *206/325-6537. Bus: 2, 10, 11, or 12. Map p 139.*

★ **Neighbours** CAPITOL HILL   This long-time favorite disco is gay-friendly but attracts a mixed group to bump and grind on its large, popular dance floor. *1509 Broadway.* ☎ *206/324-5358. Bus: 2, 10, 11, or 49. Map p 139.*

Re-bar BELLTOWN   There's always something going on at this funky club, which attracts a mixed straight/younger gay (some in drag) clientele. There's dancing every night. *1114 Howell St.* ☎ *206/233-9873. Bus: 70, 71, 72, 73, or 83. Map p 138.*

The Wild Rose CAPITOL HILL   Everyone is welcome at Seattle's only real lesbian bar, as long as they're tolerant and don't gawk at the ladies. The drinks are strong,

the bar food is good, and the atmosphere is laid-back. *1021 E. Pike St.* ☎ *206/324-9210. Bus: 2, 10, or 11. Map p 139.*

Live Jazz and Blues
★★★ **Dimitriou's Jazz Alley** BELLTOWN   With consistently great acts from around the globe, this beautiful club is Seattle's premier jazz spot. *2033 6th Ave.* ☎ *206/441-9729. Ticket prices vary; check website (www.jazzalley.com). South Lake Union Street Car 98. Bus: 25, 66, 70, 73, or 250. Map p 138.*

Fans of jazz should plan to spend an evening at Dimitriou's Jazz Alley.

★★ **New Orleans** PIONEER SQUARE   The New Orleans is hopping every night with live jazz, zydeco, and blues. Chow down on some Cajun food while you listen. Kids are allowed 'til 10pm. *114 1st Ave. S.* ☎ *206/622-2563. www.neworleanscreolerestaurant.com. Cover $0–$8 (more for special band) Fri–Sat. Bus: 99, 143, 157, 158, or 159. Map p 137.*

★★★ **The Triple Door** DOWNTOWN   This former vaudeville theater attracts an upscale, friendly crowd. Hear music from around the world upstairs in the Musiquarium (a bar with a huge fish tank) or buy a ticket to watch the show in the Mainstage Theatre. Shows that start before 9pm are open to children. *216 Union St.* ☎ *206/838-4333. Ticket prices vary; check website (www.tripledoor.com). Bus: 143, 157, 158, 159, or 162. Map p 137.*

★ **Tula's** BELLTOWN You'll find live jazz any night of the week at this intimate club, and a taste-tempting Mediterranean menu. It's an all-age venue until 10pm. *2214 2nd Ave.* ☎ *206/443-4221. www.tulas.com. Cover $5–$15. Bus: 19, 21, 24, or 56. Map p 138.*

Piano Bars

★ **88 Keys Dueling Piano Sports Bar** PIONEER SQUARE An unlikely combination of dueling pianists and sports makes this a unique and entertaining spot. The show starts at 9pm. *315 2nd Ave. S.* ☎ *206/839-1300. Cover $0–$10. Bus: 13, 99, or 522. Map p 137.*

★ **Chopstix** QUEEN ANNE The fun starts at 8pm, when dueling musician/entertainers play their hearts out on a pair of grand pianos. *11 Roy St.* ☎ *206/270-4444. Cover $0–$7 Bus: 1, 2, 8, 13, or 15. Map p 138.*

Sports Bars

Floyd's Place QUEEN ANNE Savor some of the best barbecue in town while you watch a game on one of many TV sets at this neighborhood hangout. Pool tables are in the back. *521 1st Ave. N.* ☎ *206/284-3542. Bus: 1, 2, 8, 13, or 15. Map p 138.*

★ **Jillian's Billiard Club** LAKE UNION There's lots to do at this fun, roomy sports bar. Tons of pool tables, arcade games, ping-pong tables, air hockey, even snooker tables. *731 Westlake Ave. N.* ☎ *206/223-0300. South Lake Union Street Car 98. Bus: 26, 28, 70, 71, or 72. Map p 138.*

★ **Slugger's** PIONEER SQUARE Across from Qwest Field, this convenient location draws lots of pre- and post-game fans. The walls are lined with Seattle sports memorabilia. *538 1st Ave. S.* ☎ *206/654-8070. Bus: 13, 70, 85, 99, or 522. Map p 137.*

★ **Spitfire** BELLTOWN Lots and lots of TV sets airing lots and lots of events. Grab a bowl of yummy tortilla soup, loaded with avocado, or a pulled pork sandwich, and settle in. *2219 4th Ave.* ☎ *206/441-7966. Bus: 1, 13, 17, 56, or 202. Map p 138.*

★ **Sport Restaurant & Bar** QUEEN ANNE If you get a booth, you can control your own TV set. If not, don't worry, you'll have plenty of options, including the gargantuan HD screen over the lounge. *140 4th Ave. N., Ste. 130.* ☎ *206/404-7767. Bus: 3, 8, 13, 16, or 30. Map p 138.*

★ **Temple Billiards** PIONEER SQUARE A friendly place with great pool tables and sticks, Temple also has a DJ and dancing downstairs. And it's open for lunch. *126 S. Jackson St.* ☎ *206/682-3242. Bus: 10, 13, or 99. Map p 137.* ●

Spitfire is proof that even sports bars can be funky when they're done right.

Arts & Entertainment **Best Bets**

Most **Jaw-Dropping Show With Dinner**
★★★ Teatro ZinZanni *222 Mercer St. (p 150)*

Best **Place to Go for a Chuckle**
★ The Comedy Underground *109 S. Washington St. (p 148)*

Best **Family Entertainment**
★★ Zootunes *N. 59th St. & Evanston Ave. (p 148)*

Best **Popular Music**
★★★ Showbox *1426 1st Ave. (p 152)*

Best **Orchestra**
★★★ Seattle Symphony *200 University St. (p 148)*

Most **Eclectic Theater Calendar**
★★ The Moore Theatre *1932 2nd Ave. (p 151)*

Best **Place to Hear Chamber Music One Night and a Talk on Religion in Politics the Next**
★★ Town Hall *1119 8th Ave. (p 148)*

Best **Theater to Take Your Date Before Popping the Question**
★★★ Paramount Theatre *911 Pine St. (p 152)*

Best **Place to Watch an Arabesque**
★★★ Pacific Northwest Ballet *321 Mercer St. (p 149)*

Most **Eclectic Musical Lineup**
★★★ The Triple Door *216 Union St. (p 150)*

The Pacific Northwest Ballet.

Seattle **Arts & Entertainment**

ACT (A Contemporary
  Theatre) **4**
Can Can **10**
The Comedy
  Underground **12**
Dimitriou's Jazz Alley **1**
Experience Music
  Project **21**
5th Avenue Theatre **6**

Intiman Theatre **17**
The Moore Theatre **2**
Pacific Northwest Ballet **19**
Paramount Theatre **3**
The Pink Door Cabaret **11**
Seattle Gilbert & Sullivan
  Society **16**
Seattle Opera **20**
Seattle Repertory Theatre **15**

Seattle Symphony **7**
Showbox **9**
Teatro ZinZanni **18**
Town Hall **5**
The Triple Door **8**
UW World Series **14**
Zootunes **13**

Arts & Entertainment A to Z

Classical Music

★★★ Seattle Symphony
DOWNTOWN The 85-person orchestra is beloved in the community, and has been going strong for more than a century. The internationally respected symphony is known for pushing the envelope musically and showcasing contemporary, as well as classical works. It performs in the beautiful and acoustically outstanding Benaroya Hall. *200 University St. ☎ 206/215-4800. www.seattle symphony.org. Ticket prices vary. Bus: 212, 216, 217, 218, or 225. Map p 147.*

Comedy Clubs

★ The Comedy Underground
PIONEER SQUARE Comics from around the country keep the audience in stitches here every night of the week. The roster includes winners of regional comedy contests, late-night TV guests, and up-and-comers. The historic club is headquarters for the Seattle International Comedy Competition. *109 S. Washington St. ☎ 206/628-0303. www. comedyunderground.com. Ticket prices vary. Bus: 85 or 99. Map p 147.*

Concert Venues

★ Experience Music Project
The EMP hosts live concerts in its beautiful Sky Church auditorium; check the website (www.empsfm. org) for the calendar of events. *325 5th Ave. N. ☎ 206/770-2700. Ticket prices vary; check website (see above). Monorail or Bus: 3, 16, 30, or 82. Map p 147.*

★★ Town Hall
FIRST HILL From chamber music to science lectures to political discussions, you never know what you might hear at Town Hall, Seattle's cultural gathering place—despite the name, it is *not* connected to city government. The beautifully restored Roman-revival building houses two performance halls. *1119 8th Ave. ☎ 206/652-4255. www. townhallseattle.org. Ticket prices vary. Bus: 2 or 12. Map p 147.*

★★ Zootunes
FREMONT Every summer, the locals head to Woodland Park Zoo one evening during the week to lounge on a grassy meadow and hear concerts by old favorites and hot new groups. You might hear anyone from Art Garfunkel to the Indigo Girls. The concert

The Seattle Symphony Orchestra.

starts at 6pm, just inside the northern zoo gate. Lots of folks bring picnic baskets and low chairs or towels, but food is also available. You can buy tickets at the zoo, but many concerts sell out, so check the website in advance. *N. 59th St. & Evanston Ave.* ☎ *206/548-2500, ext.1164. www.zoo.org/zootunes. Prices vary but are reasonable; kids 12 & under free. Bus: 5 or 82. Map p 147.*

Dance

★★★ Pacific Northwest Ballet

QUEEN ANNE One of the country's largest and most acclaimed ballet companies, the PNB gives more than 100 performances a year, mostly at the beautiful Marion Oliver McCaw Hall, culminating in the beloved *The Nutcracker*—complete with spectacular Maurice Sendak sets—over the holidays. *321 Mercer St.* ☎ *206/684-7200. www.pnb.org. Ticket prices vary. Bus: 3, 16, or 82. Map p 147.*

★★ UW World Series

UNIVERSITY DISTRICT The University of Washington brings in world-class dancers, musicians, and other artists from around the globe to perform at Meany Hall on the UW campus. The season runs October through May. UW Arts Ticket Office: 3901 University Way NE. Meany Hall is on the west side of the UW campus. *15th Ave. NE & NE 40th.* ☎ *206/543-4880. www.uwworldseries.org. Tickets $30–$55; $20 students (advance). Bus: 25, 43, 49, or 70. Map p 147.*

Dinner Theatre

★ Can Can

PIKE PLACE MARKET This avant-garde cabaret venue is for the daring and open-minded. It's on the cutting edge of neo-burlesque. Dinner/show packages are available, and there is also a happy hour

The Paramount Theatre.

menu. Can Can brings in local and national acts, and also has its own house cabaret troupe. Almost anything can happen here! *94 Pike St.* ☎ *206/652-0832. www.thecan can.com. Show $5–$10. Bus: 19, 99, 113, 121, or 122. Map p 147.*

★★ The Pink Door Cabaret

PIKE PLACE MARKET There's almost always something out of the ordinary going on here, be it a trapeze artist or accordion player. But Saturday nights are reserved for the fun and naughty burlesque show in the lounge, which starts at 11pm and incorporates cross-dressing and elements of striptease. Come earlier and you can enjoy a delicious Italian meal in the dining room before the show. *1919 Post Alley.* ☎ *206/443-3241. www.thepinkdoor.net. Cover for burlesque show: $15. Bus: 10, 99, 113, 121, or 122. Map p 147.*

If you're feeling daring, head to Can Can. You won't regret it!

A performer at Teatro ZinZanni.

★★★ **Teatro ZinZanni** QUEEN ANNE Talk about overstimulation! This incredible spectacle of sights and sounds, set inside a huge tent, is accompanied by a first-class five-course meal by none other than legendary Seattle Chef Tom Douglas. This 3-hour mix of acrobatics, circus acts, cabaret, comedy, and audience interaction must be experienced to be believed. Teatro is housed in a spectacular building just across from McCaw Hall. *222 Mercer St.* ☎ *206/802-0015. www.zinzanni. com. Showtimes 6:30pm Thurs–Sat*

Dimitriou's Jazz Alley hosts some of jazz's finest acts.

(and some Weds); 11am and 5:30pm Sun. Tickets $105 Wed–Fri & Sun evenings, $125 Sat. ($10/ticket more in Dec; $175/ticket for New Year's Eve). Bus: 1, 2, 8, 13, or 15. Map p 147.

Jazz
★★★ **Dimitriou's Jazz Alley** BELLTOWN If you're a jazz-lover, don't miss Dimitriou's while you're in town. The lineup of world-class performers at this large, yet somehow intimate, dinner/jazz club never fails to amaze. *2033 6th Ave.* ☎ *206/ 441-9729. www.jazzalley.com. Ticket prices vary; check website. South Lake Union Street Car 98. Bus: 25, 123, 250, or 252. Map p 147.*

★★★ **The Triple Door** DOWNTOWN Jazz is just part of the attraction at this hot club, known for its eclectic roster of performers. Its offerings even include chamber music by a group of musicians from the Seattle Symphony. *216 Union St.* ☎ *206/838-4333. www.tripledoor. com. Ticket prices vary. Bus: 143, 157, 158, 159, or 161. Map p 147.*

Opera
★ **Seattle Gilbert & Sullivan Society** FIRST HILL This is an amateur group, but it does the Victorian

151

opera writers proud. The shows are fun, colorful, and fast-paced. Various venues and ticket prices; check website. ☎ 206/682-0796. www.pattersong.org. Map p 147.

★★★ **Seattle Opera** QUEEN ANNE   Housed in the elegant Marion Oliver McCaw Hall, this fine company performs contemporary American compositions and traditional European works with panache. 321 Mercer St. ☎ 206/389-7676. www.seattleopera.org. Ticket prices vary. Bus: 3, 16, or 82. Map p 147.

Plays
★★ **ACT (A Contemporary Theatre)** DOWNTOWN   The focus at this energetic venue is on newer plays and playwrights, rather than the classics. 700 Union St. ☎ 206/292-7676. Ticket prices vary. Bus: 306, 312, or 522. Map p 147.

★★★ **5th Avenue Theatre** DOWNTOWN   This elegant playhouse produces some of the liveliest theater in Seattle, including original and Broadway-bound shows and Broadway musicals. 1308 5th Ave. ☎ 206/625-1900. www.5thavenue.org. Ticket prices vary. Bus: 250, 252, 257, 260, or 261. Map p 147.

A performance by the Seattle Opera.

The Triple Door features a broad range of acts.

★★ **Intiman Theatre**   Serious drama-lovers will love the Tony award-winning Intiman. This gem of a regional theater, on the north side of Seattle Center, has produced international classics as well as contemporary plays—including some world premieres—for 3 decades. Prices vary; check box office and website. 155 Mercer St. ☎ 206/443-2222. www.intiman.org. Bus: 1, 2, 8, or 13.

★★ **The Moore Theatre** DOWNTOWN   Seattle's oldest theater, the Moore hosts some of its edgier acts.

Cheap Tickets

If you decide to catch a show in town and don't have tickets, you could try the theater box office—they will sometimes give you a great deal an hour before a performance. But first try www.goldstar.com (click on "Seattle" at the bottom of the page), where you can get discounted deals on many local shows, as well as on lake and harbor cruises.

It's always a diverse lineup; you might see anyone from cross-dressing Dame Edna to Ladysmith Black Mambazo— perhaps with a children's play scheduled in between. *1932 2nd Ave.* ☎ *206/467-5510. www.stgpresents. org. Ticket prices vary. Bus: 10, 25, 99, 113, or 121. Map p 147.*

★★★ Paramount Theatre

DOWNTOWN   From Broadway to rock shows, the Paramount offers superb entertainment in a glamorous historic setting. *911 Pine St.* ☎ *206/467-5510. www.stgpresents. org. Ticket prices vary. Bus: 10, 11, 14, 43, or 49. Map p 147.*

★★ Seattle Repertory Theatre

The Rep's offerings tend to be important, beautifully performed literary and artistic productions. The theater itself is an elegant venue,

located at Seattle Center. ☎ *206/ 443-2222. www.seattlerep.org. Prices vary; check with box office or website. Bus: 1, 2, 8, 13, or 15.*

Popular Music

★★★ Showbox PIKE PLACE

MARKET   One of Seattle's premier music clubs, the legendary Showbox has a lot going for it: great bands, elbow room, acoustics, and lots of all-ages shows. (The under-21s have their own section.) Around since 1939, the ballroom has hosted everyone from Duke Ellington to Pearl Jam. There is also a Showbox in the Sodo district. *Market location: 1426 1st Ave. Sodo: 1700 1st Ave. S.* ☎ *Info line for both: 206/628-3151. www. showboxonline.com. Ticket prices vary by event; check website. Bus: 99, 113, 121, 122, or 143. Map p 147.* ●

A performance of The Women *at ACT.*

Downtown Lodging

Alexis **25**

Arctic Club Hotel **27**

Best Western Pioneer
Square Hotel **26**

Courtyard by Marriott
Lake Union **2**

Crowne Plaza **19**

The Edgewater Hotel **4**

Fairmont Olympic
Hotel **18**

Four Seasons Hotel
Seattle **23**

Grand Hyatt Seattle **12**

Hilton Seattle **17**

Hotel Max **9**

Hotel Monaco **22**

Hotel 1000 **24**

Hotel Vintage Park **20**

Hyatt at Olive 8 **10**

Inn at the Market **6**

Marriott Seattle
Waterfront **5**

Mayflower Park
Hotel **14**

Mediterranean Inn **1**

Paramount Hotel **11**

Ramada Seattle
Downtown **3**

Red Lion Hotel
on Fifth Avenue **16**

Renaissance Madison
Hotel **28**

Roosevelt Hotel **13**

Sheraton Seattle Hotel **15**

Silver Cloud Hotel
Broadway **30**

Sorrento Hotel **29**

W Seattle Hotel **21**

Warwick Hotel Seattle **7**

The Westin Seattle **8**

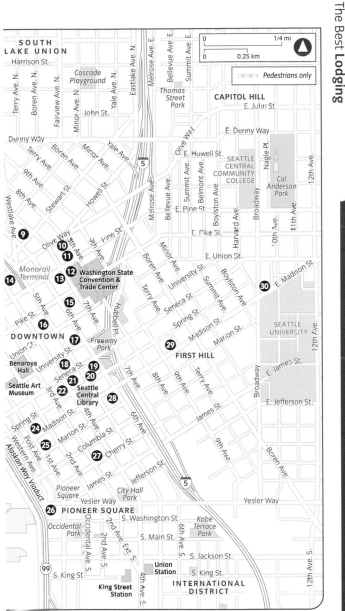

Lodging **Best Bets**

Most **Authentic Seattle Experience**
★★★ The Edgewater Hotel $$$–$$$$ *2411 Alaskan Way (p 157)*

Best **Panoramic City Views**
★★★ The Westin Seattle $$–$$$ *1900 5th Ave. (p 162)*

Most **Romantic**
★★★ Inn at the Market $$$–$$$$ *86 Pine St. (p 160)*

Most **Traditionally Elegant**
★★★ Fairmont Olympic $$$–$$$$ *411 University St. (p 157)*

Most **Whimsical Fun**
★★★ Hotel Monaco $$–$$$$ *1101 4th Ave. (p 158)*

Most **Elegant European Style**
★★★ Sorrento $$–$$$ *900 Madison St. (p 161)*

Best **Location**
★★★ Alexis. $$–$$$$$ *1007 1st Ave (p 157)*

Best **Choice for Wine-Lovers**
★★★ Hotel Vintage Park $$–$$$$ *1100 5th Ave. (p 159)*

Greenest **Hotel**
★★★ Hyatt at Olive 8 $$–$$$$ *1635 8th Ave. (p 159)*

Hippest **Hotel**
★★★ W Seattle Hotel $$–$$$$ *1112 4th Ave. (p 161)*; and ★★★ Hotel 1000 $$–$$$$$ *1000 1st Ave. (p 159).*

Newest **Hot Hotel**
★★★ Arctic Club $$–$$$ *700 3rd Ave. (p 157)*

Most **Stunning Lobby**
★★★ Grand Hyatt Seattle $$–$$$$ *721 Pine St. (p 158)*

Artsiest **Hotel**
★★ Hotel Max $$–$$$ *620 Stewart St. (p 158)*

Best **Seattle History**
★★ Best Western Pioneer Square Hotel $$–$$$ *77 Yesler (p 157)*

Best **Pool View**
★★★ Marriott Seattle Waterfront $$–$$$$ *2100 Alaskan Way (p 160)*

The Edgewater Hotel brings Seattle's unique style to each of its guest rooms.

Seattle Hotels **A to Z**

★★★ kids **Alexis** DOWNTOWN
Just north of Pioneer Square, this cozy boutique hotel is luxurious and romantic, pampering guests with 300-thread count sheets, feather beds, flat-screen TVs and a spa. Jetted tubs and wood-burning fireplaces are available in some suites. Dine at the charming Library Bistro & Bookstore Bar. *1007 1st Ave. (at Madison).* ☎ *866/356-8894 or 206/624-4844. www.alexishotel.com. 121 units. Standard doubles $195–$410. AE, DC, DISC, MC, V. Bus: 12, 16, 66, or 99. Map p 154.*

★★★ **Arctic Club Hotel** DOWNTOWN Once an exclusive club for gold prospectors who struck it rich, this historic building now houses the luxurious Arctic Club Hotel. The period warmth and glamour remain, from the beautiful Alaskan marble to the sculpted walruses that wrap around the outside of the building. Ask to see the dramatic Northern Lights Dome Room, with its spectacular restored stained-glass dome. *700 3rd Ave. (at Cherry St.).* ☎ *800/600-7775 or 206/340-0340. www.arcticclubhotel.com. 120 units. Standard doubles $149–$289. AE, DC, DISC, MC, V. Bus: 11, 15, 18, 121, or 122. Map p 154.*

★★ **Best Western Pioneer Square Hotel** PIONEER SQUARE Set in the midst of Seattle's charming historic district, this hotel brings history to life in a century-old Romanesque Victorian building. *77 Yesler Way.* ☎ *800/800-5514 or 206/340-1234. www.pioneersquare.com. 72 units. Standard doubles $125–$250 w/deluxe continental breakfast. AE, DC, DISC, MC, V. Bus: 99, 143, 157, 158, or 159. Map p 154.*

★ kids **Courtyard by Marriott Lake Union** LAKE UNION This hotel on Lake Union is not in the heart of downtown, but a nearby streetcar runs downtown every 15 minutes, costs $1.75 for adults, and runs until 9pm Monday through Thursday, 11pm Friday through Saturday, and 7pm Sunday. The hotel also has a pool. *925 Westlake Ave N.* ☎ *800/321-2211 or 206/213-0100. www.courtyardlakeunion.com. 250 units. Standard doubles $99–$199. AE, DC, DISC, MC, V. Bus: 26 or 28. Map p 154.*

★★ **Crowne Plaza** DOWNTOWN Two blocks from the convention center and a few blocks from Pike Place Market, this comfortable, inviting hotel is also near the theaters and downtown shops. *1113 6th Ave.* ☎ *800/770-5675 or 206/464-1980. www.cphotelseattle.com. 415 units. Standard doubles $112–$263. AE, DC, DISC, MC, V. Bus: 3, 5, 16, or 82. Map p 154.*

★★★ **The Edgewater Hotel** WATERFRONT This landmark Seattle inn has the woodsy feel of a mountain lodge, and it's the only hotel in town directly on the waterfront. Perched over Elliott Bay, the Edgewater affords stunning sunset views. The Beatles once stayed here, and fished in the sound from their window. *2411 Alaskan Way, Pier 67.* ☎ *800/624-0670 or 206/728-7000. www.edgewaterhotel.com. 223 rooms. Standard doubles $202–$449. AE, DC, DISC, MC, V. Bus: 19, 24, or 99. Map p 154.*

★★★ kids **Fairmont Olympic Hotel** DOWNTOWN Traditional elegance is the theme at this classic luxury hotel. The rooms have down pillows and duvets and come with PlayStations. A welcome package is

The lushly elegant lobby at the Fairmont Olympic.

available for children; the hotel will also childproof your room. *411 University St.* ☎ *800/257-7544 or 206/621-1700. www.fairmont.com/seattle. 450 units. Standard doubles $249–$349. MC, V. Bus: 85, 143, 150, 157, or 158. Map p 154.*

★★★ Four Seasons Hotel

DOWNTOWN   One of Seattle's newest hotels, the chic and luxurious Four Seasons features floor-to-ceiling windows in its guest rooms, looking out on expansive bay or city views. The rooftop pool shimmers beside a toasty-warm fireplace. *99 Union St.* ☎ *206/749-7000. www.fourseasons.com/seattle. 149 rooms. Standard doubles $375–$415. Bus: 12, 99, 121, 122, or 125. Map p 154.*

★★★ Grand Hyatt Seattle

DOWNTOWN   This high-tech hotel has comfy beds and oversized bathrooms with soaking tubs. Check out the local art throughout the hotel, including a glass "waterfall" sculpture in the lobby. Adjacent to Ruth's Chris Steak House. *721 Pine St.* ☎ *888/591-1234 or 206/774-1234. www.grandseattle. hyatt.com/hyatt/hotels/index.jsp. Standard doubles $190–$320. AE, DC, DISC, MC, V. Bus: 10, 11, 14, 43, or 49. Map p 154.*

★ kids Hilton Seattle DOWN-

TOWN   Conveniently connected by tunnel to both the convention center and 5th Avenue shopping area, the Hilton is especially popular with business travelers. The staff is multi-lingual. The rooms have great views, and they come with large HDTVs with music channels and Nintendo systems. *1301 6th Ave.* ☎ *800/HILTONS or 206/624-0500. www.seattle hilton.com. Standard doubles $209–$360. AE, DC, DISC, MC, V. Bus: 2, 250, 306, 312, or 522. Map p 154.*

★★ Hotel Max DOWNTOWN

Don't have time to stop at the art museum? At this unique hotel, where you get a menu of pillow choices, the original works of hundreds of local artists and photographers are showcased in the lobby and guest rooms. There's a sushi (and more) restaurant, the Red Fin, on site. *620 Stewart St. (at 6th Ave.).* ☎ *866/833-6299 or 206/728-6299. www.hotelmaxseattle.com. 163 units. Standard doubles $134–$209. AE, DISC, MC, V. S. Union Street Car 99. Bus: 25, 123, 250, 252, or 257. Map p 154.*

★★★ kids Hotel Monaco

DOWNTOWN   The whimsical decor at this lovely boutique hotel makes it an inviting place for kids and adults alike. Kids get their own welcome gift, and Guitar Hero is available on Fridays. There's plenty of pampering for grown-ups, too, including hosted evening wine receptions. Oh, and a fortune-teller (Wed and Sat). You can bring your dog—and even order dinner and a free pillow for him—or just borrow a goldfish overnight. The restaurant, Sazerac, injects a delightful dash of New Orleans to its dishes. *1101 4th Ave.* ☎ *800/715-6513 or 206/ 621-1770. www.monaco-seattle.com. 189 units. Standard doubles $186– $369. AE, DC, DISC, MC, V. Bus: 202, 210, 214, 215, or 554. Map p 154.*

★★★ **Hotel 1000** DOWNTOWN This modern, sophisticated hotel offers sleek beauty and the latest in technology (read: 40-in. flat-screens, free Wi-Fi everywhere). And check out the artsy tubs: They fill from the ceiling down. The technology is impressive, but excellent service is also part of the mix here. The BOKA Kitchen + Bar offers creative cuisine and a lively lounge scene. *1010 1st Ave.* ☎ *877/315-1088 or 206/957-1000. www.hotel1000seattle.com. 120 units. $179–$419. AE, DC, DISC, MC, V. Bus: 12, 16, 66, or 99. Map p 154.*

★★★ kids **Hotel Vintage Park** DOWNTOWN A lush, jewel-tone decor tips guests off to the fact that they will be treated like royalty here. In-room spa services are available, and an elegant wine reception is held nightly. Each room is dedicated to a Washington winery. Still, this is a Kimpton property and kids are welcomed warmly. Dine at the wonderful Tulio Ristorante. The Fifth Avenue Theatre and shops are steps away. *1100 5th Ave.* ☎ *800/853-3914 or 206/624-8000. www.hotelvintage park.com. 125 units. $170–$329. AE, DC, DISC, MC, V. Bus: 12, 143, 157, 18, or 159. Map p 154.*

★★★ **Hyatt at Olive 8** DOWNTOWN One of Seattle's newest hotels, this is also one of the greenest—it's LEED certified for energy efficiency. For instance, the lights only come on when your card-key is in its slot. The rooms may be a bit smaller than at the Grand Hyatt around the corner, but the prices are lower and the service is equally unsurpassed at this modern, beautiful hotel. Don't miss breakfast or brunch at Urbane. *1635 8th Ave.* ☎ *206/695-1234. www. olive8.hyatt.com. Double $170–$305. Bus: 10, 11, 14, 43, or 49. AE, DC, DISC, MC, V. Map p 154.*

The cozy Hotel Monaco is pet-friendly, so bring Fido.

Relax in the classy Urbane and Bar at the Hyatt Olive 8.

★★★ Inn at the Market PIKE

PLACE MARKET A romantic hide-away right across from Pike Place Market, this friendly hotel offers spectacular views of Elliott Bay and the mountains. Best-kept secret: the 5th-floor roof garden. Take a bottle of wine and a couple of glasses and enjoy! Room service is from the nearby Café Campagne. *86 Pine St.* ☎ *800/446-4484 or 206/443-3600. www.innatthemarket.com. 70 units. Standard double $215–$320. AE, DC, DISC, MC, V. Bus: 10, 99, 113, 121, or 122. Map p 154.*

★★★ kids Marriott Seattle

Waterfront WATERFRONT A short walk from Pike Place Market and across the street from the waterfront, this hotel was built with dramatic views in mind: water, cityscape, mountains. To showcase them, half the rooms have balconies, and the indoor/outdoor pool has a sweeping view of Elliott Bay and the Olympic Mountains. *2100 Alaskan Way.* ☎ *800/455-8254 or 206/443-5000. www.marriott.com/hotels/travel/seawf-seattle-marriott-waterfront. 358 units. Standard doubles $149–$319. AE, DC, DISC, MC, V. Bus: 99. Map p 154.*

★★ kids Mayflower Park Hotel

DOWNTOWN This elegantly restored grand dame has been operating since 1927. A wine reception is served at 4:30pm Wednesdays, and the rooms have lots of modern touches. It connects to Westlake Center shopping mall (and the monorail). Oliver's Lounge and Andaluca Restaurant are located here. *405 Olive Way.* ☎ *800/426-5100 or 206/623-8700. www.mayflowerpark.com. 171 units. Double $139–$229. AE, DC, DISC, MC, V. Bus: 25, 79, 123, 202, or 355. Map p 154.*

★ Mediterranean Inn QUEEN

ANNE A sunny yellow building in a quiet neighborhood houses this moderately priced hotel. Rooms come with kitchenettes. A short stroll takes you to Seattle Center, where you can catch the monorail downtown. *425 Queen Anne Ave. N.* ☎ *866/525-4700 or 206/428-4700. www.mediterranean-inn.com. Doubles $159–$169. AE, DC, DISC, MC, V. Map p 154.*

★★ kids Paramount Hotel

DOWNTOWN Across the street from the Paramount Theatre, this European-style hotel is also near the convention center and Pacific Place. Video games available. *724 Pine St.* ☎ *800/663-1144 or 206/292-9500. www.paramounthotelseattle.com. 146 units. Standard doubles $129–$199. AE, DC, DISC, MC, V. Bus: 10, 11, 14, 43, or 49. Map p 154.*

★ Ramada Seattle Downtown

DOWNTOWN With views of the Space Needle and the downtown cityscape, this is a reasonably priced choice. While not right in the heart of the shopping core, it's just a few blocks away, and within the free bus zone. Max's Café serves breakfast and lunch. *2200 5th Ave. (at Blanchard St.).* ☎ *206/441-9785. www.ramada.com/Ramada/control/Booking/property_info?propertyId=00015. Standard doubles $109–159. AE, DC, DISC, MC, V. Bus: 56 or 202. Map p 154.*

★★ **Red Lion Hotel on Fifth Avenue** DOWNTOWN
The Red Lion's location is just about perfect, an easy walk from Pike Public Market and the downtown shops. There's a roomy outdoor dining patio and the Elephant and Castle pub downstairs. *1415 5th Ave.* ☎ *206/971-8000. www.seattlered lionlifthavenue.com. 297 units. Standard double $103–$159. AE, DC, DISC, MC, V. Bus: 143, 150, 157, 306 or 312. Map p 154.*

★★★ **Renaissance Madison Hotel** DOWNTOWN
This upscale luxury property offers great views and a homey Northwestern decor. Maxwells serves breakfast, lunch, and dinner on site. *515 Madison St.* ☎ *800/546-9184 or 206/583-0300. www.marriott.com/hotels/travel/ seasm-renaissance-seattle-hotel. 553 units. Standard doubles $135–$215. AE, DISC, MC, V. Bus: 12, 124, 250, 252, or 257. Map p 154.*

★ **Roosevelt Hotel** DOWNTOWN
This lovely old hotel has personality, and it's right across from Pacific Place, in the heart of downtown. Don't miss the martinis at Von's Grand City Café, attached to the hotel. *1531 7th Ave.* ☎ *206/621-1200. www.roosevelthotel.com. 151 units. Standard doubles $149–$249. AE, DC, DISC, MC, V. Bus: 10, 11, 14, 43, or 49. Map p 154.*

★★★ kids **Sheraton Seattle Hotel** DOWNTOWN
One of the city's largest—and greenest hotels, the Sheraton has a pool and workout center. Near the convention center and downtown shops, it offers both views and convenience. The beds are oh-so-comfy. Dine and relax at the Pike Street Cafe and the Gallery Lounge. Cribs, video games. *1400 6th Ave.* ☎ *206/621-9000. www. starwoodhotels.com/sheraton/seattle. 1,258 units. Standard doubles*

$139–$199. AE, DC, DISC, MC, V. Bus: 306, 312, or 522. Map p 154.

★★ kids **Silver Cloud Hotel Broadway** CAPITOL HILL
Situated in the funky Capitol Hill district, the Silver Cloud has its own indoor pool and fitness center. A shuttle gets you downtown. *1100 Broadway.* ☎ *800/590-1801 or 206/325-1400. www.silvercloud.com/14home. htm. 179 units. Standard doubles $119–$209. AE, DC, DISC, MC, V. Bus: 12. Map p 154.*

★★★ **Sorrento Hotel** FIRST HILL
This luxury boutique's first guest was Teddy Roosevelt, and it's been pampering travelers ever since with European style and service. Spacious bathrooms feature Italian marble, and rooms come with thoughtful extras like a French press for coffee. The hotel is located in a quiet neighborhood, walkable from downtown. The Hunt Club is one of Seattle's finest restaurants. *900 Madison St. (at Terry).* ☎ *800/426-1265. www.hotel sorrento.com. 76 units. Doubles $155–$265. AE, DC, DISC, MC, V. Bus: 12. Map p 154.*

★★★ **W Seattle Hotel** DOWNTOWN
Sleek, contemporary, and youthful, the W is trendy in a great way. The rooms are warmly inviting,

The Inn at the Market has one of the best locations in town.

The Best Lodging

and you can choose from a "Wonderful" room to an "Extreme Wow" suite (on the 24th floor with more than 1,000 sq. ft. of space). Get a shiatsu massage in your room—or most anything (legal!) your heart desires, via the Whatever/Whenever service. Dine at the palate-pleasing Earth & Ocean. *1112 4th Ave.* ☎ *206/264-6000. www.Whotels. com/Seattle. 417 units. Doubles $178–$399. AE, DC, DISC, MC, V. Bus: 202, 210, 214, 215, or 554. Map p 154.*

★★ **kids** **Warwick Hotel Seattle**
BELLTOWN   This moderately priced, French-owned property is in Belltown, an easy walk from downtown and Pike Place Market. It features an indoor pool, accommodating staff, and a balcony on each room. Dine at the excellent Brasserie Margaux. *401 Lenora St.* ☎ *206/443-4300.*

www.warwickwa.com. 230 units. Doubles $89–$229. AE, DC, DISC, MC, V. Bus: 116, 118, 119, 120, or 202. Map p 154.

★★★ **kids** **The Westin Seattle**
DOWNTOWN   Located in landmark round towers, the 47-story Westin offers breathtaking views of the Space Needle, sound, and cityscape. Rooms come with the Westin Heavenly Bed that makes you want to stay in bed a little longer in the morning. Kids get a special welcome kit, and you can request a Heavenly Crib for the baby. Cool off in the roomy indoor pool; enjoy outstanding regional cuisine at the Coldwater Bar and Grill. *1900 5th Ave.* ☎ *800/ WESTIN or 206/728-1000. www. westin.com/seattle. 891 units. Doubles $178–$228. AE, DC, DISC, MC, V. South Lake Union Street Car 98. Bus: 25, 79, or 123. Map p 154.* ●

Check out the Space Needle from your room—views from the Westin are spectacular.

Tacoma

1 Tacoma Art Museum
2 Hello, Cupcake
3 Tacoma Union Station
4 Washington State History Museum
5 Chihuly Bridge of Glass
6 Museum of Glass
7 Point Defiance Zoo & Aquarium

True, it has no Space Needle, but the town of Tacoma, 30 miles south of its glitzy northern neighbor, has spruced up its image by redeveloping its downtown into a charming area with free light rail, an esplanade along the Thea Foss Waterway, a convention center, and major cultural facilities as anchors. It's worth checking out. START: **1701 Pacific Ave.**

---

1 ★★ kids Tacoma Art Museum. The building is itself a work of art, with a ramp spiraling up through galleries, arranged around an atrium with a stone garden. The museum houses a fine collection of works by Northwest artists, including the world's largest collection of Tacoma native Dale Chihuly's glass. In addition to American art, you'll find European and Asian works. ⏲ 1 hr. 1701 Pacific Ave. ☎ 253/272-4258. www.tacomaartmuseum.org.

$9 adults, $8 seniors & students, $25 family (2 adults & up to 4 children), free ages 4 & under. Wed–Sun 10am–5pm, 3rd Thurs 10am–8pm (free 5–8pm).

2 Hello, Cupcake. Just look for the pink bicycle outside. This charming little spot serves the tastiest cupcakes around. Try the red velvet and the vanilla vanilla. Mmm! *1740 Pacific Ave.* ☎ *253/383-7772. $.*

③ Tacoma Union Station.

The former terminus of the Northern Pacific Railroad, this grand station was abandoned for many years, then renovated in the 1990s. There are no more trains, but it's worth a stop to admire the magnificent 90-foot-tall rotunda dome, now decorated with a splendid 20-foot Chihuly chandelier. ⏱ *15 min. 1717 Pacific Ave. ☎ 253/863-5173, ext. 223. www.unionstationrotunda.org. Free to the public. Mon–Fri 8am–5pm.*

④ ★★★ kids Washington State History Museum.

History comes to life here via high-tech interactive displays. Engaging for all ages, these exhibits make learning history not only painless but terrific

World-famous glass artist Dale Chihuly designed the glass bridge that now connects downtown to the waterfront.

fun. "Meet" characters from Washington's past—like Lewis & Clark—in the Great Hall of Washington history. ⏱ *1½ hr. 1911 Pacific Ave. ☎ 253/272-3500. www.wshs.org. $8 adults, $7 seniors, $6 ages 6–17, $25 families (2 adults & up to 4 children). Wed–Sun 10am–5pm, third Thurs 10am–8pm (free 2–8pm).*

⑤ ★★★ Chihuly Bridge of Glass.

Connecting the revitalized downtown to Tacoma's waterfront is a spectacular 500-foot walking bridge by Chihuly. It rises 70 feet into the air as it crosses Interstate 705, and features a ceiling of "sea-form" glass, blue crystal towers, and a variety of glass sculptures. *1801 Dock St.*

⑥ ★★ Museum of Glass.

Here you'll find works by world-famous contemporary glass artists, and you can stop at the hot shop to watch artisans at work. ⏱ *1hr. 1801 Dock St. ☎ 253/284-4750. www.museumofglass.org. $12 adults, $10 seniors, $5 ages 6–12, $36 families (2 adults & up to 4 children). Summer: Mon–Sat 10am–5pm, Sun noon–5pm, third Thurs 10am–8pm (free 5–8pm). Fall/Winter: Wed–Sat 10am–5pm, Sun noon–5pm, third Thurs 10am–8pm (free 5–8pm).*

⑦ ★★ Point Defiance Zoo & Aquarium.

This terrific little zoo is best known for its marine exhibits, including its beluga whales. I once saw one retrieve a piece of litter thrown in its tank by a guest and deliver it to a docent. ⏱ *1½ hr. 5400 N. Pearl St. ☎ 253/404-3689. www.pdza.org. $13.50 adults, $12.50 seniors, $11.50 ages 5–12, $7.50 ages 3–4. Daily 9:30am (8:30am July–early Sept), closing hours vary.*

San Juan Islands

1 Friday Harbor Ferry Dock
2 Whale Watch
3 San Juan Roasting Co.
4 Pelindaba Lavender Gallery
5 Whale Museum

Just a few hours from Seattle, these small islands feel much, much farther away. The quaint portside town of Friday Harbor, at the tip of San Juan Island, is lined with interesting shops, art galleries, and cafes. The islands are a popular getaway for tourists and local residents. You won't need a car, unless you want to drive around the islands and do some exploring. Even then, you can rent bikes or mopeds when you get there. START: **Friday Harbor Ferry Dock.**

1 **kids Friday Harbor Ferry Dock.** This landing, with its stunning views of the surrounding hilly islands, is where your adventure begins. You can get here from the Seattle waterfront, via the *Victoria Clipper* (☎ 206/448-5000; www. victoriaclipper.com), or you can drive up I-5 to Anacortes (about a 2-hr. trip), then follow the signs to the Washington State ferry dock. You can take your car on the boat, but it costs quite a bit more.

Long-term parking at the dock is cheaper, and you can walk right onto the boat. Car lines get long in the summertime. For Anacortes–San Juan Islands ferry schedules, check the website (www.wsdot. wa.gov/ferries). This 1½-hour ferry ride is arguably the prettiest in the world, winding its way among enchanting emerald islands. It's spectacular on a sunny day, but dreamy in the mist as well. ⏱ *2 hr., 45 min. each way on Victoria Clipper* from Seattle (round-trip $75 adults, $37.50 children; discounts if purchased in advance); or 2 hr. by car, then about 1½ hr., excluding wait time on Washington State ferry, each way (current Anacortes–Friday Harbor round-trip Washington State ferry fares: passenger-only $10.10–$13.45 adults, $5.05–$6.70 seniors, $8.10–$10.80 ages 6–18. For car under 20 ft. long, add $35.05–$52.55, which includes driver's fare).

② ★★★ **kids** Whale Watch. A number of whale-watch cruises leave from Friday Harbor. If you get there via the *Victoria Clipper*, whale-watch tickets can be purchased as a package. Most companies won't guarantee you'll see sleek black-and-white orcas leaping out of the water, but chances are good in the summer. Most boats have knowledgeable guides who recognize the individual whales in the resident pods. *Victoria Clipper:* 🕐 2½ hr. from the port. Friday Harbor Port. ☎ 800/888-2535. Prices vary, depending on date, how far in advance purchased, and whether purchased separately or as package from Seattle. Check website (www.clippervacations.com). Victoria Clipper whale-watch only: $40 adult, $20 ages 1–11.

③ **kids** San Juan Coffee Roasting Co. For a great cup of island-roasted coffee, made with estate-grown beans from around the world, pop into San Juan Coffee and sample their smooth java. While you're there, give in to your sweet tooth; their chocolates are the melt-in-your-mouth variety. The shop is right beside the ferry dock. *18 Cannery Landing.* ☎ 800/624-4119. $.

Watch for the lighthouse as you head out to find whales.

④ ★ Pelindaba Lavender Gallery. Who knew there were so many uses for lavender—from a cooking ingredient to pet-odor spray? Pelindaba grows its own lavender right on San Juan Island. *150 1st St., Friday Harbor.* ☎ 866/819-1911. www.pelindabalavender.com. AE, MC, V.

⑤ ★ **kids** Whale Museum. Three blocks from the harbor, this unusual little museum is chock-full of information on these huge sea mammals, especially the three orca pods that spend their summers around the San Juans. Exhibits include a whale skeleton. 🕐 1 hr. *62 1st St. N.* ☎ 360/378-4710. www.whalemuseum.org. $6 adults, $5 seniors, $3 ages 5–18. Daily 10am–5pm.

Bellevue

148th Ave. NE
148th Ave. SE

NE 8th St.
Main St.
SE 8th St.

140th Ave. NE
140th Ave. SE

1/4 mi
0.25 km

Glendale Country Club

Kelsey Creek Park

Lake Hills Connector Road

Bellevue Redmond Rd.

NE 12th St.

NE 8th St.

Wilburton Hill Park

Main St.
Bellevue Botanical Garden

118th Ave. SE

116th Ave. NE

118th Ave. SE

405

112th Ave. NE
112th Ave. SE
SE 8th St.

Mercer Slough Nature Park

Surrey Downs Park

110th Ave. NE

112th Ave. SE

DOWNTOWN BELLEVUE
108th Ave. NE

Bellevue Way
NE

NE 2nd St.
Main St.

NE 12th St.

NE 4th St.
Downtown Park

100th Ave. NE

Lake Washington

1 Rosalie Whyel's Museum of Doll Art
2 Elements Gallery
3 Bellevue Square Mall
4 Bellevue Arts Museum
5 Cupcake Royale
6 Mercer Slough Nature Park
7 Bellevue Botanical Garden
8 Bellevue Aquatic Center

S hooting for the stars across the lake from Seattle is the city of Bellevue, which has quietly boomed from a sleepy Eastside suburb into one of the richest towns in Washington, with an overall per capita income nearly twice that of Seattle. Along with a thriving population comes high-end shopping, skyscrapers teeming with shops and offices, and lots of great activities. As elsewhere in the Northwest, there is a reverence for all things outdoors: Bellevue boasts miles of beautiful parks and waterfront. Just a short drive from downtown Seattle—across Lake Washington on either of two floating bridges—Bellevue has its own personality: less eccentric and more well-heeled than its westside counterpart. **START: Bus 233, 234, or 249 to NE 10th Street & 110th Ave., walk to 108th Ave. NE, or drive across SR 520 floating bridge, left on NE 12th Street, right on 108th Ave. NE, to 1116 108th Ave. NE.**

❶ ★ **kids** **Rosalie Whyel's Museum of Doll Art.** Visiting a doll museum might not be everybody's idea of a fun afternoon, but this eclectic collection has something to interest just about anyone. It runs the gamut from the first Barbie to a mass-produced Homer Simpson doll. The rooms are filled with dolls from around the world, many of them antique. There are also elaborate Victorian dollhouses, furnished with detailed miniatures, and other toys: trains, rocking horses, mechanical displays. Adults are sure to feel a tug of nostalgia. When you've had your fill of dolls, take a stroll in the English garden. ⏱ *1 hr. 1116 108th Ave. NE.* ☎ *425/455-1116. www.dollart.com. $10 adults, $9 seniors, $5 ages 5 to*

17, free 4 & under. Mon–Sat 10am–5pm; Sun 1–5pm.

❷ **Elements Gallery.** Visitors can take home a treasured souvenir or just enjoy gazing at the exquisite art, much of it created in the Northwest. Brilliantly colored glass, elegant sculptures, gleaming carved wood, and stunning jewelry share the space here. ⏱ *30 min. 10500 NE 8th St.* ☎ *425/454-8242. www.elementsglassgallery.com. Mon–Sat 9:30am–8pm; Sun noon–5pm.*

❸ ★ **kids** **Bellevue Square Mall.** A shopping excursion at Bellevue Square is not your ordinary mall experience. With about 200 shops and restaurants to wander through, I still occasionally get

Cupcake Royale will entice even the most reluctant cupcake converts.

lost—which usually translates into more shopping bags. Tenants include a new Microsoft outlet, giving the existing Apple Store a little competition; a Nordstrom, Crate & Barrel, Harry and David (yum!), Macy's, Once Upon a Time (quality toys), Something Silver, True Religion, Zumiez, and Tiffany & Co. If the little ones get antsy, head up to the Kids' Cove play area on the third floor. Mom and Dad can grab a latte while the tots scramble across a Washington ferryboat and other brightly colored climbing toys. Parking at the mall is free. Try to find *that* in Seattle. ⏱ *1 hr. 1086 Bellevue Sq.* ☎ *425/646-3660. www.bellevue collection.com. Mon–Sat 9:30am–9:30pm, Sun noon–5pm.*

④ ★★ kids Bellevue Arts Museum. With a focus on fine crafts and design, BAM is appropriately housed in an eye-catching red building by contemporary architect Steven Holl. Exhibits are inventive and thoughtful, and often showcase Northwest artists. A favorite was the U.S. premier of a dazzling collection of women's shoes by Beth Levine,

Exhibits at the Bellevue Arts Museum are thought-provoking and kid-friendly.

designer of Nancy Sinatra's legendary go-go boots ("These Boots are Made for Walkin' "). The museum often hosts Saturday craft classes in conjunction with exhibits, so kids can create some art of their own; check the schedule. Free docent tours are offered daily at 1pm. ⏱ *1 hr. 510 Bellevue Way NE.* ☎ *425/519-0770. www.bellevuearts.org. Admission $10 adults, $7 students and seniors, free for kids 5 & under. Mon–Thurs 11am–5pm, Fri 11am–8pm, Sat–Sun noon–5pm.*

⑤ kids Cupcake Royale. Even if you don't love cupcakes (but who doesn't?), you'll change your mind when you bite into one of these. My favorites are lavender, with real flower buds stirred into the buttercream, and peppermint patty—but a case could also be made for the chocolate orange. Or save yourself the agonizing and get the baker's-choice dozen. ⏱ *15 min. 21 Bellevue Way NE.* ☎ *425/454-7966. $3 each; $33 per dozen.*

⑥ ★ kids Mercer Slough Nature Park. Explore 320 acres of hiking trails, wetlands, and wildlife habitat along beautiful Lake Washington. Be sure to stop by the environmental education center's visitor center, where you'll find interpretive displays, libraries for adults and children, trail maps, and nature-inspired art exhibits. The treehouse offers a bird's-eye view of the park, and free nature walks leave from the center at 2pm every Saturday. From May to September, 3-hour **guided canoe trips** (☎ **425/452-6885;** $14 per person; children must be 5 or older) leave at 8:45am every Saturday from Enatai Beach Park, 3519 108th Ave. SE. Advance registration is recommended. ⏱ *1 hr. Environmental Education Center, 1625 118th Ave. SE. Daily 10am–4pm.*

Mercer Slough Nature Park is an oasis of hiking trails and wildlife.

7 ★ **kids** **Bellevue Botanical Garden.** No one loves flowers like Northwesterners. It would be hard not to, surrounded as we are by an ever-changing natural palette: delicate cherry blossoms, outrageous azaleas, rhododendrons in every hue imaginable, tulips, daffodils, forsythias, camellias . . . and let's not forget roses, bursting with color, which grow untended in everyone's backyard. Here at the Botanical Garden, everything *is* tended—to perfection. In addition to the splashy floral displays, there's a rock garden, a waterwise garden, and a trail for meandering through the woodlands. Just about the time of year when the colors seem to be gone, **Garden d'Lights** brings back the bling. Between Thanksgiving and New Year, more than a half-million bulbs lend a festive glow to the garden from 5 to 10pm daily. It is not to be missed. Garden d'Lights costs $5; no charge for children 10 and under. Otherwise, admission to the garden is free. ⏱ *1 hr. 12001 Main St.* ☎ *425/452-2750. www. bellevuebotanical.org. Admission free except $5 for 11 and older for Garden d'Lights. Daily dawn–dusk, plus 5–10pm during Garden d'Lights.*

8 **kids** **Bellevue Aquatic Center.** With two large indoor pools, the Blue Lagoon and Warm Springs, this is a great place for a refreshing workout, rain or shine. You can also dive into the tank or head down the 10-foot slide. Warm Springs is heated to a balmy 91 degrees for therapy, but it's often open to the public—and perfect for the younger set. *601 143rd Ave. NE.* ☎ *425/452-4444. www.ci.bellevue.wa.us/ aquatic_center.htm. Open swim sessions $6 adults, $5 12 & under. Mon–Fri 8am–8pm, Sat 8am–2pm, Sun 9am–2pm.*

Mount Rainier National Park

- **1** International Mountain Guides
- **2** Visitor Center
- **3** Paradise Inn
- **4** Snowshoeing
- **5** Hiking
- **6** Longmire
- **7** Comet Falls

Seattleites can go for weeks without seeing the sun, and they're pretty okay with that. What gets them down is when the gray skies blanket their beloved Mount Rainier, which soars—on a clear day—a mile-and-a-half above the surrounding Cascade peaks. When it breaks through the clouds, you're likely to hear someone say, "The mountain's out!" Less than 3 hours from the city, Mt. Rainier is considered somewhat of a backyard by Seattleites, who love to hike it, climb it, picnic on it, and marvel at its wildflowers. START: **The Nisqually Entrance.**

1 ★ Go Mountain Climbing. Several mountain-climbing organizations offer programs for various levels of climbers (including novices). A popular one is International Mountain Guides. *31111 S.R. 706, Ashford.* ☎ *360/569-2609. www.Mountain Guides.com. Prices start at $180 for a one-day mountaineering school.*

2 Paradise Jackson Visitor Center. From Seattle, drive south on I-5, east on SR 512, south on SR 7 to Elbe, then east on SR 706 through Ashford to reach the Nisqually Entrance of Mount Rainier National Park. This entrance is open year-round, as is the ride along the Nisqually-Paradise Road to Paradise. The drive is spectacular, winding through old-growth forest as the road climbs the mountain. At Paradise, stop at the Visitor Center for maps of the park and its many trails.

Free nature walks also leave from the center. *At Paradise.* ☎ *360/569-2211, ext. 3314.*

3 **The stunning Paradise Inn,** a national historic building made of Alaskan cedar, is a beautiful hotel with a huge fireplace and the feel of a woodsy lodge. In the dining room (closed in the winter months), you can grab a buffalo burger, smoked salmon Caesar salad, or a creamy crab mac 'n cheese. ☎ *360/569-2275. $.*

4 ★★ **kids** **Try Snowshoeing.** Snowshoeing is a popular sport on Mount Rainier, and no wonder: The variety of trails is endless, from very easy to super challenging. Beginners might want to try the half-mile Myrtle Falls trail, which starts near the Paradise Inn and leads to a lovely view of Myrtle Falls and the Paradise Valley. From mid-December through March, rangers lead free 2-hour snowshoe walks for kids and adults, with snowshoes provided. ⏱ *2 hr. Visitors Center.* ☎ *360/569-2211, ext. 3314. Free. Walks leave from Visitors Center at 12:30 & 2:30pm daily mid-Dec–early Jan; Sat–Sun early Jan–early Apr.*

5 ★★ **kids** **Take a hike.** The park maps will help you decide which trails best suit your needs. There are plenty of easy hikes, and lots of tougher ones as well. Watch for wildlife and dramatic mountain vistas. Or continue driving up the Nisqually-Paradise Road to Kautz Creek, where you can park and enjoy the view of Mount Rainier. You can also hike along the Kautz Creek trail to Indian Henry's Hunting Ground.

6 ★ **kids** **Longmire.** Nisqually-Paradise Road takes you next to Longmire, a town about 12 miles from Paradise, where you will find the **Longmire Museum** (☎ *360/ 569-2211, ext. 3314; year-round. 9am–4:30pm; free to all*) with exhibits about the land's history and geology, as well as the **National Park Inn** (☎ *360/569-2275*) and more trails near mineral springs, which are worth checking out even though you can no longer soak in them.

7 ★ **kids** **Comet Falls.** About 10 miles from the entrance to the park, Nisqually-Paradise Road takes you to a 300-foot waterfall, Comet Falls. You can hike there or drive to the viewing area, just past Christine Falls.

A view of Mt. Rainier.

Vancouver, BC

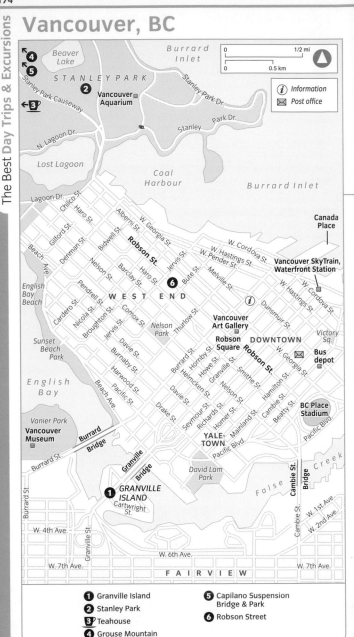

Burrard Inlet

Beaver Lake

STANLEY PARK

❷ Vancouver Aquarium

Stanley Park Dr.

❹
❺

Stanley Park Causeway

←❸

N. Lagoon Dr.

Lost Lagoon

Stanley Park Dr.

Coal Harbour

Burrard Inlet

| 0 | 1/2 mi |
| 0 | 0.5 km |

ⓘ Information
✉ Post office

Lagoon Dr.

Chilco St.

Haro St.

Gilford St.

Alberni St.

W. Georgia St.

Robson St.

Jervis St.

W. Cordova St.

W. Hastings St.
W. Pender St.

Canada Place

Vancouver SkyTrain, Waterfront Station

Bidwell St.

Denman St.

Haro St.

Barclay St.

Bute St.

Melville St.

W. Hastings St.

W. Cordova St.

English Bay Beach

Beach Ave.

Nelson St.

Pendrell St.

Cardero St.

Nicola St.

Broughton St.

Comox St.

WEST END

Nelson Park

Thurlow St.

Jervis St.

❻

Dunsmuir St.

ⓘ

Vancouver Art Gallery

Robson Square

DOWNTOWN

Robson St.

W. Georgia St.

Victory Sq.

✉

Bus depot

Sunset Beach Park

Davie St.

Burnaby St.

Burrard St.

Hornby St.

Howe St.

Helmcken St.

Harwood St.

Pacific St.

Davie St.

Seymour St.

Richards St.

Homer St.

Granville St.

Nelson St.

Smithe St.

Hamilton St.

Cambie St.

Beatty St.

BC Place Stadium

English Bay

Beach Ave.

YALE-TOWN

Pacific Blvd.

Cambie St.

Burrard Bridge

Vanier Park

Vancouver Museum

Burrard St.

Granville Bridge

David Lam Park

False Creek

Cambie Bridge

W. 1st Ave.

W. 2nd Ave.

Burrard St.

❶ *GRANVILLE ISLAND*

Cartwright St.

Granville St.

W. 4th Ave.

W. 6th Ave.

W. 7th Ave.

W. 7th Ave.

FAIRVIEW

❶ Granville Island
❷ Stanley Park
❸ Teahouse
❹ Grouse Mountain
❺ Capilano Suspension Bridge & Park
❻ Robson Street

So close to Seattle it's considered a neighbor, Vancouver is a sophisticated city with lots to offer. Set on the Pacific Ocean, with the majestic Coast Mountains looming in the background, this is breathtaking country. To get there, drive 2½ hours north from Seattle along I-5, over the Canadian border at Blaine or take the 4-hour **Amtrak Cascades** ride (☎ **800/USA-RAIL;** www.amtrak.com). Passports are a must. Getting around town is a breeze—by light rail (the Vancouver Sky Train), bus, or ferry.

START: GRANVILLE ISLAND. Take the #50 False Creek bus from Gastown (downtown area), which stops just off Granville Island; walk toward the sign. Other city buses will take you to Granville & 5th Ave., and you can walk to the island. You can also take a ferry (continuous runs 7am–10:30pm in the summer; 'til 8:30pm in the winter).

The Public Market at Granville Island rivals Pike Place Market.

❶ ★★★ kids **Granville Island.**
If you have time for only one stop, make it lively, picturesque Granville Island. The public market is an experience of colors, smells, and tastes (free samples!). Meanwhile, entertainers of some sort are usually performing on the deck. The Kids Market is an entire building of children's shops surrounding a three-story climbing ball pit. ⏱ *2 hr.* www.granvilleisland.com/public-market.

❷ ★★★ kids **Stanley Park.**
One of the most magnificent parks in the world, Stanley is a 1,000-acre

paradise of meadows, forests, and gardens. As if the natural beauty weren't enough, there's plenty to do here. The **Vancouver Aquarium** is open daily (☎ **604/659-3511;** www.vanaqua.org; $21 adults, $16 ages 13–18, $13 ages 4–12; summer: 9:30am–7pm; winter: 9:30am–5pm). The Variety Kids Water Park is free—and teeming with little ones cooling off in water sprays, from the end of May 'til Labor Day. For more water fun, take a plunge into the heated pool or bask on two bathing beaches. If you want to get around in style, take a horse and carriage (C$30 adults, C$28 seniors and

Stanley is considered one of the world's great urban parks.

The Best Day Trips & Excursions

Olympic Gains

Vancouver and environs spruced up to the tune of $6 billion for the 2010 Winter Olympics. That included improvements to the Sea to Sky Highway (99), a formerly challenging—and sometimes scary!—route from Vancouver north to the breathtaking ski town of Whistler. Now wider and safer, the road takes you there in less than 2 hours. You'll need an early start to fit this into your day trip, but it's worth it for the spectacular alpine scenery.

students with ID, C$16 children 3–12, free 2 & under). Enter the park on Georgia Street, and turn left. ⏲ *2 hr. Georgia St., north end.* ☎ *604/257-\8400. www.stanleypark.com. Bus: 19.*

3 **Teahouse in Stanley Park.** Elegant but never stuffy, the Teahouse serves lunch, brunch, or dinner—or just a pick-me-up treat, like the gingerbread cake. *Ferguson Point, Stanley Park Drive.* ☎ *604/669-3281. $–$$$.*

4 ★ kids **Grouse Mountain.** Just a 15-minute drive from the city, Grouse Mountain offers snowshoe-ing, ice skating, and sleigh rides in

If you're afraid of heights, you may want to skip the Capilano Suspension Bridge, though you should still check out the park.

the winter. In the summer, take the **SkyRide cable car** (C$40 adults, C$24 ages 13–18, C$14 ages 5–12) up to the top and enjoy the pan-oramic view. Work up an appetite, then enjoy fine dining at the Obser-vatory Restaurant, or a casual bite at the cafe or bistro. ⏲ *2 hr. 6400 Nancy Greene Way.* ☎ *604/980-9311. www.grousemountain. com. Take bus 232 from Phibbs Exchange or bus 236 from Lonsdale Quay. Or drive north across Lions Gate Bridge, take the North Vancou-ver exit to Marine Drive, then 3 miles up Capilano Road. Daily 9am–10pm.*

5 ★ kids **Capilano Suspen-sion Bridge & Park.** This 443-foot swinging bridge gives you a breathtaking view of the rainforest and the Capilano River rushing along below. In the park, you can watch First Nation carving demonstrations and go on the Treetops Adventure, which takes you far above the forest floor on a separate series of suspen-sion bridges. ⏲ *1½ hr. 3735 Cap-ilano Rd.* ☎ *604/985-7474. www. capbridge.com. C$28 adults, C$17 ages 13–16, C$10 ages 6–12. Daily times vary; check website.*

6 ★ **Robson Street.** The Rodeo Drive of Vancouver, this is where you'll find upscale shops with trend-setting fashion, shoes, and jewelry. *Btw. Burrard and Jervis sts.* ●

The
Savvy Traveler

Before You Go

Tourist Offices

Need more information about Seattle? You can get all the details your heart desires by contacting **Seattle's Convention and Visitors Bureau,** 701 Pike St., Ste. 800, Seattle, WA 98101 (☎ **206/461-5800;** www.visitseattle.org), which operates the **Seattle Visitor Center and Concierge Services** inside the Washington State Convention and Trade Center, 7th Avenue and Pike Street, Upper Pike Street Lobby (☎ **206/461-5840**); and the Market Information Center, Southwest Corner of 1st Avenue and Pike Street in the Pike Place Market (☎ 206/461-5840). For information on other parts of Washington, contact **Washington State Tourism** (☎ **800/544-1800;** www.experiencewashington.com).

The Best Times to Go

Summer arrives with a bang in Seattle around the Fourth of July. From then through the end of September, the rain (for the most part) goes away and Seattleites come out to play. The picture-perfect weather means hotels and restaurants are crowded, so book as far in advance as possible. If you're not afraid of the rain—usually more of a mist than a downpour—come in the winter months, when rates are lower, crowds are thinner, and the theatres are churning out top-notch productions. With Seattle's temperate climate, it will probably be warmer than wherever you started out.

Festivals & Special Events

SPRING April brings the **Skagit Valley Tulip Festival** (☎ 360/428-5959; www.tulipfestival.org), in and around La Conner. An hour north of Seattle, acres and acres of tulips

and daffodils blanket the Skagit Valley with a living quilt for weeks, accompanied by festivities. May starts with a splash the first Saturday of the month, **Opening Day of Boating Season** (☎ 206/325-1000; www.seattleyachtclub.org). It's held on Lakes Union and Washington. Next comes the first big street fair, the **U District StreetFair** (☎ 206/547-4417; www.udistrictstreetfair.org), in the lively University District. Also in mid-May is Giant Magnet's **International Children's Festival** (☎ 206/684-7338; www.giant magnet.org), at Seattle Center, celebrating cultures from around the world. Then comes the world-famous **Seattle International Film Festival** (☎ 206/324-9996; www.seattlefilm.com), held at area theaters, mid-May through early June. On Memorial Day weekend, the **Northwest Folklife Festival** (☎ 206/684-7300; www.nwfolklife.org) at Seattle Center honors the many cultures that come together in the Northwest.

SUMMER The third weekend in June is time for the wackiest festival of all, the **Fremont Fair** (☎ 206/694-6706; www.fremontfair.com), which sees in the summer solstice with a quirky parade, complete with political satire and bicyclists in the buff. At the end of the month comes **Seattle Pride** (☎ 206/322-9561; www.seattlepride.org), a gay, lesbian, bisexual, and transgender festival. On the Fourth of July, head for **Lake Union** (☎ 206/281-7788; www.familyfourth.org) to ooh and ahhh at fireworks over the lake. The biggest event of the season is **Seafair** (☎ 206/728-0123; www.seafair.com), which starts in early July and lasts for a month. Highlights are the hydroplane boat races, the Navy's

SEATTLE'S AVERAGE TEMPERATURE & DAYS OF RAIN

	JAN	FEB	MAR	APR	MAY	JUNE
Temp. (°F)	46	50	53	58	65	69
Temp. (°C)	8	10	12	14	18	21
Rain (days)	16	17	14	10	9	5

	JULY	AUG	SEPT	OCT	NOV	DEC
Temp. (°F)	75	74	69	60	52	47
Temp. (°C)	24	23	21	16	11	8
Rain (days)	7	9	14	18	20	19

Blue Angels show, and the Torchlight Parade. At **Bite of Seattle** in mid-July, crowds head to Seattle Center to hear live bands and sample treats and wine from local restaurants. Wrapping up the summer is **Bumbershoot, the Seattle Music & Arts Festival** (☎ 206/281-7788; www.bumbershoot.org), at Seattle Center on Labor Day weekend. It's a little bit crazy and a lot of fun.

FALL Issaquah Salmon Days Festival (☎ 425/392-0661; www.salmon days.org) welcomes the salmon on their return to the lakes and streams. Issaquah, 15 miles east of Seattle, the first full weekend in October.

WINTER Throughout December, the **Argosy Cruises Christmas Ships Festival** (☎ 888/623-1445 or 206/622-8687; www.argosycruises.com) takes place at various waterfront locations. Boats decked out with Christmas lights parade past a number of beaches. What better way to ring in the new year than with **New Year's at the Needle** (☎ 206/905-2100; www.spaceneedle.com), Seattle Center, December 31?

In January, Seattle celebrates the Chinese New Year in a big way, with dragon kites, music, and dance. The **Chinatown/International District Lunar New Year Celebration** (☎ 206/382-1197; www.cidbia.org), is held at Hing Hay Park (423

Maynard Ave. S.).The next month, gardening buffs head to the **Northwest Flower & Garden Show** (☎ 253/756-2121; www.garden show.com), at the Washington State Convention and Trade Center.

The Weather

Okay, so Seattle doesn't come to mind when you think of sunny destinations. But if you're here in July, August, or September, when those glorious summer days stretch lazily on 'til 10pm, you might think the city has an undeserved rap. Come back in November and you might change your mind. But even then, the rain is generally more drizzle than downpour. When they run the numbers, it turns out that Seattle get 19 inches less rain every year than Miami—though it rains here 29 more days. Theirs is torrential downpour; ours is gentle mist. So Seattle has less rain but more gray days. No matter when you visit, bring an umbrella or hooded jacket for chilly nights. Winters seldom bring below-freezing temperatures in temperate Seattle, and snow is a rarity in the city.

CAR RENTALS

All the major car-rental agencies have offices in Seattle and at or near Seattle-Tacoma International Airport. These include the following.

- **Advantage** (☎ 800/777-5500 or 206/824-0161; www.advantage. com)

The **Savvy** Traveler

Useful Websites

- Seattle's Convention and Visitors Bureau (www.visitseattle.org)
- Seattle-Tacoma International Airport (www.portseattle.org/seatac)
- *Seattle Times* (www.seattletimes.com)
- *Seattle Weekly* (www.seattleweekly.com)
- Universal Currency Converter (www.xe.com/ucc)
- Visa ATM Locator (www.visa.com), MasterCard ATM Locator (www.mastercard.com)
- Washington State Ferries (www.wsdot.wa.gov/ferries)
- Weather (www.intellicast.com and www.weather.com)

- **Alamo** (☎ **877/905-5555** or 206/433-0182; www.goalamo.com)

- **Avis** (☎ **800/331-1212** or 206/433-5231; www.avis.com)

- **Budget** (☎ **800/527-0700** or 206/444-7510; www.budget.com)

- **Dollar** (☎ **800/800-3665** or 206/433-5825; www.dollar.com)

- **Enterprise** (☎ **800/261-7331** or 206/246-1953; www.enterprise.com)

- **Hertz** (☎ **800/654-3131** or 206/248-1300; www.hertz.com)

- **National** (☎ **877/222-9058** or 206/433-5501; www.nationalcar.com)

- **Thrifty** (☎ **800/847-4389** or 877/283-0898; www.thrifty.com)

Cellphones

It's a good bet that your phone will work in major cities, but take a look at your wireless company's coverage map on its website before heading out. If you need to stay in touch at a destination where you know your phone won't work, **rent** a phone that does from **InTouch USA** (☎ 800/872-7626; www.intouchglobal.com) or a rental car location, but beware that you'll pay by the minute for airtime.

Getting **There**

By Plane
The **Seattle-Tacoma International Airport** (☎ **206/433-5388;** www.portseattle.org/seatac) is served by about 30 airlines.

International carriers that fly from Europe to Los Angeles and/or San Francisco (continue to Seattle on a domestic carrier) include **Aer Lingus** (☎ **0818/365-000** in Ireland; www.aerlingus.com) and

British Airways (☎ **0870/850-9850;** www.britishairways.com). The latter also flies directly to Seattle from London.

From New Zealand and Australia, there are flights to San Francisco and Los Angeles on **Qantas** (☎ **13-13-13** in Australia; www.qantas.com.au) and **Air New Zealand** (☎ **0800/737-000** in New Zealand; www.airnewzealand.co.nz).

From Los Angeles, you can continue on to Seattle on a regional domestic carrier.

Seaplane service between Seattle and the San Juan Islands; and Victoria, BC, is offered by **Kenmore Air** (☎ **866/435-9524** or 425/486-1257; www.kenmoreair.com), which has its Seattle terminals at the south end of Lake Union and at the north end of Lake Washington.

By Car

There are two main exits from the airport: From the loading/unloading area, take the first exit if you're staying near the airport. Take the second exit (Wash. 518) if you're headed to downtown Seattle. Driving east on Wash. 518 will connect you to I-5, where you'll then follow the signs for Seattle. Generally, allow 30 minutes for the drive between the airport and downtown—45 minutes to an hour during rush hour.

By Taxi, Shuttle, or Bus

A taxi into downtown Seattle will cost you about $32 to $52. There are usually plenty of taxis around, but if not, call **Yellow Cab** (☎ **206/622-6500**) or **Farwest Taxi** (☎ **206/622-1717**). **Gray Line Airport Express** (☎ **800/426-7532** or 206/626-6088; www.graylineofseattle.com) is a good way to get downtown. They leave the airport every 30 minutes from 6:20am (5:30am from

downtown) to 9pm. Passengers are picked up outside the baggage-claim area, on Level Three of the parking garage, Island Two. Shuttles stop at the following downtown hotels: Madison Renaissance, Crowne Plaza, Fairmont Olympic, Seattle Hilton, Sheraton Seattle, Grand Hyatt, Westin, and Warwick. Fares are $15 one-way and $25 round-trip for adults, and $11 one-way and $18 round-trip for children 2 to 12.

Shuttle Express

Shuttle Express (☎ **800/487-7433** or 425/981-7000; www.shuttleexpress.com) provides 24-hour service between Sea-Tac and Seattle and environs. Rates to downtown Seattle hotels are $32 for one to two adults, $40 for three adults, and $52 for four. Children 12 and under ride free. You need a reservation to get to the airport; to leave the airport, reservations are recommended, but walk-ups are welcome. Head to the Ground Transportation Center on the third floor of the parking garage.

The new **Link Light Rail Station** (☎ **800/201-4900** or 206/398-5000; www.soundtransit.org/Riding-Sound-Transit/Schedules) is connected to the fourth floor of the parking garage. Trains run between the airport and downtown every 7½ to 15 minutes, from 5am to 1am Monday through Saturday, and 6am to midnight Sunday, $1.75 to $2.50.

Getting **Around**

By Car

Seattle is 110 miles from Vancouver, BC, 175 miles from Portland, 810 miles from San Francisco, 1,190 miles from Los Angeles, 835 miles from Salt Lake City, and 285 miles

from Spokane. I-5 is the main north-south artery, running south to Portland and north to the Canadian border. I-405 is Seattle's eastside bypass and accesses Bellevue, Redmond, and Kirkland on the east side of Lake Washington. I-90, which ends at I-5, connects Seattle to Spokane in the eastern part of Washington. Wash. 520 connects I-405 with Seattle just north of downtown and also ends at I-5. Wash. 99, the Alaskan Way Viaduct, is another major north-south highway through downtown Seattle; it passes through the waterfront section of the city. All the major car-rental agencies have offices in Seattle and at or near Seattle-Tacoma International Airport.

Keep in mind that Seattle traffic congestion is bad, parking is limited (and expensive), and streets are almost all one-way. You'll avoid frustration by leaving your car in your hotel parking garage. You might not need a car at all. The city center is well served by public transportation. Plus, Seattle is very walkable—and parking is formidable. However, to get north of Seattle Center, east of Lake Washington, west of Puget Sound, or south of the sports stadiums is a bit tricky without a car (of course, you can take the foot ferry for a trip to Bainbridge Island). You could certainly have a very fun trip to Seattle without renting a car.

Parking

On-street parking in downtown Seattle is expensive and extremely limited. Most downtown parking lots charge $20 to $25 per day, though many offer early-bird specials. Some lots near the Space Needle charge less, and you can leave your car there, then take the monorail downtown. Some restaurants and Pike Place Market merchants validate parking permits.

By Ferry

Seattle is served by **Washington State Ferries** (☎ 888/808-7977 within Washington, or 206/464-6400; www.wsdot.wa.gov/ferries). Car ferries travel between downtown

Seattle and both Bainbridge Island and Bremerton from Pier 52, Colman Dock. Car ferries also connect Fauntleroy (in West Seattle) with Vashon Island and the Kitsap Peninsula at Southworth; Tahlequah (Vashon Island) with Point Defiance in Tacoma; Edmonds with Kingston (on the Kitsap Peninsula); Mukilteo with Whidbey Island; Whidbey Island at Keystone with Port Townsend; and Anacortes with the San Juan Islands and Sidney, BC (on Vancouver Island near Victoria).

If you're traveling between Victoria, BC, and Seattle, several options are available through **Victoria Clipper,** Pier 69, 2701 Alaskan Way (☎ 800/888-2535, 206/448-5000, or 250/382-8100 in Victoria; www.victoriaclipper.com). Ferries make the 2- or 3-hour trip throughout the year, at prices ranging from $75 to $140 round-trip for adults.

By Train

Amtrak (☎ 800/872-7245; www.amtrak.com) service runs from Vancouver, BC, to Seattle and from Portland and as far south as Eugene, Oregon, on the *Cascades.* The train takes about 4 hours from Vancouver to Seattle and 3½ to 4 hours from Portland to Seattle. One-way fares from Vancouver to Seattle or from Portland to Seattle run $23 to $50. There is also Amtrak service to Seattle from San Diego, Los Angeles, San Francisco, and Portland on the *Coast Starlight,* and from Spokane and points east on the *Empire Builder.* Amtrak also operates a bus between Vancouver and Seattle, so be careful when making an online reservation or you won't even be on a train.

By Bus

Greyhound (☎ 800/231-2222; www.greyhound.com) bus service provides connections to almost any city in the continental United States.

Seattle's Greyhound bus station is at 811 Stewart St. (☎ 206/628-5561), a few blocks northeast of downtown. Several budget chain motels are located nearby, and you can grab a free ride into downtown on a Metro bus.

By Metro Bus   The best thing about Seattle's **Metro** (☎ **206/553-3000;** http://metro.kingcounty.gov) bus system is that as long as you stay within the downtown area, you can ride for free between 6am and 7pm. The **Ride Free Area** is between Alaskan Way (the waterfront) to the west, 6th Avenue and I-5 to the east, Battery Street to the north, and South Jackson Street to the south. If you travel outside the Ride Free Area, adult fares range from $2.25 to $3, depending on distance and time of day. You do need exact change; day passes are sold by bus drivers on weekends and holidays for $4.50.

Fast **Facts**

AREA CODE   The area code is 206 in Seattle, 425 for the Eastside (including Kirkland and Bellevue), and 253 for south King County (near the airport).

ATMS   Nationwide, the easiest and best way to get cash away from home is from an ATM (automated teller machine), sometimes referred to as a "cash machine." The **Cirrus** (☎ 800/424-7787; www.mastercard.com) and **PLUS** (☎ 800/843-7587; www.visa.com) networks span the country.

BUSINESS HOURS   The following are general guidelines. Banks are open Monday through Friday from 9am to 5pm (some also on Sat 9am–noon). Stores are open Monday through Saturday from 10am to 6pm and Sunday from noon to 5pm (malls usually stay open until 9pm Mon–Sat). Bars can stay open until 2am.

CURRENCY   The most common bills are the $1 (a "buck"), $5, $10, and $20 denominations. There are also $2 bills (seldom encountered), $50 bills, and $100 bills. Coins: 1¢ (1 cent, or a penny); 5¢ (5 cents, or a nickel); 10¢ (10 cents, or a dime); 25¢ (25 cents, or a quarter); 50¢ (50 cents, or a half-dollar); the gold-colored Sacagawea coin, worth $1; and the rare silver dollar.

U.S. currency can be used in most places in Vancouver, BC, but the exchange rate is more favorable if you buy Canadian currency before you leave the U.S., or if you use credit cards while visiting Canada. The most common Canadian paper bills are $5, $10, $20, $50, and $100. The $1 coin is called a loonie; the $2 coin is a toonie.

DENTIST   Contact the **Dental Referral Service** (☎ 800/510-7315).

DOCTOR   To find a physician, check at your hotel for a referral, contact Swedish Medical Center (☎ 800/833-8879; www.swedish.org), or call the referral line of the Virginia Mason Medical Center (☎ 888/862-2737; www.virginiamason.org).

DRINKING LAWS   The legal age for purchase and consumption of alcoholic beverages is 21; proof of age is required and often requested at bars and restaurants. Do not carry open containers of alcohol in your car or any public area that isn't zoned for alcohol consumption. And nothing will ruin your trip faster than getting a citation for DUI ("driving under the influence"), so don't even think about driving while intoxicated.

EMBASSIES & CONSULATES All embassies are located in the nation's capital, Washington, D.C. Some consulates are located in major U.S. cities, and most nations have a mission to the United Nations in New York City. If your country isn't listed below, call for directory information in Washington, D.C. (☎ **202/555-1212**) or log on to www.embassy.org/embassies.

The embassy of **Australia** is at 1601 Massachusetts Ave. NW, Washington, DC 20036 (☎ **202/797-3000;** www.usa.embassy.gov.au). There are consulates in New York, Atlanta, Chicago, Denver, Honolulu, Houston, Los Angeles, and San Francisco.

The embassy of **Canada** is at 501 Pennsylvania Ave. NW, Washington, DC 20001 (☎ **202/682-1740;** www.canadianembassy.org). Other Canadian consulates are in cities including Buffalo (New York), Detroit, Los Angeles, New York, and Seattle.

The embassy of **Ireland** is at 2234 Massachusetts Ave. NW, Washington, DC 20008 (☎ **202/462-3939;** www.embassyofireland.org). Irish consulates are in Boston, Chicago, New York, San Francisco, and other cities. See website for complete listing.

The embassy of **New Zealand** is at 37 Observatory Circle NW, Washington, DC 20008 (☎ **202/328-4800;** www.nzembassy.com/usa). New Zealand consulates are in Los Angeles, Salt Lake City, San Francisco, and Seattle.

The embassy of the **United Kingdom** is at 3100 Massachusetts Ave. NW, Washington, DC 20008 (☎ **202/588-6500;** www.ukinusa.fco.gov.uk/en). Other British consulates are in Atlanta, Boston, Chicago, Cleveland, Houston, Los Angeles, New York, San Francisco, and Seattle.

EMERGENCIES For police, fire, or medical emergencies, phone ☎ **911.**

HOLIDAYS Banks, government offices, post offices, and many stores, restaurants, and museums are closed on the following legal national holidays: January 1 (New Year's Day), the third Monday in January (Martin Luther King, Jr., Day), the third Monday in February (Presidents' Day), the last Monday in May (Memorial Day), July 4 (Independence Day), the first Monday in September (Labor Day), the second Monday in October (Columbus Day), November 11 (Veterans' Day/Armistice Day), the fourth Thursday in November (Thanksgiving Day), and December 25 (Christmas). The Tuesday after the first Monday in November is Election Day.

HOSPITALS Hospitals convenient to downtown include **Swedish Medical Center,** 747 Broadway (☎ **206/386-6000;** www.swedish.org), and **Virginia Mason Medical Center,** 1100 9th Ave. (☎ **206/583-6433** for emergencies or 206/624-1144 for information; www.virginiamason.org).

INTERNET ACCESS First, ask at your hotel to see if it provides Internet access. Alternatively, you can head to the **Seattle Central Library,** 1000 4th Ave. (☎ **206/386-4636**), which has hundreds of online computer terminals.

LOST & FOUND Be sure to tell all of your credit card companies the minute you discover your wallet has been lost or stolen and file a report at a police precinct. Your credit card company or insurer may require a police report number or record of the loss. Most credit card companies have an emergency toll-free number to call if your card is lost or stolen. **Visa**'s U.S. emergency number is ☎ **800/847-2911. American Express** cardholders and traveler's check holders should call ☎ **800/528-4800. MasterCard** holders should call ☎ **800/627-8372.** For other credit cards, call the toll-free number directory at ☎ **800/555-1212.** You can have money wired to you via Western Union (☎ 800/325-6000; www.westernunion.com).

MAIL   At press time, domestic postage rates were 28¢ for a postcard and 44¢ for a letter. For international mail, a first-class letter of up to 1 ounce costs 98¢ (75¢ to Canada and Mexico); a first-class postcard costs 98¢ (75¢ to Canada and Mexico). For more information go to www.usps.com and click on "Calculate Costs."

If you aren't sure what your address will be in the United States, mail can be sent to you, in your name, c/o General Delivery at the main post office of the city or region where you expect to be. (Call ☎ 800/275-8777 for information on the nearest post office.) Always include zip codes when mailing items in the U.S.

NEWSPAPERS & MAGAZINES   The *Seattle Times* is Seattle's daily newspaper. *Seattle Weekly* is the city's free arts-and-entertainment weekly.

PHARMACIES   Conveniently located downtown pharmacies include **Rite Aid,** with branches at 319 Pike St. (☎ **206/223-0512**) and 2603 3rd Ave. (☎ **206/441-8790**). For 24-hour service, try **Bartell Drug Store,** 600 1st Ave. N. (☎ **206/284-1353**).

POLICE   For police emergencies, phone ☎ 911.

RESTROOMS   There are public restrooms in **Pike Place Market, Westlake Center, Pacific Place, Seattle Center,** and the **Washington State Convention and Trade Center.** You'll also find restrooms in most hotel lobbies and coffee bars in downtown Seattle.

SAFETY   Although Seattle is a relatively safe city, it has its share of crime. The most questionable neighborhood you're likely to visit is the Pioneer Square area. By day, this area is quite safe (though it has a large contingent of street people), but when the bars are closing, stay aware of your surroundings. Also take extra precautions with your wallet or purse when you're in the crush of people at Pike Place Market. Try to park your car in a garage at night. If you must park on the street, make sure there are no valuables in view.

SMOKING   Smoking is banned in public indoor spaces throughout the state of Washington, even in bars.

TAXES   Seattle has a 9.5% sales tax. In restaurants, there's an additional .5% food-and beverage tax. The hotel-room tax in the metro area ranges from around 10% to 16%. On rental cars, you pay an 18.6% tax, plus, if you rent at the airport, a 10% to 12% airport concession fee (plus other fees for a whopping total of around 45%!).

TELEPHONES   Hotel surcharges can be astronomical, so use your cellphone or a public pay telephone. Many convenience groceries sell prepaid calling cards; for international visitors these can be the least expensive way to call home. Many public pay phones at airports now accept American Express, MasterCard, and Visa credit cards. For calls within the United States and to Canada, dial 1 followed by the area code and the seven-digit number. For other international calls, dial 011 followed by the country code, city code, and the number you are calling.

Calls to area codes 800, 888, 877, and 866 are toll-free. For local directory assistance ("information"), dial 411; for long-distance information, dial 1, then the appropriate area code and 555-1212.

TIME   The continental United States is divided into **four time zones:** Eastern Standard Time (EST), Central Standard Time (CST), Mountain

Standard Time (MST), and Pacific Standard Time (PST). Alaska and Hawaii have their own zones. For example, when it's 9am in Los Angeles (PST), it's 7am in Honolulu (HST),10am in Denver (MST), 11am in Chicago (CST), noon in New York City (EST), 5pm in London (GMT), and 2am the next day in Sydney. Seattle is on Pacific Standard Time (PST), making it 3 hours behind the East Coast.

Daylight Saving Time is in effect from 1am on the second Sunday in March to 1am on the first Sunday in November, except in Arizona, Hawaii, the U.S. Virgin Islands, and Puerto Rico. Daylight Saving Time moves the clock 1 hour ahead of standard time.

TIPPING Tips are the standard way of showing appreciation for services provided. In hotels, tip bellhops at least $1 per bag ($2–$3 if you have a lot of luggage) and tip the chamber staff $1 to $2 per day (more if you've left a disaster area). Tip the doorman or concierge only if he or she has provided you with some specific service. Tip the valet-parking attendant $1 every time you get your car. In restaurants, bars, and nightclubs, tip service staff 15% to 20% of the check, tip bartenders 10% to 15%, tip checkroom attendants $1 per garment, and tip valet-parking attendants $1 per vehicle. Tip cab drivers 15% of the fare; tip skycaps at airports at least $1 per bag ($2–$3 if you have a lot of luggage); and tip hairdressers and barbers 15% to 20%.

TRANSIT INFO For 24-hour information on Seattle's **Metro** bus system, call ☎ **206/553-3000** or go to http://metro.kingcounty.gov. For information on the **Washington State Ferries,** call ☎ **888/808-7977** within Washington, or 206/464-6400; www.wsdot.wa.gov/ferries.

TRAVELERS WITH DISABILITIES For anyone using a wheelchair, the greatest difficulty of a visit to Seattle is dealing with the city's steep hills. One solution for dealing with downtown hills is to use the elevator at Pike Place Market to get between the waterfront and 1st Avenue. There's also a public elevator at the west end of Lenora Street (just north of Pike Place Market). This elevator connects the waterfront with the Belltown neighborhood.

Organizations that offer assistance to travelers with disabilities include **MossRehab** (☎ **800/CALL-MOSS;** www.mossresourcenet.org); the **American Foundation for the Blind (AFB)** (☎ **800/232-5463;** www.afb.org); and **SATH (Society for Accessible Travel & Hospitality)** (☎ **212/447-7284;** www.sath.org). **AirAmbulanceCard.com** is now partnered with SATH and allows you to preselect top-notch hospitals in case of an emergency.

WEATHER Check the *Seattle Times* or *Seattle Post-Intelligencer* newspapers for forecasts. If you want to know what to pack before you depart, go to www.wrh.noaa.gov/seattle, www.cnn.com/weather, or www.wunderground.com/US/WA.

A Brief History of Seattle

1792 Briton George Vancouver explores and names the Puget Sound.

1851 The Denny party makes land at Alki Point (now West Seattle)

and endures a harsh first winter with the help of local Indian tribes.

1852 Denny and gang move their town to the more temperate east side of the Puget Sound; "Doc"

Maynard names the town after Chief Sealth of the local Duwamish tribe.

1853 The Washington Territory is officially created; it includes what is now Idaho and part of Montana.

1853 Henry Yesler opens the first of many sawmills to be built in the Puget Sound area.

1855 The U.S. government signs treaties with several Native-American tribes in the Washington Territory, giving much of their land to the federal government.

1861 The University of Washington (then called Territorial University) opens its doors to students.

1863 Idaho Territory is separated from the Washington Territory.

1863 The *Gazette*, later to become the *Seattle Post-Intelligencer*, publishes its first newspaper.

1864 Cross-country Western Union telegraph line reaches Seattle.

1869 The City of Seattle incorporates.

1871 The Indian Appropriations Act says Indians are no longer sovereign but federal "wards."

1878 Seattle gets its first telephones.

1885 Chinese immigrants are forced out of Seattle.

1889 Twenty-five blocks of Seattle burn to the ground in the Great Fire, prompting a frenzy of building—several feet higher than the original shops had been.

1889 Washington becomes the nation's 42nd state.

1893 Transcontinental Great Northern Railway reaches Seattle.

1893 Great Panic delivers a punch to Washington's economy.

1896 Col. Alden Blethen buys *The Seattle Daily Times*. (The Blethen family still owns *The Seattle Times*.)

1897-99 Seattle booms as a stopping-off point for Klondike gold-seekers.

1901 John Nordstrom opens his first shoe store.

1907 Pike Place Market brings farmers and customers directly together.

1910 Seattle women win their on-again-off-again right to vote once and for all.

1914 Smith Tower is completed in Seattle, becoming the tallest building west of Ohio.

1915 William Boeing goes for his first flight.

1916 A long, violent longshoremen's strike takes place.

1917 Construction is complete on the Lake Washington Ship Canal.

1917 Boeing Airplane Co. is launched.

1919 The nation's first general strike causes mayhem in Seattle.

1919 First international airmail delivery by Boeing and Hubbard.

1919 Eddie Bauer's first store opens.

1921 The Alien Land Law is passed in Washington, restricting Asian immigrants' rights to own or lease property.

1924 Native Americans are made U.S. citizens.

1926 Seattle elects the first woman mayor of any major U.S. city.

1940 Lake Washington Floating Bridge becomes the first of its kind in the world.

1940 Sen. Henry "Scoop" Jackson wins election to Congress, and later to the U.S. Senate.

1942 FDR signs order sending Japanese Americans from the West Coast to internment camps; thousands in the Seattle area are forced to abandon their homes and businesses.

1942 Seattle native Jimi Hendrix is born.

1949 Sea-Tac International Airport opens.

1951 Washington State Ferries begin service on the Puget Sound.

1954 First successful passenger jet, Boeing 707, takes off.

1962 Seattle builds Space Needle and monorail for the World's Fair.

1966 Boeing builds 747 assembly plant.

1970s Boeing layoffs devastate the local economy.

1971 Starbucks opens its first shop, and the rest is history.

1975 Microsoft is founded by Bill Gates and Paul Allen in Albuquerque; 3 years later, it moves to Seattle area.

1976 First woman governor of Washington, Dixy Lee Ray, is elected.

1976 The new Seahawks football team plays its first game.

1977 The new Mariners baseball team throws its first pitch.

1979 The Seattle SuperSonics win the NBA Championship.

1999 A World Trade Organization conference in downtown Seattle prompts riots, property damage, and accusations of police misconduct.

2001 The Nisqually Earthquake causes extensive damage to many older Seattle buildings.

2004 Washington elects Christine Gregoire in tightest governor's race in U.S. history, giving Washington state three women in its powerful political positions—two U.S. senators and the governor.

2005 Smoking is banned in all public places in Washington.

2006 Starbucks CEO Howard Schultz sells the Seattle SuperSonics team to an Oklahoma group after the city refuses to expand the basketball arena or build a new one. This leaves the Sonics' future in Seattle in doubt.

2007 The Washington state Legislature legalizes same-sex unions.

2008 Seattle voters approve $73 million worth of renovations to their beloved but aging Pike Place Market.

2009 The Link light rail station opens at Sea-Tac Airport, providing rapid mass transportation from downtown Seattle to the airport.

2010 A new law makes it a primary offense to text-message or hold a cellphone to your ear while driving.

2010 The Seattle Storm women's basketball team wins its second WNBA championship.

Index

See also Accommodations and Restaurant indexes, below.

Photo **Credits**